Don't Ask Me to Believe

CLARE NONHEBEL launched her novel-writing career by becoming the joint winner of the first Betty Trask Award for *Cold Showers* in 1984. Since then she has written three highly praised novels, *The Partisan*, *Incentives* and *Child's Play*. Her latest novel, *Eldred Jones, Lulubelle and the Most High* is equally brilliant (Lion, 1998).

Born in 1953, Clare was educated in London and Salisbury. She graduated in French Studies from Warwick University and has worked in social work, public relations and journalism. She lives in London with her husband Robin, a history teacher.

Also by Clare Nonhebel

FICTION

Cold Showers

The Partisan

Incentives

Child's Play

Eldred Jones, Lulubelle and the Most High

NON-FICTION

Healed and Souled
(by Ashuli: co-written with Joseph Stefanazzi)

for David
with best wishes,

CLARE NONHEBEL

Clare Nonhebel

Don't
Ask
Me
to
Believe

A LION BOOK

Published by
Lion Publishing plc
Sandy Lane West, Oxford, England
ISBN 0 7459 3930 9

First edition 1998
10 9 8 7 6 5 4 3 2 1 0

A catalogue record for this book is available
from the British Library

Typeset in 11/14 Goudy Old Style
Printed and bound in Great Britain by
Caledonian International Book Manufacturing, Glasgow

A brief introduction

A friend's seven-year-old boy, walking through the woods while on holiday with his family, looked around him at the sun streaming through the trees and said aloud, 'Okay, God, I know you are real.' His family looked at him, a bit surprised, and he added very firmly, 'And I'll believe anything you like, but don't ask me to believe in the resurrection – all right?'

So thank you, James, for providing the introduction to this book, because you may have voiced what a lot of people feel: yes, I do see signs of God's existence, and yes, I'm prepared to believe at least some of the things that God seems to teach but... to believe in Jesus Christ rising from death? Isn't that asking too much of any normal, solid and reasonable human being?

What I'd like to do in this book is to take a look at why people persist in believing this, and why they don't. The division between these groups of people isn't simple. There are plenty of people, like James, with a natural religious sense, who have no trouble in perceiving a creator behind creation, a higher intelligence surpassing us in understanding, and who can even accept that a good God could send a loving son into a cold and lonely world and allow him to experience all its agonies, before recalling him home to be consoled. But they gag on the supposition that this son could physically return to life on earth after his death, or that this resurrection has somehow 'saved the world'.

Other people, who have never shown any signs of being

religiously inclined and whose lives are firmly earth-bound, may suddenly claim to have met a person called Jesus Christ who has changed all their priorities and their life – and it's clear to everyone around them that they really have been changed by something. They're as stunned and awed as a first-time lover, and it's as though the old platitudes that everyone takes for granted have suddenly gained meaning and come alive for them. They'll spout phrases that seem to come straight from the Bible – even if they've never read it – as though these were new revelations delivered to them alone, and their behaviour changes; they may give their money away, patch up old feuds, give up a lucrative job to do menial service work, or they stop swearing or getting drunk or having a sex life… They either won't stop talking about what has changed their life, or else they become thoughtful and withdrawn.

So what's happened to them? How can they seriously claim that some minor figure in history who died a bloody death a long time ago has 'met' them and changed their life?

It seems that what we're being asked to believe in is a transformation or 'coming alive' of the essential person, taking place here and now in a present-day individual, as the result of some kind of intervention by a person they firmly believe to be Jesus Christ. This is asking more than a faith in the resurrection of Jesus Christ as a symbolic myth. It's even asking more than belief in Jesus Christ as a real figure in history, who was seen alive by a number of witnesses after being crucified and buried – though in itself that's quite a lot to believe. Listen to this:

There was this man who, according to contemporary accounts, lived a physically demanding life, constantly preaching, healing, besieged by large crowds, travelling long distances on foot in extreme heat, staying up all night and hardly eating, and who – according to his critics – looked 'barely fifty' when he was in his early thirties.

He upset just about everybody's ideas and was finally arrested, tortured and treated abusively, and had his emaciated form – hardly a picture of health in the first place – nailed to a cross, where he not surprisingly died in a short space of time. The execution squad, not knowing much about his way of life, did find it surprising, so to make good and sure that he was really dead, they speared him through the side.

After that, because he'd talked about rising to life, they secured a massive stone across the mouth of his burial cave, sealed it around the edges, and posted shifts of four armed soldiers at a time to make sure that no one came and stole the body in order to claim miraculous powers on his behalf. But at dawn, the tomb was found empty.

His followers – who had been so scared that they'd all run away as soon as he'd been arrested and most of whom had been hiding in a locked attic ever since – suddenly came out, speaking in foreign languages they'd never been taught, not caring whether or not they were caught, on fire with enthusiasm, and claiming they'd seen this man alive and even eaten with him and that he'd promised he was still with them and always would be. And they were so carried away by this conviction that they began upsetting everyone as well, and travelling not only around the country but around the world, trying to tell perfect strangers about what had happened to them that had taken away their fear and their common sense and made it worth their while losing their homes, careers, reputations, their families and their normality.

And it still seems to be happening, doesn't it? All in the name of this same minor historical figure, and not just as a ritualistic memorial of some holy hero in history, but as a contemporary event taking place in the lives of present-day 'disciples'. Other 'prophets' of that time, and at other times since, have drawn bigger crowds than Jesus Christ, have been reported to have more astonishing powers and have set up organizations more efficient and reputable than any Christian church – and have disappeared, either within a few centuries or a few years.

So why – WHY? – are some tens of thousands of people every year, 2,000 years after any verifiable historical event, still being infected with this reckless form of faith? Why, for them, has Jesus 'come alive', and what has caused them to redefine their lives and feel so convinced that the life they've lived up till now isn't real or satisfying and that there's some other way of life that's worth any sacrifice – relationships, security, health, and perfectly normal ambitions?

And why are so many other people dubious about this phenomenon – not only hardened cynical people who don't believe anything real or good can happen to anyone, but also some deeply religious people who have no hesitation in believing in a good God and a life that goes way beyond the limits of this one?

I don't know the answers myself, but I'd like to. All I do know is that I've met a lot of people in my life who've seemed genuine: some of them have undoubtedly 'come alive' with some inner conviction related to Jesus Christ, and some have had genuine reservations and doubts and have been honest enough to express them.

I've met other people who've been complacent about their faith and not interested in hearing the alternatives – whether their faith is in Jesus, in science, in personal heroes, political solutions, or in their own abilities – and many more people whose religion is cynicism, who aren't prepared to see any goodness in human beings or to forgive any human failings. But you'll have met plenty of those people yourself, and they don't need more space to preach their philosophies.

What I'd like to do in this book is to tell you about my experience of Jesus coming to life, and the times in my life he failed to come alive. Like most lives, mine has had its dark side as well as its flashes of insight and faith, so it's not an inspiring account of someone who's 'seen the light' and lived happily ever afterwards –

but if you're prepared to listen, I'm prepared to be as honest as I know how about the ups and downs of my own relationship with this person called Jesus Christ. There may be something in my life that you can identify with, or you may decide that your experience has little in common with mine.

So I'd also like to introduce some other people and let them tell you about a wide variety of lives in which Jesus came alive – usually at some time when their life seemed to be well and truly crucified and sealed in a cold, dark cave, with a troop of hostile pickets outside to prevent them from emerging into the sunlight – as well as a few people for whom Jesus' reality has stayed hidden or remained a theory.

The people I interviewed were asked to contribute because of their willingness to talk bluntly about the good, the bad and the ugliness of their lives. I felt I could trust them not to manipulate the facts or to peddle their own theories at the expense of truth or to do a whitewash job on the reality of their reservations and doubts.

To be that truthful about some intimate details of life can make a person feel vulnerable, so I offered them the option of changing their names if they liked, as long as they didn't compromise on the truth.

So here we are – Mark and Bernadette, Dean, Alan, Kiran, myself, and a number of others. Maybe somewhere among these very different personalities and lives you'll catch a glimpse of your own individual experience of Jesus Christ – whether it's an experience of his reality or of his absence. And maybe you'll catch a glimpse of another person as well, someone closely involved with all these histories but with a life and personality of his own, beyond them all.

1
∙∙∙∙∙∙∙∙∙∙∙∙∙

I didn't at first connect God with church, because home was where most of the praying took place.

My mother had been left on her own with two small children, destitute. She didn't have a high opinion of men and hardly ever prayed directly to Jesus but usually through his mother, Mary; I think she trusted her more to understand the needs of the family and to make the appropriate requests to her son.

The prayers were practical and made aloud: 'Our Lady, give me strength to finish the ironing,' or 'The children need new vests and there's no money; please ask God to help.' My sister and I took this method of praying for granted, and because it worked so efficiently I assumed all other families went about getting their needs met in the same way.

The clearest example I remember was when my mother had washed and ironed us a clean dress each, polished our shoes and told us to put on clean white socks, because we'd been invited to tea by an aunt who was rather particular about 'keeping up standards'. Mum was sensitive to criticism about her children's appearance because evidence of poverty was considered shameful and embarrassing, a sign of being 'common' or 'not properly brought up'. Any childish misbehaviour on our part might also be regarded as the consequence of coming from a 'broken home'. So tea with this aunt meant spotless clothes and best behaviour!

My sister, who was dressed and ready before me, went out into the garden while she was waiting, and accidentally tore her dress on a rose bush. I remember Mum sitting down on the stairs saying, 'Oh Lord, that's a punishment on me for my pride: I shouldn't be so worried about what people think of me.'

As she opened the mending basket and began to work on patching the torn dress, the doorbell rang and one of the neighbour's children stood there with a bag of clothes, saying, 'Mum said she hopes you won't be offended and would you like some cast-offs?'

I can still remember my mother tearing open the bag as soon as the door closed behind the child, taking out the ironing board and telling my sister to find something in the bag that would fit her, all the time praising Our Lady for helping her out yet again, understanding a mother's concerns and not despising them but putting in a good word for her to God – who, I assumed, was above such things.

Although the family, and some of our schoolteachers, seemed to fear and despise poverty, I didn't find it a barrier in my relationship with God. From an early age, we learned about God's son born in a stable because no one wanted to take the family into their own house, a reality that seemed so similar to our own that I felt quite close to that other child, Jesus Christ – though God the Father was a distant figure.

My father left home at the time I was born, a fact that weighed on me terribly because I believed for years that it must have been my fault.

I have one memory of him, and I can't be sure if it's accurate because I can't have been more than a few days old. The memory is of lying in a hospital cot, in a separate room; the door opens in front of me and my father comes in and puts his hand on me. His thumb is just under my right collarbone and I seem to feel all the love and strength in me flow out and into him, through that thumb.

He lets go of me and goes abruptly out of the room and I feel drained and cold, and there's a terrible sadness at seeing him go and not knowing when I'll see him again. The patch below my collarbone aches, on and off, for years and I wear a threadbare patch in all my clothes, stroking it whenever I feel tired or sad.

I could never make sense of this memory, because I couldn't imagine a scene in which a newborn baby would be left alone with a father whose wife had reported him as violent. But years later, at the age of thirty-six, I met my father and although I never mentioned the memory, he told me that he had seen me once for two minutes in the hospital where I was born, and that had only been allowed because he'd applied for a court injunction giving him the right to do so.

However accurate or distorted this memory may be, my main interest in God the unseen Father was that he was the only person who might have either the ability or the desire to bring my earthly father back, as soon as my father felt able to cope with having me as a daughter. By the time I was five, we had had eight homes and I worried each time we moved that my father wouldn't be able to find us. And as God didn't bring him back, I believed what I was often told – that I was a difficult child, uncontrollable, disobedient and impossible to like. I reasoned that no father would want to come back to a child like that.

One of my worst memories is of locking myself in the toilet, away from my mother who was trying to catch me to smack me, crying and digging my fingernails into my hands to avoid making any noise, while my mother shouted through the door, 'You're a horrid little girl; I love you because I'm your mother but I don't like you and nobody ever could.'

Years and years later, a Christian who hardly knew me told me, 'You don't need to be told God loves you, because you've always known it, but I feel he's asking me to let you know that he also likes you,' and I burst into tears because only God could have known I still needed to hear that.

I did often have a sense of him being near me, often at the most desolate times of a fairly desolate childhood. Living with an elderly great-uncle I found terrifying, I had hiding places all over the house and would often stay crouched for hours in the spare room wardrobe, keeping quiet while everyone shouted and searched for me. It was my insurance policy: if no one could find me, then this was a place I could go to when the time came that I dreaded – the time when my great-uncle would get his hands on me and no one would be around to hear me scream and come running to tell me off for making a noise and annoying him.

It was in those hiding places – in the cupboard or under a bed or behind the low garden wall that shielded the compost heap from sight, or locked in the toilet, that I felt safest and, inexplicably, least alone. Something or someone was there, and knew where I was.

At school I was taught that God expected children to be good, to obey their good and loving parents who made selfless sacrifices in bringing them up, but that we could never earn heaven, not even if we became like the holy saints who let tyrants cut off their hands rather than sign a paper saying they didn't believe in God. I lived in fear of getting my hands cut off, and greater fear that when God got around to asking this tiny favour of me in return for his vast goodness, I would lose my nerve and deny that I ever knew him. I made fervent prayers pleading with him that I wouldn't let him down, when the time came, by doing any of the bad things I did at home – running away, hiding, screaming, crying or demanding my own way.

I never really identified Jesus with God. Jesus was someone I knew – the child born to a poor mother, who didn't have his real dad living at home, who came here because he loved us and who was abused and rejected and nailed to a cross so he couldn't cause any more trouble.

God was a bit like Father Christmas, I thought – a sham who

loved little children only as long as they were sweet and nice; he gave all the big toys and special treats to rich kids who boasted about them in front of poor kids who had tried to be good for months and still never got Sindy dolls or roller skates or a chance to go on school trips.

I believed that God was also like my great-uncle, because I was told it was thanks to God that we ended our succession of moves from one live-in job to another and went to live with Uncle. It was clear to me that God and Uncle were on the same side, because we were expected to be grateful to them both for providing a lovely home. So it never occurred to me to tell God I was unhappy.

Uncle knew that I didn't want to live with him and wasn't grateful for the privilege, and he resented it. When my mother and sister were there, he was the jovial uncle making jokes; when he was alone in the room with me he would sit and stare at me with a hard unpleasant smile till I lost my nerve and ran out.

He had been the youngest child of a large family, ignored and bullied as much as he was indulged, and he harboured a great deal of bitterness. Now there was another 'youngest child' and he was in charge.

He played on my fear of the dark, refusing to let me have a light on in the bedroom in the long waiting time till my elder sister came to bed, turning off the landing light every time he came upstairs, standing outside the door in the dark till I pleaded with him to switch the light on again. He told me there were goblins on top of the wardrobe and a creature called Jack Frost, with a long blue icicle for a nose, scrabbling outside the window pane trying to get in at me.

If Uncle was upstairs in the evening and heard me coming up the unlit stairway, he'd wait in his bedroom doorway till I reached the landing, then just as I was fearfully stretching up for the light switch he'd step forward and grip his hands round my neck and laugh at my soundless shrieks for help.

He stole my sweets and dared me to tell my mother. He gave me pocket money and later demanded it back from me as a penalty for some misdemeanour. He would taunt me and call me names, and ask me catch questions that had no right answers, ridiculing any response and calling me 'mentally deficient' if I stayed silent. If my mother came in while this was going on he'd roar with laughter, say, 'I'm only teasing!' and tell her I couldn't take a joke against myself and had no sense of humour. He'd suggest we all played a happy family game, at which he would cheat and then accuse my sister and me of being bad losers if we so much as exchanged glances. If I refused to play, he'd call me a spoilt brat who spoiled everyone's fun. The punishment for spoiling everyone's fun was a day shut in the bedroom with no one speaking to me until next morning and no food except dry bread and water. I remember this happening twice, till a friend's mother found out about it and made a shocked protest to my mother; then it stopped.

He would praise me publicly for helping him with the gardening then take me aside in private and tell me I'd made a mess of everything. He thanked me for birthday presents I chose for him and later called me into his bedroom to witness him throwing them in the bin. 'God-awful rubbish,' he'd say, tearing up the calendar or emptying out the packets of seeds.

He came into the bedroom while I was undressing, saying he was going to 'discipline' me because my mother had told him I'd been a bad girl today. I remember hearing his footsteps on the stairs and trying frantically to hide under the bed, only the gap was too small, and then trying to pull the corner of the bedspread across my lap, but it caught on the blankets and wouldn't cover me. And then the lurch of fear as he came into the room, and the carpet burning the back of my leg as he dragged me across the floor by the arm and held me, hanging, allowed neither to sit or stand, while the 'discipline' began.

The terror was clear, and the humiliation, and the sense that something was very unfair. My mother's philosophy on smacking children limited it to three times, so it was only when he reached four that I'd start to yell for her, knowing he had gone beyond her authority. But the other things he did a child has no name for and only the vaguest concept of what is wrong. The real harm done by sexual abuse is not experienced by the child at the time, but in the adolescent and adult years, when all that groping and fumbling and heaving, all the furtive avoidances of being found out, and the threats ('If you keep on being impudent and fighting me you'll be sent away from this lovely home and never see your mother or sister again'), suddenly acquire significance, in the context of raw new knowledge about adult sexuality.

That's when the real betrayal begins: when the child, no longer a child now, learns the meaning of innocence and knows it was stolen from her by someone who had lost his own, long ago. Then there seems to be no choice – no time to enjoy a gradual awakening from childish to adolescent relationships or to formulate one's own ideas about rights and wrongs, joys and limits. Instead of curiosity and excitement, there is only a sick realization that all decent boundaries have been breached before the child had the maturity to set any for herself, and a sense of alienation from her friends – because surely no other child in the world has ever been involved in such defilement. The isolation can only be healed, along with the shock and horror, when the child – or adolescent or adult that he or she becomes – can tell someone, but the barriers against telling are the hardest ones in the world to breach, both because of the threats the abuser has made, whether spoken aloud or implicit, and because of the shame and guilt the child feels. To be involved in evil, even so blamelessly, is like being pushed into a muddy pool; it can never be the fault of the one who is pushed, but the dirt attaches itself to the victim, not to the bully who has done the pushing.

God knew everything, we were taught, so I reasoned that he must even know about the things that Uncle did, things that no one else knew or took any notice of. And God still left me in that house with that tormented, unbalanced man, even though I pleaded to leave, packed my teddy bear and left home on several occasions, and screamed and cried so often and so loudly that I hoped eventually Uncle would do as my mother warned he'd do if I kept on being a nuisance, and throw us all out in the street, where I would be safe from him.

Yet we were constantly taught that God is good and kind and cares about everyone, even children.

The nearest I came to an image of a God who listened was the family doctor, an irritable and hard-drinking man, who seemed to have a genuine soft spot for children. He came to the house when I had measles and, for some reason, told my mother to wait downstairs while he went into the bedroom. My mother had told me the doctor would need to examine me and warned me 'not to be silly and make a fuss if he wants to have a look at you'.

I can remember my fear and despair as I heard him come up the stairs and say to my mother, 'I'll be down in a few minutes.' He opened the door and stood there, a stranger with a bag containing secret torture implements like the needle he'd stuck in my arm once, while telling me to watch a non-existent butterfly on the ceiling of his surgery, and no doubt a full range of nasty medicines that he'd force down my throat 'for my own good', like Uncle's 'punishments'. And the reason he didn't want my mother upstairs must be the same reason Uncle didn't – so she wouldn't hear me crying and come in to tell me off for being insolent to him, and so stop him from abusing me.

The doctor came towards the bed, and I hid under the bedclothes, clutching on to the blankets till he detached them, gently, from my hand and said, 'I'm just going to have a look at you; I won't hurt you.'

At that point, I gave up hope, and to get it over with quickly, I pulled my pyjama trousers down, not waiting for him to do it. He looked shocked for a minute and then such sadness came into his eyes that I had never seen in an adult, and for the first time in my life I felt that I was a child, not a terror or a nuisance or an aggravation to adults, but only a very small child, entitled to be protected.

He pulled the bedclothes back over me and said, 'I'm going to look at your chest, that's all, to see if there's any rash on it. Is that all right with you?' When I nodded consent, he knelt down, unbuttoned my pyjama top, took a brief look and said, 'Yes, you have measles; I'll give you some medicine to make you better.' He buttoned the jacket up again – although I was old enough to dress myself – then said, 'Are you afraid of your uncle?'

The question was so unexpected that I stared at him and said nothing, because the lump that came into my throat was the only thing stopping me crying out loud and 'making a fuss', but I felt my face puff up with the effort of staying quiet, and tears rolled out of my eyes.

He stood there looking at me, then he said, 'All right', and went out abruptly. I felt he was angry, but not with me. When he'd gone out, it took me a while to stop crying, but I felt such a sense of peace. I knew God was good after all and that he'd visited me.

Later on, my mother said, 'The doctor says I must get you away from Uncle, that we should all leave,' and I felt a great hope, and also guilt, because she'd always said if we had to leave it would be because of my naughtiness. Then she said, 'He doesn't understand, does he? This is our security.'

And that's when I felt that God was well-meaning but not, after all, all that powerful. After that I only prayed that he'd either send my father home or let me live with my grandfather, or arrange it so that I'd very soon be dead.

What a barrier it is, in the relationship with God, to want to forgive and forget and thank God for where I am now, while still being troubled by these memories – still a victim, not of the people any longer, but of the memories. Pushing them 'out of sight and out of mind' isn't the answer, because denying the past is to deny the present reality as well.

Many families have a hidden history, and even when the events were not so bad in the first place, once they are surrounded by shame and concealed by lies they grow into something overwhelming – like a tiny mushroom spoor left in a dark, damp cellar. At the root of the secrecy is someone claiming that they never did anything wrong. That leaves everyone around them in conflict. How can I forgive someone who makes themselves unforgivable – because the perfect don't need to be forgiven, and will interpret any offer of it as a veiled condemnation? I felt as though a great pack of guilt was unloaded on to me, which I had to carry until I could find a safe place to lay it down.

Even hearing Jesus say, 'Come to me, all you who are overburdened; give me everything you can't cope with' may cause further distress, when this invitation conflicts with a whole upbringing which calls it disloyalty to talk about the family, or to call on any 'outsider' for help. He's asking me to treat him as an insider, and unless I decide to take that risk, he'll stay outside my life and not intervene in it. That's my choice, and this is the conflict I have to deal with: if I believe the gospel Jesus who says, 'Come as you are and tell me everything,' I become an inadequate person who reveals my own shameful history and my inability to outgrow its effects unaided and move forward into maturity. And I become a bad person who tells tales about other people – perhaps even about the father and mother that God in his commandments has told me to honour. And those people, of course, may go to God with their own version of events, in which they are fully justified and I am a liar, or at best a person possessed of an unbridled imagination. Maybe that's why Jesus emphasized that the reason he came here was 'not for the virtuous or the respectable people but for sinners'. Even if I don't feel like much of a sinner before I approach him, the nearer I get to accepting his invitation, the more light he will shine on the darkest corners of my life, and the more shameful and needy I'm going to become, at least in my own eyes.

I don't doubt that he can cope with this torn and fearful history that has formed me and influenced my decisions and actions, or that he can still welcome me as the person I have become – but can I?

2

....

I met Mark Anderson, thirty-six, after I heard him make a charity appeal for an organization which gives financial support to clergy who lose their livelihood as a result of leaving one Church to join another.

He explained that because they can't immediately be re-ordained in the Church they join, they lose both their job and their home at once – and many of them have families to support.

In order to explain the inner conviction that draws someone to change from one Christian denomination to another, even when it means losing so much, Mark gave a brief account of his own experience – and at this point his talk ceased to be an appeal for money for yet another good cause and became a real account of the cost of someone following his conscience.

His audience went very still and began to listen with both ears instead of one as he told of his nagging doubts, over a period of eight or nine years, during which he became a deacon and then was ordained a priest in the Church of England.

Mark's account struck me as a story of faith because of his persistence in following a personal conviction about his individual route to a deeper relationship with Christ, and his willingness to take risks in the course of doing what he believed to be right. I reasoned that, for him, Jesus had to be someone who's alive. No one risks their security and their whole lifestyle for an abstract theory. So I asked him if he'd be willing to talk to me about who Jesus is for him. This is how he describes the growth of his own relationship with the person called Jesus Christ.

Mark

The scripture text that has always meant most to me is a line from one of Peter's letters that says, 'Make your conversion a daily experience.' Since teenage I'd been a communist. I was a member of a Trotsky group and we believed in constant revolution. I was looking for a just, egalitarian system that did something about the world's poverty and resources.

It was when I was at university that I first picked up the Bible. I was struck by the Acts of the Apostles: the first followers of Jesus 'holding all things in common' – sharing everything. That's what I'd been looking for in Marxism.

Before I went to university, I was a nurse and my training included geriatric nursing. One old man, Jack, came in with nothing – tatty clothes, wild beard. His wife was taken into another ward on the same day and died within a week. His clothes were taken away; his wife was taken away; even his beard was shaved off; even his mind had gone. He had nothing.

Sunday afternoons, after the shift, I would take six of the old men back to my flat and give them tea, and I took him, on a lovely spring day, and he knelt down and smelt the daffodils and thanked God. That really struck me. I had everything and never thanked God for anything. But I did nothing about it at the time.

I didn't ever totally stop believing in God. I'd been to Church of England schools. The teaching in school was a very gentle faith – social conscience. Jesus was only the Christmas play and Victorian pictures – gentle Jesus. I remember the priests telling us about their vocations. God had called them to be a priest. I expected that a voice would come.

I became very cynical and hard against the Church in my teens, when it seemed that God really only called people who were white, middle-class, highly educated and male. I didn't come from a middle-class background and didn't do all that well at school; I never expected to do more than work in the local bread factory. I couldn't really divorce the two – God and the Church's attitude. For me, the priests represented God – the white, English, middle-class God. Later, by becoming middle-class and educated myself, I couldn't help wondering at times – 'Is that why I was accepted for ordination?'

When I was working in the hospital, caring for the dying or for people in pain or young people who were very ill, or laying out a dead body, I felt there had to be something – that there was a God and he was involved in the suffering in some way. I saw different reactions to suffering, on the part of people and their relatives. I'm generalizing, but if someone had faith, they died more easily, on the whole, than those who didn't. The ones who didn't have faith fought death. I knew which way I'd rather die. I sometimes wandered into an empty church and sat there, but I never went to any services.

I did a diploma in social studies, then I went on to university. At university, there was more time to think, and I met people I'd never normally meet. The eighteen- and nineteen-year-olds asked me about my nursing years and talking about it helped me to reflect on those three years too.

It was at that time that I went to a High Church Anglican Mass for the first time since the age of eleven. At school I was already so cynical that I'd avoided confirmation, but my faith had come back and I wanted to talk to the university chaplain about being confirmed now. I made several attempts to go and see him, but I was very nervous and the chaplaincy was always full of people. When I did finally get to see him, the priest who was there was really welcoming and open and I found I could talk to him about how I felt.

I felt in love with Jesus, because of the realization that he loved me. He loved that old man who had nothing, and that old man loved him back. And I wanted to love him back too; I wanted to give Christ everything, so it seemed clear he would want me to be a priest. My life, my weaknesses and faults: God loved me with all those, not despite them. The chaplain made a difference as well, to how I saw myself. I'd half-expected him not to take me seriously – a communist and all that.

I really felt a presence of Christ in those days – the freshness of the newly-wed – like a hand of God on my shoulder. I rarely feel that now, but it doesn't matter because of this ongoing conversion. Some religious experiences consist of God feeling very far away. It's like being in the desert, like Christ crying out on the cross: 'My God, my God, why have you forsaken me?' It's not an experience of the intimacy of God but of his otherness. There are times when he feels a long way off; he's the Creator and we're only the creatures. At those times I wonder, 'Is it me that moved away, or is it him?' But he's just as real when he's far off. To know him in his absence is still to know him.

Marxists talk about 'alienation': man creates because he's a creative being but he's alienated from his creations because, for us, creation becomes a means of profit. Christians talk about alienation from the creator too: the 'cloud of unknowing' that separates us from God. That separation gives us some insight into God's vastness, which our minds can't comprehend. But then at the times when he's near, God is minute: he's in my genes and in my atoms. We can make him far away by dwelling too much on his mightiness.

During my confirmation classes with the Anglican chaplain, he suggested I went to the Roman Catholic chaplain. It seemed an odd thing to suggest, but he must have thought even then that I might have more in common with Catholic teaching. The Anglo-Catholic movement, which I was brought up in, always considered itself still part of the Roman Catholic Church – a reformed version, not a breakaway group. But the more I thought about it, the more that didn't make sense to me. It's a complex issue and I won't go into it here, but for one thing, forty Catholics from England and Wales were martyred by the very Church that's claiming to be still one Church with theirs; we can't just write off history like that.

Also, I'd always had a very catholic outlook on the Church: most of my friends live in Europe, and a Church that has national boundaries makes very little sense to me. Anglican churches I'd visited in other European countries were mainly for ex-pats. As a Marxist I was used to thinking in international terms – the world proletariat, world revolution and so on – not one country. I realized that once I stepped off the ferry onto the continent, I was out of communion with the Anglican Church. The Church, for me, had to be universal.

I went and talked to the Catholic bishop and he was encouraging, but it just wasn't the right time for me. I had reservations about changing from the familiar Church I'd always known and it had already been a big step coming back to it. So I went ahead within the Anglican Church, went to theological college, became a deacon and was finally ordained. Part of my training was to do three months' work in a parish, and friends in Germany arranged for me to work in their parish, which was Catholic.

I enjoyed my time in Germany, and found the German people generally very welcoming and kind. That's why I went back there when I left the priesthood and lost my home and my job all in one go.

As an Anglican priest, the eucharist always meant a lot to me. It's three years now since I left the Anglican Church and I miss that priestly role terribly. There's a relationship of intimacy at that altar, between Christ and the priest. The wonder of holding Christ in my hands – it's something really special.

I used to giggle sometimes, when I said Mass: I would blush and giggle nervously and didn't understand why. My spiritual director said it was because it felt like making love in public, and he was right.

It was a difficult decision to leave the Anglican Church but eventually it had to be made. Like all clergy who leave, I had to vacate my flat; in my case, within four weeks. There was no compensation from the Church and no state benefit; clergy who leave because they join another Church are still usually considered to have made themselves voluntarily unemployed.

It wasn't as bad for me as for clergy who have families; at least I only had myself to support, but I had financial commitments and in order to clear those I had to contact a house-clearance firm, who totally stripped my flat. I was very upset at seeing my home go – every picture, the kitchen clock, blinds from the window, rugs, literally everything. I was penniless and owned nothing. But a few days later I felt light as a feather; I had nothing to hold me any more; I've never felt freer in my life.

I decided to go back to Germany to become a Catholic and to explore the religious life; the Franciscans agreed to take me and the family I knew there sent me the air ticket, but two days before my departure date the Franciscans contacted me and said they didn't feel able to guide me through this process of change after all!

I went anyway, and stayed with my friends first of all, then they arranged for me to go to a Benedictine monastery that specialized in counselling and guiding people on their spiritual journey. It was three hours' drive away from anyone I knew and my German wasn't very good, so I felt quite alone.

I studied for reception into the Catholic Church, and one of the old monks gave me German lessons every afternoon, and I worked on their farm and in the carpentry shop, doing the menial work because I didn't have any skills.

At first I had a room in the guest wing, but the monastery was a popular place to stay and they needed it for visitors. One afternoon, two of the students came to me, laughing, and said, 'You have to move – and guess where you're going!' It was a room above the huge covered pigsty. In a Bavarian winter, it was probably one of the warmest places to live. It was certainly the smelliest! I felt like the Prodigal Son in reverse: he was living with the pigs when he decided to go home to the Father; in my case I decided to get closer to the Father and then ended up living with pigs!

I was received into the Catholic Church, my German had become fluent, and the Franciscan community I'd originally wanted to go to had more members now and were willing to take me, so I went there. I was thinking of joining but they didn't want to rush me, because I'd already gone through so many changes, so I just lived with them, worked on the farm, and also did some of the begging; like St Francis in the beginning, these Franciscans still begged for their food.

Most of it was given by the local chest hospital – the patients' leftovers – and local farmers brought bread or cheese. Some days there was very little food for us, but the monks were inventive at spinning it out and spicing it up with garlic or herbs and we never really went hungry.

I'd been in Germany nearly a year when I could no longer ignore the fact that I was ill. I'd been having a lot of pain: with hindsight, it must have begun before I left England, but I didn't admit it to myself, or perhaps there was so much going on that it just didn't seem important. I didn't know how serious it was, but from my nursing training I thought it was probably cancer.

My form for medical treatment in the European Community was no longer valid and I couldn't get treatment without payment, so it seemed best to go back to England, to my parents. My GP was part of a Christian medical practice – I didn't know such a thing existed – where the doctors offered to pray with patients if they wanted it. I did. I had to wait three months for an appointment with the consultant, then there were tests, which confirmed that it was a tumour, and I was operated on, then had four weeks of radiotherapy every weekday.

The day I was told it was cancer, the first time the word was mentioned, I remember feeling quite frightened; there's something about the word 'cancer' when it's applied to you. I'd dealt with it as a nurse, but I'd never been a patient in my life. That first night, I couldn't sleep and I had a direct chat with Jesus, just like you'd chat with a friend – along the lines of, 'This is it, then; this is what the doctor told me – thanks a lot!' I didn't ever really feel, 'Why me?' If it hadn't been me it would have been some other poor bugger. But it was frightening. During the talk with Jesus, though, it was as if he said to me, 'Don't you know who you're talking to here? Don't you realize you're afraid of the worst possible outcome of this illness?'

I realized that what I was seeing as the worst outcome for me was death, and how could I call myself a Christian and be frightened of dying? I was talking to Jesus, so obviously I had belief, and if I believed in him, why on earth was I afraid of dying?

In the early hours of the morning, I felt I dumped the whole situation at his feet and said, 'All right, then, you have it.' I fell asleep then and when I woke up in the morning I found the fear had totally gone. And it never came back. I mean, I wondered how much pain there'd be when I came round from the operation, and things like that, but I had no fear at all about the outcome of the illness; in fact, it felt quite strange to be without the fear.

I reacted badly to the radiotherapy; I was sick all the time, every twenty minutes; you could set your watch by me. By that time I was under the care of the hospital and out of the hands of the GP, but I think the doctor praying with me was more help than anything. Sure, God gives the skills for the operating theatre and the radiotherapy but prayer goes far deeper. I had a sense I was being healed of more than the cancer.

During the period of radiotherapy, for four weeks I lay on the sofa and did nothing, apart from the trips to the hospital. I was dependent on other people, and it seemed to deepen the relationships. I'd never 'done nothing' before, never had time. The biggest healing was just slowing down, just being. The dependence made me feel that everything really was in God's hands. I felt like a child again, being cared for by my father – my heavenly Father as well as my earthly one.

God works through our experiences, and because this experience was a big change for me, there was a big revelation to go with it. The image of God as a loving Father was one I'd forgotten really. I know the concept of God the Father is a difficult one for a lot of people, especially in our politically correct world, but it was really helpful and enlightening at that time. The illness took me back to the simplicity of spirit that you have in childhood.

It sounds naff, but I really thank God now that I had this illness. I'm not grateful for the illness, but for the revelation that came with it. I've come closer to God in the last three years than I ever was before, even as a priest. Priesthood isn't necessarily a deeper relationship with Christ; it's just different.

After the radiotherapy I felt very weird for a while, even though I started working for this society almost immediately, as charity appeals organizer within the diocese. While I was doing appeals, talking about the need for financial support for clergy who leave the Anglican Church, I began to include a few details of my own experience, to make it more relevant for the people listening, but it was a great therapy for me as well, to talk about it, and I've been amazed by the generosity of people's response, emotional as well as financial.

I joined the society just before the rush of Anglican clergy into the Catholic Church. People have different motives for joining the Catholic Church, but in a way it's not relevant, because God invites people in different ways and works through all kinds of attitudes.

I'm hoping to join an order that does missionary work in the poorest areas of this country; I've been having talks with them. I long to be a priest again. There's a risk in ministry; there has to be. I want to see the Church taking risks all the time, because we have nothing to lose. Christ took amazing risks in his ministry, especially in the people he chose to be his friends. Peter, in today's world, would be a rough man with tattoos and an earring and swearing like a trooper. Matthew, the tax-collector, would be the Establishment figure.

And Jesus was seen to be enjoying life – having meals and going into people's homes for a drink; he clearly lived life to the full. God doesn't call dead people: he calls live people, and he calls people to live a full life.

A lot of people are put off Christians by their caution. There's a story about the devil's disciple suggesting ways of tempting people away from faith in God. He says, 'We'll tell people there's no God,' and the devil says, 'No, that won't do. They'll see a baby being born and they'll know God exists.' So the disciple says, 'Well, we'll tell them you don't exist,' and the devil says, 'No, they'll see war and they'll know I'm real.' So the disciple finally hits on a good idea: 'I know!' he says. 'We'll tell them there's no rush; there's always tomorrow!'

As priests and as Christians we should err on the side of risk. It's better to make mistakes than to get too cautious. Intolerance puts people off too. There's a hymn that goes, 'They'll know we are Christians by our love,' and it would probably be more truthful to sing, 'They'll know we are Christians by our intolerance.' I get angry about the Church because I love it; that's why.

My family aren't churchgoers; like many people, they're put off by what they see as hypocrisy in the Church, and exclusiveness – though I know the Church is trying hard now to make better provision for groups that feel excluded: the remarried, for example.

There are some saintly people out there, but the general criticism of the Church is still that it's wealthy, distanced, and has nothing to say to our world. If we're really going to follow Christ, we have to take risks, make mistakes, and make changes – and first we have to do it in our own lives, and all in the context of our own relationship with Christ. Then it makes sense.

3

•••••••••••••

The God my mother prayed to for the family's needs seemed different from the God that the nuns at school had given their lives to. They seemed in awe of him and constantly concerned to please and not to offend him. I had the impression that God wasn't easy to please.

The religion they taught was devotion to God and a strict code of morality which drew little distinction between the laws made by God (love your neighbour; thou shalt not steal), laws defined by the Catholic Church (don't miss Mass on Sunday without a good reason), and laws devised by the school (don't chew gum or give in homework with messy handwriting).

This lack of priority made even the Ten Commandments seem like one more item in a chain of nit-picking, and the practice of rote-learning deprived the subject of meaning. A child who confused the Ten Commandments with the Seven Sacraments or the Twelve Disciples or the Seven Deadly Sins was ridiculed and rebuked. Religious education classes inspired anxiety rather than love of God.

Some things, though, were unexpectedly inspiring. I remember one nun, in the middle of giving a maths lesson, suddenly beginning to talk about Christ's love in accepting undeserved punishment on the cross, on behalf of people like us whose lives would have led them to spiritual death if he hadn't taken the consequences of our actions in place of us – people he didn't even know, who would come to earth a long time after him and never even thank him or recognize the significance of his sacrifice. There were tears in her eyes.

Sunday Mass was not inspiring – the priest mumbled in Latin, with his back to us – but communion was. It meant a lot to me that Jesus consented to become part of my life, even physically. I was so convinced I was difficult to live with that it seemed he did more for me, in letting me receive him in the eucharist, than he did for anyone else. The other children were better, nicer, less full of rage and hatred than I was; it wasn't so much of a sacrifice for him to live with them. That he chose to live with me as well was an act of supreme love. I used to be afraid, every week, that I'd be turned away by the priest. When I was older I sometimes turned myself away, not confident after all that Jesus would want me. I devised painful penances, said long prayers and cried at night over my sins, feeling I would never be good enough to stop causing that tortured figure on the cross even more suffering.

Of the church services, I preferred Benediction, an optional devotion on Sunday evenings. The blessed sacrament – a small unimpressive disc of bread embodying the presence of God – was displayed on the altar, making Christ physically as well as spiritually available, and vulnerable, to his people; the hymns and prayers were moving, and the long silences refreshing.

At school too, a few times a week during lunch-break, the school chapel or parish church would expose the blessed sacrament on the altar. The nuns who were not on school duties would spend an hour there, while little groups of children dropped in for a couple of minutes, bobbed up and down in front of the altar in a hasty mark of respect, lit candles, whispered breathless prayers, and rushed back to their friends in the playground. It must have been extremely distracting for the nuns, engaged in silent prayer, but they usually managed to smile at us and even thanked us for giving up part of our playtime to spare a thought for God.

As teachers and as people, the nuns had limitations: their perception of family life was idealized; they tended to typecast their pupils into 'good girls' and 'bad girls' and blame the 'bad ones' for everything, regardless of evidence; their methods of correcting children were insensitive, the punishments were often humiliating, and their teaching of religious doctrine was mixed in with dollops of sentiment, prejudice and superstition. Yet their faith in God was real. They had no doubt about the ultimate triumph of good over evil, never seeing it as an even-handed battle; they believed in a root of goodness in every human being and were willing to exhaust themselves in the process of nurturing it.

Their pupils complained about them, laughed at them and hated them at times, but the underlying feeling of most of the children towards the nuns was a grudging respect. It was clear that they tried, at least, to live what they taught and that they taught what they personally believed: religious knowledge was never just another academic subject to them, as it was to some of the lay teachers.

If I felt that the nuns' view of God was different from the one at home, it didn't surprise me, because their view of me was different too. At school I was one of the 'good girls' – a bit too quiet, according to the nuns, and worryingly pale and nervy, but a hard worker and useful for taking care of the shyer new pupils.

At home I was a problem. Five years after going to live with Uncle I still cried, screamed, rebelled, argued, and refused to sleep without the light on; according to my mother I had 'bad blood' in me, 'got the devil' in me or 'had a black dog sitting on my shoulder'; I was often unwell, felt constant nausea, and had fits of shaking and being sick at night; medical tests revealed no physical cause, and I was put on tranquillizers at the age of nine.

And in church I was different again, often bored with the

services but feeling that I was entitled to be there, part of the family of God with all its faults, all my faults, and all the disappointing aspects of a God who was faultless.

The local church was dingy, the priest impatient and the people mainly poor and devoid of much hope, but even in those surroundings there were occasional glimpses of a reality beyond anything I could imagine. It's hard to find words to describe it, but there were moments in that church when I felt the touch of God and had a sense of being part of something without boundaries.

There were other peaceful times as well – holidays at an aunt and uncle's house and visits from our cousins; a whole year in which an older cousin lived with us; long summer days spent playing endless 'pretend' games with my sister; parties; friends; trips to the park; coming home with a stack of new books from the library; 'holy days' celebrated in school time with processions and flowers and cakes which the nuns smilingly plied us with while eating none of the feast themselves.

But I'd like to say to anyone – child or adult – living in a situation where they're routinely abused or intimidated, that I know now what I never suspected then: that it isn't the will of God for that situation to continue. No matter what the rewards may be of staying in an abusive household – a 'lovely home', 'a quiet life', or 'security' – and no matter how many good points the abuser has or how valid the excuses for his or her behaviour, there can be no peace in a household where intimidation is allowed to occur and never gets dealt with.

It wasn't that God didn't care or wanted me to submit without making a fuss; it wasn't that he considered this a good training ground for my character; it wasn't even that he sent no one to help me. There were a number of occasions over the years when teachers at school or friends' parents asked me if everything was all right at home, because I looked so white and anxious, and I said yes, that things were all right, thanks. Perhaps if there had been one episode of stark cruelty in an otherwise normal family existence, it would have been easier to tell somebody, but the individual incidents seemed so minor that it was only the constantly repeated pattern of sarcasm, ridicule, invasion of privacy, intimidation and episodes of violence or molestation that added up to living in fear.

After a while, even the most bizarre situation begins to seem normal. It's hard, especially for a child, to stand back from an everyday situation and describe it by comparison with a normal family life that you haven't personally experienced. What could I say that could convey to a stranger the essence of our system of survival at home? And there was always that fear that if someone outside the family looked into the circumstances, they might conclude that it was deserved, that I was indeed an unpleasant child who needed to be disciplined with abuse and ridicule in order to be kept from 'getting above herself'.

The nuns offered to take me as a boarding pupil, and I thought seriously about it, till I found it was being regarded at home as a solution to my being so 'uncontrollable', and that the intention was to send me alone and keep my sister at home because she 'knew how to behave'. I couldn't separate the nuns' invitation, which had been kindly meant, from my mother's assessment that I was too much to cope with and my great-uncle's threats to send me away till everyone forgot about me. My sister was equally horrified at the idea of our being separated, and the offer was never taken up.

So it seems, looking back, that God was present not only in those rare moments when a breath of peace seemed to waft through from a wider world, but in more ordinary ways as well, and that he wasn't, as I believed as a child, a kind of super-adult who always took the side of adults. I began to suspect that he was behind the kind impulses that sometimes motivated people and that there might be another way of achieving peace – by bringing the turmoil out into the light and letting it show, not stifling it for the sake of a quiet life.

As Mark Anderson said, when God seems far away, is it that he is turning away from us, or are we turning away from him?

Did I refuse the help that was offered me because I sensed that the people weren't really willing to help and, if they'd known the situation, would have turned away, not wanting to get involved beyond expressing disapproval or offering vague sympathy? Or had I come to believe that I was too much to cope with, not only for my family but for anybody, and even perhaps for God?

Did I believe the extended family turned a blind eye, wanting to see my mother's situation as her uncle's housekeeper as ideal because it relieved them of responsibility for two difficult family members, the rich but grumpy old man who had to be humoured for the sake of the money he would leave in his will, and the penniless woman with two small kids to support?

Or was I being cynical and refusing to trust anyone because of my fear that all of it was my fault, that I shouldn't have been born and that, whatever I did with my life I could never redeem it from the sin of being here where I only caused trouble?

Did I really believe that God didn't want to know, or would only accept the version of some adult who was more qualified to speak to him? Or was I afraid that my own harsh perception of myself was also his, so that I never came near enough to his people to take the risk of finding out how he saw me?

Or was it safer, perhaps, to believe that it was my fault and that every furious silence or bitter attack was a punishment for some wickedness on my part, so that at least I had some hope that I could change it – that tomorrow I might learn to be better behaved and earn some respect and tenderness? Was that less frightening than believing I was trapped in a house with adults who released their tension and bitterness at random, triggered by no worse fault than that my presence irritated their raw nerves?

Forty years on, I feel I'm still only halfway to learning that the love that God offers, and that only Jesus really knows how to accept, comes without strings and is more valid and more real than any fears or sense of guilt.

4

·············

I'd like to introduce you to two women who faced up to their own fears and sense of guilt and found the courage to admit their difficulties and appeal to other people for help.

Bernadette is a young grandmother of nine children, who works full-time in a job that involves dealing with troubled people. She came face to face with Jesus as a reality when her life hit its lowest ebb and she felt there was no one who understood what she was going through.

Ann is single and in her early forties. For her, meeting Christ presented her with a very difficult choice; hers is a heartfelt account of the cost of being a disciple.

Bernadette

I saw God as someone to be feared: I was scared of him. When I was about fourteen I heard a sermon in church that scared the life out of me; we were told that we would go on living for ever and ever. From that moment, I stayed away from church. I was married in church because it was the thing to do, but I wasn't going to any of the services.

Through childhood, there was no love. My mother went to church, for whatever reason, but it was a bleak, dark, horrible childhood; everything seemed black.

From the age of two, there were beatings with a stick and later with a strap – the buckle end, and I could never understand what I'd done that was bad enough to deserve it.

My father moved out and my uncle moved in, and he beat me as well. My brother was never beaten. My father used to come and go; I was the result of one return visit, and he finally left home when I was three.

One day when she wasn't well, my mother cursed me in and out of hell, and to me that was it: that was where I was going to go. I was ten or eleven then. I wanted to get away from home. As my brother got older, he beat me too; he locked me in the coalshed and left me; he tried to smother me, many times, with a pillow – as a game. It's no wonder I'm claustrophobic.

My cousin, who was younger than me, could tell the time, so my mother would ask me what the time was and beat me if I didn't know. That's how I learned to tell the time. My childhood was a real isolated experience, completely alone. Nobody ever mentioned Jesus; it was just God – someone to be feared.

A few years ago, someone told me about that exercise where you imagine yourself as a child but you see Jesus there. When I tried it, I saw myself running into his arms, over and over again, like an action replay – and I knew he'd always been there, but I never knew it at the time.

During my first marriage, I lived overseas. My husband was having affairs, and by the law of the country we were in, if the woman stayed in the house, she was condoning her husband's behaviour. I went to a solicitor and was told I had to leave the marital home, so I decided to come back to England. The Department of Social Security insisted I start divorce proceedings or they wouldn't give me any money. I had three children by then and I'd been ill and had to have a hysterectomy after the third one. I was twenty-six.

When I came back to England with the children, we were staying with different people, lodging where we could, sleeping four to a bed, then someone told me I could go to the Council, and they found me somewhere to live.

I met my second husband and that marriage lasted eighteen months. He was so jealous that when I walked into a pub with him I had to keep my head down or I was accused of flirting. He got drunk and beat me. One time, he was pulling me up the stairs by my hair, and my son, aged nine, ran to the kitchen for a knife, to try and make him leave me alone.

I didn't know at the time, but my husband was also hitting my son, and he was getting into the girls' beds and even my mother's one time, when he was drunk. It was eighteen months of hell. Then he started an affair with someone at work, and the day just came that I said: 'Get out – I've had enough.' But I didn't find out till just recently what the children had gone through. After my husband left, I went into myself, lost a lot of weight and all my confidence. I made myself go out and get a job.

While my marriage was breaking up I'd gone to the doctor and told him what was going on, and he'd given me tranquillizers, and I carried on taking them. One day, I realized the tablets were actually causing the symptoms; they seemed to be making me panicky rather than keeping me calm, and I was like a zombie. I'd been on them six years. I tried to stop taking them, but all hell broke loose, and my boss's wife took me to the doctor – who put me on stronger tranquillizers.

I tried everything to come off them, including acupuncture, but I went into fits while I was having it. I felt terrible. I wanted to walk under a bus. One day I was sitting at home, so depressed I didn't know what to do. I rang my local church and asked to see a priest right now. The woman who answered the phone asked me if I wanted to see a young priest or an old one and I said I didn't mind, but it had to be now. The one who came was very young; it was his first posting in a parish. But he was the first person who ever believed me and accepted me for the person I was and the state I was in, and he offered to pray with me. I agreed – reluctantly.

He knelt down beside me in the living room, held my hands and started to pray, and I looked at his face and it changed, and I knew it was Jesus – I knew. But at the time I wondered what on earth was going on; it scared me as well. His features changed.

He said he was going to say a 'house Mass' – a Mass in someone's house – and he'd like me to come. I said I'd go, but that I didn't want him to come and pick me up for it – because I didn't want to go and I didn't intend to turn up. He also gave me the phone number of someone he wanted me to meet, a lady who prayed with people. I didn't feel so afraid of that, so I phoned her and made an appointment. Then she cancelled it because she wasn't well, and I found I was really disappointed, though I'd been scared about it, at the same time.

The priest did call for me, on the day of the house Mass. I was crying because I was so scared. I was suffering from agoraphobia as well, at the time, and it was hard just to go out of the front door, let alone into a room full of strange people. I said, 'Will you look after me?' and he said, 'Yes, I will,' and I said, 'Well, if I'm going to die I'm in good hands then.' I did feel as though I was going to die; I was so frightened.

At the Mass, I wanted to run away, but I didn't. I was in withdrawal from the drug and I didn't like doors and windows being shut; I needed an escape, wherever I was. But I managed to stay there somehow.

Then I made another appointment with this lady, to be prayed with. A friend took me there, to her house, and she prayed with me. I was shaking when I went in. My friend said he could smell the fear on me. I was absolutely terrified. Afterwards, he couldn't believe the change in me. I was calm; the fear had gone. The lady laid hands on me. She asked my friend to stay in the room with me but he said he didn't want to be involved. I didn't feel a big change, myself. I wanted my miracle there and then, but I still had the drug withdrawal to go through.

The woman left it to me to phone her if I wanted to go back, but I was scared even to get out of bed or go to the bathroom. One day, I was in bed and I just screamed at the Lord: 'I'm frightened!' – and immediately I heard him say, 'So was I.'

It was such a shock. I sat with my mouth open, and it dawned on me that Jesus was human, and he'd suffered, and what he'd suffered – that he'd gone through the same kind of suffering. I saw him as a human being, for the first time – someone I could relate to.

I started going to prayer meetings, where this priest and the lady who prayed with people went – though I was very nervous, especially if the door was closed. At first, I thought I was someone special, and I did go spouting off about the Lord Jesus and what he'd done for me. People did get tired of me and I was a big embarrassment to my family. I was just so thrilled that I'd been found – but I was jumping ahead of myself: I saw myself as different from other people. Then I came to see I wasn't: that we all have gifts, though maybe not the same ones.

I was with people who were praying and healing people, and I thought I could do it too. What I didn't realize was that I had an awful lot to learn. I thought I could heal anyone, but this lady said to me, 'It's quality, not quantity, Bernadette!' I thought I could pray with everyone; I didn't realize you had to sit back, listen to the Lord, see what he wanted you to do, what to pray for, and so on. I became caught up in the excitement of it all.

But it's like the Lord's a teacher: you have to be taught, and I wasn't waiting for the teaching, initially. I had to learn that I didn't know what a person needed; I assumed I knew, but I hadn't asked the Lord. Now I see him as a loving Father, someone who's with me all the time, who's promised never to leave me. Because I'm always rabbiting on to him about things, I have to remember that I need to listen to him as well.

Jesus has helped me with everything, even getting the job I'm in now. I'd been out of work for three years when I found this job; I wasn't young; it's full-time work and it involves a lot of responsibility, dealing with people who are often very upset and angry. But I'm not doing it on my own. I can call on him any time of the day for guidance in my job; I can go out to the car, at work, and have a cigarette and ask him for help, and he guides me. Everything takes time, though. It doesn't happen overnight. I expected healing to happen overnight, but it's ten years now since the priest first came to my house.

Ann

I was brought up Catholic, but by my early twenties I hadn't been going to Mass for some time. At about that time, though, I picked up the Bible and found the Psalms, and I thought they were good because they seemed to be about real people talking about their rebellion against God – but talking to him about it. I felt I was in rebellion against God, because I'd been living with a man for several years. I'd drifted away from God, as I'd drifted into the relationship, and I didn't know if there was a way back.

The line in the Psalms that meant most to me was about God being 'slow to anger, full of compassion and love, abiding in mercy'. Also during this time, my father was taken seriously ill, and I had some physical symptoms myself, and I got a lot of fear of dying. I wasn't sure what would happen to me if I died.

Through my teenage years, God was a person I heard about but didn't know personally, but there was a longing that I couldn't really place. I was at an all-girls' school and like everybody else I was thinking about boys, but I remember the head teacher saying once: 'We all need God. Some of you will marry, so you might be thinking what you need is a man, but you don't just need a man – you need God more.'

That sounded right to me, but till my early twenties, I didn't think about my spiritual needs. Even then, it wasn't easy to talk to my boyfriend, Peter, about my need for God. For him God was 'somebody that you have in your head to use as a reference, but you don't let him take over'. He didn't see a need to pray or go to church to worship him; you just got on with things the way you thought. He thought it was wrong to let God get in the way of our relationship; a relationship was between two people.

But as my dad's illness made me think more about God, I became more uneasy with the way I was living. Once, I thought of leaving but I didn't have the courage. I'd often wake up in the night feeling really uneasy, and I read that passage in the gospels about not worrying about tomorrow, or about what you would eat or what you would wear.

I went back to church and I was praying – saying set prayers – and also spending an hour or two sometimes just sitting in the church, which felt peaceful and safe.

But then I used to feel really angry; it often came out while I was doing the ironing! I thought about what it would be like to have the Holy Spirit in you so much that it would become natural to do things like helping people – so that it would be part of me, instinctive.

Then, when Peter and I and another couple were on holiday I had a dream, in which Jesus appeared. There was this terrific white light, and I felt this love coming from him. It was as though Love came up and gave me a big hug. I could feel it physically. And he said, 'This is how I want to love you, but first you have to leave the man beside you.'

I remember waking up and having no doubt it was Jesus. I felt relieved and calm and confident. I sat up in bed, in the dark, and thought, 'This is what I'm going to do.' In fact, it took me four years to leave.

Finally, I went to confession, but I didn't tell Peter till afterwards. I felt really peaceful for the first time in ages, and strong. There was no argument; he just said, 'You do realize what you're doing, don't you?' I knew that it might mean we'd split up; he'd warned me before that if we stopped sleeping together it would be the beginning of the end.

At Mass one Sunday, the reading was about Jesus going out looking for the lost sheep and leaving the other ninety-nine, and I knew it was me – I was only in that church because he'd reached out and come looking for me. I felt, 'Wow! He knows I exist; he knows where I am; he's done something in my life.'

My relationship with him grew in a private way; I was going to church but I didn't really get to know any of the people. I joined a Christian meditation group; I thought it might help me to be more open to God's will for me. Although I knew what he wanted, I didn't know how to go about it, or didn't feel strong enough to do it. I didn't think of just packing a suitcase and leaving.

I met people, through the meditation group, then started going to a prayer group, and the experience of forming other relationships gave me some security. It helped me to get enough strength to say to Peter that I wanted us to split up totally. It seemed God had been really patient with me, in preparing the way and changing me and my circumstances so I could do it.

A few days after my dad died, I had a real sense that he was around, and praying for me. All he'd ever wanted for me was to be happy and I'd always gone along with what friends thought or I thought would make me happy, but what I needed was peace of mind. When I had it, I realized how much energy it takes, not having peace of mind: how tiring it is.

From the time when I started searching for God till the time I moved out and lived on my own for the first time, it wasn't a straight path; I knew what I was going to have to give up. Although at first I thought the only problem was that I was sleeping with a man I wasn't married to, once we stopped I became aware there was more wrong than that: it was the relationship that wasn't right. It wasn't the kind of marriage I'd want; I wasn't in love with him.

It was hard to face that. We had been going to get married, at one time, but Peter became nervous and we didn't go ahead with it; I felt he had a fear of commitment. Looking back, though, I could see I'd drifted into the relationship: he'd moved into my rented flat when the girl from work I'd been sharing with moved out at short notice. I never gave myself time to sit down and think out the consequences. Then we bought a flat together, then a house; it just seemed to be the next stage.

Even once I knew I wasn't committed to sharing my life with Peter, there was a lot to lose by leaving; it wasn't easy. I wasn't in love with him but I did love him, I liked him, we had friends we both knew, we had a good standard of living, I felt like part of his family, there was the status of being a couple – and it was hard to close the door on a whole part of my life.

We were both getting older too, and I had to face the possibility that if I left I might never marry or have another relationship, and I did accept that that might be the cost of wanting God first. Peter said once, 'If we ever split up, I reckon we'd both be married within six months.' As it turned out, for him it was less than a year and now, ten years on, I'm living alone.

I'm in a new job but it's beginning to seem similar to the old one, and sometimes I don't think I've learned much in ten years, but the Lord has been leading me to look deeper within and at least I believe now that what I decide is important: that's a big change from wanting the Holy Spirit to do everything. It's no good praying, 'Do whatever you want, Lord'; I have to keep the dialogue going and ask what he does want, and look at what I want, even if I end up doing something different.

I do sometimes pray, 'Let your will be done': I did it when my dad was ill; I'd been praying every day for a year for him to get well, and one day I thought, 'I can't pray like this any more,' and I prayed for God's will for him to be done. But at other times that may be copping out; I may need to make a decision.

I pray for things that don't happen; I prayed for my mother to be healed and she wasn't either. Sometimes I think I understand – she was tired, missed Dad, she felt her life wasn't full enough – but maybe I won't really understand it all till I see God face to face.

All this has had an effect on the way I see Jesus. I used to feel he was very strong and judgmental: that he had black-and-white ideas about right and wrong, and that if you got it wrong, he didn't want to know. I thought he'd only love me if I got it right. Some of the prayers I was saying were a bit of an insurance policy; I thought God wouldn't be pleased if I didn't say them all.

After that experience in the church, that God had gone out looking for me, and finding how patient he was with me when I took years to split up with Peter, I saw that God was far more rounded than my idea of him.

As a child, I'd been afraid of walking on the cracks in the pavement, in case something awful happened to me, and that attitude stayed with me in regard to God. I wish I'd been more mature and realized God was different. Even when I wanted the Holy Spirit to be in me and guide me, it was because I thought that was the only way I'd get it right: if I was completely taken over.

When I had the dream, though, Jesus said I had to change the situation. I knew that he knew the struggle it would involve, and that he accepted me as I was: there was no condemnation. He was telling me what to do, out of love, like an elder brother might do, not like a judge.

Then it became clear to me that Jesus struggled, in his own way. I'd thought, in my younger years, it was different for Jesus because he was God – he was bound to do everything right! Later, I could see he had spent forty days praying and fasting and being with the Father, and that's why he got it right. It didn't strike me that way till I started praying myself, not as an insurance policy but to ask for God's help to do his will, to be myself, to do what was right – not in the black-and-white way, but the best thing – for other people, but for me too.

I saw that, although I'd done good things for people in the past, I couldn't do the best for them unless I was right with God. It had to start with him because on my own I could never love enough, or I might do a good thing for the wrong motives, or it would be done my way, not his way. The way to lead the most fruitful life was to let God be the centre of it, whatever it cost.

Sometimes it feels like all Jesus has ever done is take things away from me. I give up the polite prayers when I feel like that and get angry with him. Then, when I go off and do something else, a whole list of things he's done for me will come into my mind and I have to go back and thank him!

I get doubts at times and think, 'What if there's nothing, after we die – if we just disappear, like the Buddhists see it? What if Jesus didn't really rise from the dead, or even if he did, it doesn't mean we will?' It seems to lessen the value of human life and all creation. But then I think, 'If he's not going to be there, at the end of it all, why is he here now?' And I can't doubt that he is here now; I've met him, and I can't say he doesn't exist; it would be like saying anyone else doesn't exist, when I can see them standing in front of me.

And what he's given me in place of what I've lost is himself, a real relationship with him, and some really good close friends through whom I can experience his love and know him better. They love me without putting any conditions on it. In other friendships, there can be conditions: 'I'll be your friend if you share the same interests, or do this for me, or let me do this for you' – some kind of pay off. But the people I've met through Jesus – and our lives are too different to have crossed otherwise – want me to be myself, and they challenge me if I'm not being myself.

When I met them, God was still a hidden part of my life, but their faith and commitment to God was quite clearly lived out in their lives. For instance, one person seemed to have given up a lot of alternatives, like her career and freedom; she took the risk of doing whatever God wanted her to do every day, and I could see that was a risky thing; her house was filled with people and sometimes she didn't have any free time.

Another friend had this real enthusiasm for God that was infectious; I felt he really knew him; he talked about him with authority and it was reassuring to listen to. Another woman impressed me with her total focus on God; she had a busy life with a lot of family commitments, but if someone was in need, she'd drop everything and go. She took the risk of being seen as an irresponsible mother, but she believed if God wanted her to do something, he'd take care of everything else. I'd have been thinking, 'But what if this happens…?'

For the past few months now, I've felt Jesus calling me closer, and at times all I can do is go and pray – right now. What I'd like is to have more time, not to have to work so hard or to have so much on my mind, but he's with me and maybe all these changes are necessary. If I make time to pray in the morning, the day goes much better. I have to hand things over to him.

When I worry about my life, that's when I get resentful and feel Jesus only asks me to give things up – as though he's only there to hand things out – but when I manage to thank him, I can see how much he's doing for me. So I just have to keep my eyes on him.

5

. . . .

'The woman's hysterical; she's suffering from over-imagination' was the reaction of most of Jesus' disciples when Mary Magdalene came rushing from the cemetery to say she'd seen Jesus there – alive. When people are very upset, their perceptions can become distorted and their judgment impaired. We all know that. People with tormented pasts and tormented minds can hear voices, see visions of things that aren't really there at all, and dangerously misinterpret people's attitudes and actions towards them. What doesn't usually happen, when someone is hysterical and seriously distressed and sees or hears something not apparent to anyone else, is that what they see and hear renders them calm and able to cope with what they couldn't previously face.

There must have been something of that confident calmness in Mary Magdalene's voice, underneath the near-hysterical excitement, that made two of the disciples, Peter and John, suspect that something real had happened to her. It was these two who dropped everything and ran – the one who had been appointed founder of Jesus' church on earth, and the one who had managed to return, after running away when Jesus was taken prisoner, and stand at the foot of the cross while Jesus breathed his last breath.

And when they came to the grave and saw it open and empty, the seals broken and the massive stone rolled away, and went in and found the shrouds neatly folded, they knew she'd been speaking the truth.

They didn't have proof yet. It was going to be several days before they saw and spoke to Jesus for themselves. But something about the empty tomb reminded them of what he'd already told them, though they'd been too upset at the time to take it in: that after his death he was going to get up again; it wasn't going to be the end. Perhaps they'd thought he meant it metaphorically, some 'rising again' in an abstract spiritual form. Or more likely they just didn't register what he'd said at all; they'd heard him say he was going to allow himself to be put to death, and their minds shut off. There's something about the word 'death' that sounds horribly final.

If you're looking for truth, and really don't want to be deceived by a lot of stories or theories, however comforting, then there comes a time when you see something or hear about something, or somebody says some very ordinary sounding sentence, and your heart leaps, because this has the ring of truth. It might mean little or nothing to another person who sees or hears the same thing, and it might have meant nothing to you if you'd heard it at another time, but at this very moment you know this is significant for you and if you dismiss it you're not being true to yourself.

It wasn't the moment for those other disciples, locked in an upper room afraid to go out and almost afraid to breathe, so they dismissed what Mary said. And it wasn't the moment for the two who decided to leave the city where good men were crucified and to walk home to their own village, full of despair and bewilderment.

For them, the moment didn't come till they were halfway home and met a man on the road who asked them what they were so depressed about – a man whose face they never even looked at till they reached home and sat down to eat and he broke the bread in the same way Jesus used to, and then disappeared as suddenly as he'd arrived beside them on the road.

And it wasn't, for another week or so, the moment for Thomas, who heard all these separate accounts and, although they came from people he knew well, concluded that everyone was suffering from wishful thinking – till Jesus stood in front of him, though he'd firmly locked all the doors, and showed him the proof he'd demanded – the unhealed gashes in both hands, both feet and his side.

It seems that God is patient and reveals himself in his own time – in our own time, when we're ready to believe what we've made up our minds no one will convince us of until we see or hear or just know in our hearts for ourselves. But the patience costs him, and costs our fellow human beings.

Did Jesus' wounds have to stay open and sore just for Thomas? The Father who raised him from the dead could surely have healed them at the same time. Did Bernadette's friend who 'didn't want to be involved' in her chosen way of healing from her addiction lay an extra weight on her shoulders – one more 'don't want to know' in addition to all the others?

Does the member of a Christian congregation who attends the services but goes on leading an untruthful relationship at home, or being violent with his children, or fiddling her social security claim, drag down the spirits of the rest of the people, making it more difficult for them to pray and keep faith and keep loving? It's possible. It's acceptable. And it's worth it. Because Christ came for sinners and not for the virtuous. And anyone who follows him must do the same.

Simon Johnson was a man who got on with his work, whether or not he felt like it, who supported his family, did overtime when money was short, and went home at the end of the day feeling he hadn't shirked, hadn't cheated anyone, and owed nothing to anybody – not even God.

Then, at the end of a particularly long and wearying night shift, where nothing had gone right and there was nothing to show for all that work, when he was so cold and so hungry that he'd almost gone past wanting the breakfast he'd been dreaming about for the past four hours – almost, but not quite – along comes this man and asks to borrow his boat for a moment: Simon is part of the local fishing fleet, self-employed.

He agrees – because he's too tired to think, but then it's too late to back down. So he makes a start on checking and folding his nets up after all; he was going to leave it till later when he'd be less tired – not that he ever is less tired, these days.

And what does this bloke do but loosen the rope, push the boat away from its mooring and jump into it, and start holding some political meeting or something, using the boat as a platform, addressing a shabby huddle of no-hopers who've gathered round to hear him talk about what a blessing it is to be poor and miserable and how you're better off than the fat cats who've made life comfortable for themselves.

Simon has finished the nets by now, is exhausted, pissed off, starving, cold, lonely, bored to tears, and extremely, extremely angry with himself for letting this conman walk all over him. He tries to catch his eye, to signal, 'Time's up, mate; bring back my boat,' but the man isn't looking in his direction. Simon's not really one for praying, but by this time he's praying this bloke trips over his own verbosity and falls backwards into the water and drowns himself.

Finally Simon's had enough; he wades into the water, catches hold of the rope and begins to drag the boat back to the jetty – roughly, in the hope that the man will lose his balance.

'No,' says the man. 'Get in.' And he seizes Simon by the hand, unexpectedly firmly for someone who can't weigh much more than ten stone, and pulls him into the boat with him. 'Now,' he says, 'head out for the patch of deep water beyond the headland and you'll catch something.'

Now, Simon doesn't know who this guy is but one thing he does know – whatever he's supposed to be a leader of or an expert on, he's no expert on making money. He's dressed in clothes that are not only shabby, old, and frankly grubby, but look as though he's slept in them for a week, and judging by his gaunt face and skinny body he hasn't had a square meal for longer than that.

So by this time, this honest hardworking family man's patience has worn threadbare-thin, and he doesn't care if it shows. Johnson's normally polite to everyone, and this bloke is clearly both short of a few brain cells and seriously short of cash, but now he's had enough. So he says, 'Look mate, this is my patch; I've been fishing it dry all night and I'm telling you there's nothing out there worth catching.'

'Give it a try,' the man says. And he hands him – hands Simon, who's been rowing against the wind since yesterday evening, and it's now 9 a.m. – the oars.

What would you do? Or what would you say to a man like that? Well, Simon does and says all of that – in his mind. But his hands somehow take the oars and he starts rowing. Now he doesn't just want the man to drown, he wants to prove him wrong – then drown him.

And there, where the man said, in the patch of deep water not far out from the headland, a place that Simon knows like the back of his hand and covered, back and forth, countless times last night – is a sight that, to Simon, is all the Promised Land he needs right now. The dark smooth surface of the water is stirred up like a bubbling pot, jumping with fish – a good shoal he can get more than his usual price for.

There are so many fish that as he drags in the net he's afraid it'll rip or even that the boat may sink, so he roars across the water to his brother-in-law and his partner who are heading for the harbour in their boat, as grumpy and sleepy as Simon was himself after the long fruitless night when the fish wouldn't bite, and they come over, thinking he's sprung a leak in that creaking old boat of his.

But when they see the size of the shoal and the size of the fish, they can't believe their eyes.

The three men forget that life has dealt them a lousy hand and that they deserve a night's rest; they forget that they work too hard, earn too little and owe nothing to anyone, and they entirely understand when Simon, that down-to-earth and undemonstrative man, drops down on his knees in the boat, hugs the stranger's bony legs, and says, 'Don't have anything to do with me, sir. I've been cursing you black and blue, and look what you've done. Just go and forget you met me.'

He's afraid, you see: if this man was intuitive enough to know the deep unspoken anxiety in Simon's heart, arriving home with no catch, then he's probably also picked up Simon's curses for nicking his boat, and his prayer for him to drown. And if he knows that, who's to say he won't know all the other things Simon's done and said and felt in his life? All of a sudden, this hardworking family man doesn't feel he's such a good bloke after all – not in the presence of this one. And the man says – what?

'Don't worry. From now on, you won't be going out after shoals of fish. From now on, you're going to be fishing people out of the depths of despair, people who've lost their soul and don't know the way home any more.'

It was Simon, and people like him – people like Thomas and Mark and Bernadette and Ann, with all their faith and all their doubts and cynicism and fears and resentments – that Jesus chose to go on representing him when he moved on. Not people of perfect faith and virtue but people who say, 'Don't pick me, Lord; I might look all right on the surface and do some good things, but it's not always for the right reasons and my heart usually isn't in it; all I really want is an easy life with no one rocking the boat and I'm not prepared to believe in you or anyone else, however good or well-meaning, until you give me – me personally – definite proof that really means something to me.'

The trouble is, he does pick people who feel God is picking on them if he asks anything. He doesn't always pick the ones who stand at the front of the crowd going, 'Choose me, Lord; my life is yours!' – and I don't know why that is. His ways are very far from being our ways, as he said himself. In our terms, God often seems to do things back to front, upside down and inside out.

After all, it is quite logical to say, 'I can only believe what I understand. So prove it, explain it to me, then I might be able to believe in you.'

But God says, 'Believe. Then the understanding will come – gradually. If you don't believe, you'll think you understand, but you never will.'

And he also says, 'Ask for what you want in prayer, and you'll be given it.' But many people who spend hours or years on their knees praying for something fervently get no results, while the unspoken desire of somebody's inmost heart is often met by God when they haven't dared ask for it or even acknowledged to themselves that it is what they really want. Some prayers are answered like clockwork; some seem to be put in the pending file for eternity and no results ever show – or none that we can see.

Let's go back, for some examples of answered prayer, to childhood, because our view of God starts there, and stays there until it grows up.

As a child of seven or eight, my major desire was for a hula hoop. There was a craze for them at school; the playground was full of little girls whirling coloured plastic hoops round their waists like frantic belly dancers. They were getting more skilful every day while I waited in vain for money to be spared at home to buy one. So I prayed. I was specific and concise: 'Dear Lord, please leave a hula hoop – a red one if you've got it – under my bed in the morning. Thank you. Goodnight.'

My mother was surprised, when she woke me the next morning, that I leapt up immediately and looked under the bed.

'It's not there,' I said.

'What's not?'

'My hula hoop. I asked God to leave it for me.'

She sat down and explained. It was a good thing to ask for, she said – fun, reasonable, not too expensive. She wanted me to have one, but she couldn't afford it just now. God wanted me to have it too. But sometimes he used ordinary ways to provide things, so other people would be involved in his work of looking after his children. Would I be willing to wait till my birthday, because my aunt might like to be involved in God's work and would probably be happy to give me something she knew I wanted so much and for so long?

I was willing: a red hula hoop arrived a month or so later on my birthday, the prayer was answered and I felt I'd learned something new about how God operated.

The next prayer was not so straightforward. I was ten, in the final year of primary school, and my mother was working in the upper school, in the office. She came home one afternoon and said the head teacher had just heard that her mother had died; she asked my sister and me to pray, in our night prayers, for the mother's soul and for the head teacher's sadness.

I was dropping off to sleep that night when I remembered, and it suddenly seemed important. So I prayed for the mother to go to heaven and the daughter not to feel too sad, and followed it up by reciting every prayer I'd ever learned, one after the other.

Then I felt anxious. I didn't know all that many prayers; were these enough? As soon as I wondered that, I saw in my mind's eye two women standing side by side – the head teacher of the 'big school' and an older woman who looked quite like her – and I felt a definite presence in the room, as though they were actually there. They were both nodding and smiling at me, and I felt reassured – yes, it was enough – and fell asleep immediately.

In the morning, I told my mother I'd prayed for the head

teacher's mother and she was in heaven now. My mother frowned and said, 'You can't know that; only God knows who's in heaven and who isn't.' But I'd had the sense of a definite, affirmative answer to prayer, and I didn't have any doubt about the result.

The next time was more dramatic, and had a lasting impact on my faith. Like Simon, silently troubled about going home from a night's work with nothing to show for it, this prayer was more of a deep personal worry than a prayer, and the fact that it was answered so promptly stunned me.

My grandfather died on my tenth birthday, and shortly afterwards the glands in my neck swelled up so badly I couldn't move my head. The doctor felt it was probably a reaction to grief, but when it persisted for a couple of months, I was sent to hospital for routine tests. Nothing was found to be wrong, the symptoms eased, and I was home again within a week.

Three other children were in the ward with me, a five-year-old boy who'd been knocked down by a car, a seven-year-old girl and an eight-year-old boy, both having their tonsils out. The girl, Jeanette, lived a couple of streets away from me, but we didn't know each other, and as there was a three-year age gap and we went to different schools and had different interests and personalities, we didn't expect to meet again after we were both discharged from hospital.

A couple of months later, on our usual Saturday visit to the public library (my sister and I had to be out of the house while Uncle had his afternoon rest) the librarian was telling someone there had been a local tragedy. A seven-year-old girl had been knocked down and killed in a neighbouring street – the one Jeanette lived in. Noticing my horror, the librarian asked if it was someone I thought I knew, and I asked the name of the girl, but she didn't know. I could hear myself thinking, 'Please don't let it be her,' but I didn't consciously say it to God; afterwards I thought, 'But I didn't even pray! He just knew.'

Two days later we were shopping and my mother exclaimed, 'Oh, look who it is,' as a woman I didn't know waved at her from across the road. My mother had met her at the hospital; it was Jeanette's grandmother. I didn't dare ask her, but the woman looked cheerful enough, and eventually my mother asked whether the little girl had completely recovered from her operation. 'You can ask her yourself,' said the grandmother. 'Here she is now.'

And there she was, coming out of a shop with her mother, in a fretful mood and not at all interested in seeing some girl she'd met briefly some months ago in a hospital ward. I was so happy and relieved that she was all right that I didn't care. I couldn't find a word to say to her either and my mother said afterwards, 'You weren't very friendly!' I was awed by the timing of the meeting – I'd never met her before and never saw her again. I really felt God had arranged it; he'd known how worried I was, and took my concern seriously. He – God, who created the universe – cared about the feelings of one ten-year-old girl. Like Simon, I could have fallen to my knees in the street and cried, 'Don't come so close to me! I haven't deserved such special attention.' But, thank God, there are some requests that he doesn't listen to, and he did come close to me and planned to come closer still as I grew older.

6
....

It used to seem strange to me, at school, that a class of children all being taught the same thing could react so differently. For some, what we learned about Jesus and the way he showed everyone to live had a big impact, while for others it had no staying power at all.

I wondered if it depended on the attitude at home. While forty per cent of the children at my convent school were from nominally Catholic homes, most were non-practising, and the other sixty per cent came from non-religious backgrounds or from other denominations of Christianity or occasionally from other religions, but chiefly with parents who were non-practising.

There were a number of reasons why parents chose to send their children to a religious school, but the most usual reasons were to do with education, behaviour, discipline, the ethos of the school, and the atmosphere, which was generally gentler than the alternative choices of school in that area. Probably only a small proportion of parents were motivated by the desire for their child to be trained as a fully committed follower of Christ – in fact, some of them actively opposed it and were anxious for their daughters not to be influenced by Catholic Christianity.

I wondered, then, if each child received its religious teaching at school through a filter of implicit parental instructions: 'Listen carefully to this; it's what we sent you to this school to learn,' or alternatively, 'Ignore what the teachers tell you in religious instruction and concentrate on the important subjects.'

One of my close friends, for instance, got good results in most subjects and was exceptional at retaining facts that the rest of us had forgotten, but we could all emerge from an RE class discussing what had been taught, and she'd have no recollection of it; it seemed to have washed over her, leaving her untouched. Her father was a scientist who believed that human skill and intellect would eventually unravel every mystery, and anything that couldn't be proved by physical testing didn't exist or at least was irrelevant to human existence. Her mother believed that living a good life was important, but that it wasn't healthy to be too committed and if religious belief diverted someone from the pattern of life accepted as normal in their society, then the person had become unbalanced. They encouraged their daughter to work hard at academic subjects, and while they never actually discouraged her from taking notice of what she was taught about God at school – as some parents did – they didn't give RE the same emphasis.

My mother, on the other hand, whose parents were nominally Anglican but rarely went to church or talked about God, had converted to Catholicism at the age of twenty-one and felt she hadn't received enough instruction, so she would tell my sister and me to listen carefully to what we were taught in the RE classes so we could come home and tell her!

So obviously there would be a difference, you would expect, between the way I heard what we were taught and the way my friend heard.

But this could hardly account for all the difference, because some children from very devout families were quite disinterested, and some from non-religious families were totally absorbed by God and naturally attracted to the Church – as my mother had been in her own youth. More than that, one child in a family could be deeply religious while a brother or sister from the same family would claim that the same upbringing had 'put them off religion for life'.

It seemed to me, after a time, that each child's relationship with God had some element in it that was independent of all the influences of school and parents and experience, and was unique to that individual child. To some children, prayer seemed to come naturally and to others it did not. And among those who prayed, some had great faith in its power and some didn't expect much result.

I asked two young sisters, Krystal aged twelve and Jessica aged eight, to tell me about their relationship with Jesus Christ. They have been raised in a family where they are not taken to church unless they want to go, but where both parents believe strongly in God and, as the children know, have prayed their way through a number of crises and feel confident that God takes care of their needs – though sometimes only at the eleventh hour! One thing that affected the children personally was that, nearly a year ago, their grandfather died and they were very upset by his loss. But I'll let them tell it their own way.

Krystal

In my second year at school, I started learning about Jesus: about miracles and that. Then when my grandfather died, I was upset, and Jesus was there with me. I was really upset at school, because my teacher didn't like me. He used to make jokes about my weight, and once he closed the door on me and pretended he didn't see me. One time, he asked us to repeat something after him, and when we were doing it, he picked me out and said, 'Krystal, if I need a parrot I'll buy one, even though I can't afford to feed one the size of you.'

I was crying and I had an asthma attack, so I prayed for him to leave me alone. Then I went to the head teacher, and Mum and Dad sorted it out, and he left me alone then. I was happy because Jesus answered my prayer.

Jesus is a kind, loving, caring person who has time for everyone. He cured a sick child once; they thought she was dead but she was just sleeping and he cured her; that showed me that he cares.

I talk to him. I get the feeling sometimes he's telling me what to do, but I don't know if it's just me, if it's what I want to hear. I was praying that my dad would get the new job and I could hear Jesus saying, 'Yes, he'll get the job.' But we haven't heard yet, so I'll just have to wait and see if that was him or not.

The other week, I was wearing my grandmother's ring and I forgot to take it off when I went to school and I lost it, and I was looking everywhere. Then when I was praying to find it, I could hear Jesus saying, 'Don't worry, Krystal; you'll find it,' and the next day I did.

Jessica

I knew there was a person called Jesus, but I didn't really understand, till I started reading this Children's Bible. But when Mum first told me what Christmas Day was, I knew Jesus was a real person and not a story. And one day I was praying for my grandad to be okay, after he died, and Jesus told me he was all right. Another time, I was looking in the mirror and thinking about something – I forget what – and I thought I heard a voice saying something but I thought, 'Oh, that's just me.'

When I'm in church I can't pray like I do at home. When I'm at home I say things to Jesus, like, 'How is my grandad in heaven?' And I pray that my nan's all right, and about my auntie who fell down in the garden and nobody came to help, and about my dad getting the new job. If I'm worried about somebody, I'll say to Jesus, 'How is he, can you tell me?' and Jesus says, 'He'll be fine.'

I like Jesus because he's really nice and cares for you a lot – a lot – and he loves me; he's the most important person in the world and I love him and he's really nice to me, and when my dad was in Ireland and I was worried he was in a plane crash, he told me my dad was all right. I love Jesus the best in the world.

I know he's real because he talks to me, and I don't talk to myself! I know it's his voice because I'm always hearing it; he helps me pray, and when I did something bad once, he said, 'I forgive you and I love you.' He tells me when not to do something again, and he helps me do the things I fail at, like some of my spellings.

Many of us have faith in God, in childhood, but as we grow up the child's way of believing either has to grow into an adult faith or else we discard it and look round for another set of beliefs to replace it. There's no shortage of philosophies, and we may not be aware of what influences us. Some of the teachings of parents and teachers stay with us while others are rejected as superficial or naïve, and to that remnant we add impressions from our own experiences, but we're also affected by anything we see or hear that we accept without considering the alternatives.

There's an ongoing public debate about how much the media influences us, but no company would be spending such huge chunks of its budget on advertising and PR if we were really resistant to persuasion that their products will help fulfil our desires. Children's fantasies and games are based on the TV programmes and videos they watch and the books they read, as well as on what they see people doing and hear them saying, on their own thoughts and experiences, and on the imaginative reconstruction they place on all those events, and it seems reasonable to believe that our adult perception of reality derives from similar influences.

How do we separate what is real truth and will never change, from our own ideas based on personal experience, which seem true to us at the time but which we may, with hindsight, later change?

How do we know for sure we've made up our own minds and not been, to some extent, manipulated towards a certain slant of opinion which makes it difficult for us to view the issue from any other angle?

For instance, in my first term at university a lot of my fellow students found it hard to accept that someone of our age should be a practising Catholic. 'You've been brainwashed,' they said, when I argued against accepting some compromise: whether it was 'white lies', abortion, contraception or the right to suicide.

'How do you know you haven't been?' I countered, when they argued that the world's poverty problem could be solved by population control, or that aborting a developing embryo saved a child from being unwanted.

The truth was, we were not going to know how much those opinions were what we really believed and to what extent they'd been imposed on us from outside until, at the end of the three years at university, we made the choices that would govern our future lives. Then we would know how deeply we were really touched by certain issues and how committed to finding solutions to some of the problems we claimed to be concerned about at least in our own part of the world.

This was the acid test of truth: after three years of studying, formulating ambitions, making friendships in which we let ourselves be affected by one another and influenced by each other's ways of seeing the world, we would each make a decision about the relative importance of others' needs and the fulfilment of our own life's ambitions, and we would have to decide how much we were prepared to invest in our ideals, in terms of personal inconvenience and sacrifice.

If our ideas had been received from outside – from the media or the Church or political organizations, or wherever else – but hadn't really become our own belief, backed by our own commitment, then all our late-night discussions about life, the universe and what makes people tick would be simply a student hobby, and on graduating we would fit neatly into the place in the social system that offered itself to us, and dedicate ourselves to getting the best out of life that we could manage. If our values and opinions were our own, we would put our lives behind them. Only then would we know what we believed in.

I remember reading that if someone says, 'I don't know what I think about this,' watch what they do, and you'll know what they think.

Therefore, if someone says they believe in Jesus Christ as God's son, sent to show us who God is and to stay with us, day by day until the end of time, to fulfil the same purpose, their life must in some way bear out that belief. They must, as Jesus said, 'only do what they see the Father doing'. And what each person does with their life will reflect the way they see God and what they 'see the Father doing'.

So what do I believe God does? Sits with his arms folded while the world goes to ruin? Then I'll do the same. Or if I'm the kind of person who thunders about injustice, calls for the castration of rapists, the hanging of psychopaths and the ostracism of AIDS victims and breathes hellfire and condemnation for anyone who strays from the right path, you'll know my view of God is as that kind of tyrant.

Do I see God as a scapegoat, taking the blame, saying nothing and doing nothing to disprove the accusations against his integrity? Or as a warrior for social justice, blazing with anger about people's rights and wrongs, and frightening the more timid souls with his raging? What I see him doing is what I do.

Then, do I need Jesus Christ, the 'son of man', the 'real human being', to show me what to do? What's so wrong with finding my own way to God, who is Father of us all, whether Muslim or Hindu or atheist or humanist or Jew?

It's a question each person will find their own answer to. My belief is that one lifetime is all we get, in earthly form, and that's very little time to form all our own theories and make all our own mistakes, without reference to someone who did it all before us and had all the signs of God's approval.

If John the Baptist's witness was true and the Holy Spirit of God did indeed come down and rest on Jesus Christ, then not only was Jesus doing what he saw the Father do, but the Father, God himself, saw himself in what Jesus was doing. My test of how well I'm seeing what the Father does and intends me to do is how well I'm resembling the one his spirit came to rest on.

Not that Jesus becomes my role model – no, because a role model like that would be of no more use to me than the Ten Commandments have been, or all the wise teachings of any religious leader or prophet. All any of them do is remind me I'm inadequate and can't live up to those standards.

No, what Jesus has to do, to be of any help to me, is not to tell me or show me what to do – I know that – but to give me the ability to actually do it. If I can't earn enough to keep myself alive, then it's no use giving me a cheque-book; it's not going to help. But if you've earned enough to accumulate yourself a large fortune, then it's great if you give me a cheque-book – to your account. That's what Jesus does for me – gives me permission to enlist his help, draw on his resources and use the benefits of the knowledge, goodness, patience and resistance to malice that he accumulated during his lifetime. It's mine. For the asking. Now ask me to keep God's commandments and I might stand a chance!

What interferes with my childhood faith, either destroying it or preserving it in ice, preventing it from maturing? Jesus suggested some possibilities: the cares of the world, anxieties, physical desires and material riches – all of them, in their way, 'possessions' – not just things that I possess or my mind possesses but things that can potentially possess me, discourage my soul, weaken my conscience and harden my heart.

In my first year of senior school, as it was called then, a child was seriously injured in the playground. I wasn't there to see it happen, but several children told me about it, upset by the accident but excited to be the one who broke the news to a first-time hearer. They were disgusted by my lack of reaction, perhaps for mixed reasons, but something one of the children said did affect me. 'You're hard,' she said.

I felt distressed because there was an element of truth in it. So, the child who'd had the accident wasn't personally known to me. So, the child who brought the news was brimming with the desire to shock and impress. But still, a child in my own school was in hospital, upset and frightened and possibly permanently affected by the injury, and I felt nothing.

I'd pretended, at home, to have a hard shell around me, to show everyone that I couldn't be moulded and improved by being scolded or ridiculed. It was an act, because inside the shell somebody was crying. But by accepting the shell, even as a pretence, had I unknowingly given it a place in my life and adopted it as part of my personality?

I prayed that God wouldn't let me be hard, then, because becoming a hard person seemed more damaging than being a hurt one. I hadn't yet learned that God didn't want me to be a victim either, but an early lesson to that effect had come when I was nine.

Every summer Uncle took us away on holiday to the seaside. Rules were relaxed and though my mother was more nervous about upsetting him than in our normal routine at home, when he was at work all day and we could be sent to bed before he came back, it was generally a time for enjoyment.

I was a reluctant eater, cajoled at home and punished at school to finish what was on the plate, but on holiday my mother allowed us to eat only what we wanted. A woman staying at the same guesthouse seemed to take exception to this. Whether my mother had upset her by boasting about my prowess at school, I don't know, but this woman caught hold of me in the sitting room while I was playing with her daughter, and said, 'I've been watching you. You're a naughty little girl who doesn't eat her food.' I explained that my mother had said we didn't have to while we were on holiday, but she turned away and said to another mother, 'I can't stand a *knowing* child, can you?'

Holidays came and went, the same dates, the same place, and this woman and her family were always there. My mother didn't like her, but we children played together on the beach and Uncle liked the company of her husband. One year, my mother even persuaded Uncle to change the date of the holiday, but the woman wrote to her and asked when we were going, to make sure they booked at the same time, and my mother said, 'We're not going to be able to avoid her; we'll just have to put up with it.'

After that, the couple decided to make their permanent home at the resort, and the woman wrote to my mother every year, to be sure we arranged to meet at holiday time. My mother suggested another resort one year, just for a change, but Uncle took offence, saw it as a criticism of his choice and went ahead with the usual plans. Then one Easter, a letter arrived to say that the husband had died. My mother was full of pity for the widowed wife, and wrote back immediately. When holiday time came, instead of trying to avoid her, she said almost as soon as we'd arrived, 'We must go and see her.'

As usual, the woman and her daughter joined us every day on the beach. The woman was quieter ('Not so horrible,' my sister and I said secretly) and the little girl seemed much the same, chatty and lively, though slightly subdued around her mother. I had the feeling she was a bit afraid.

We children were going for a walk one day, and the woman said she'd come with us. We were quiet at first, as she walked along beside us, silent and withdrawn, but after a while we walked ahead together and started the usual chatting and laughter. I glanced over my shoulder a couple of times, and saw that the noise didn't seem to be bothering her; in fact, her face had brightened and she even laughed once or twice and said, 'You lot are silly!'

Encouraged by that, we raised our voices, jumped around and outdid each other in silliness. We ended up playing spooks, waving our arms and shouting, 'Whooo!' in would-be scary voices. 'I'm a ghost!' shouted my sister. I went one better. 'I'm a skeleton!' The others laughed, so we all became skeletons, teetering along the clifftop path.

'What is a skeleton?' asked the little girl.

I explained it as best I could.

'How long before a person becomes a skeleton?' she asked next.

I shrugged. 'Don't know. Couple of months?'

'And before that, what are they?'

'Don't know,' I said. 'A corpse, I suppose.'

There was a screech from behind us and the woman pounced on me, clutching me by the shoulders, swinging me round and screaming into my face: 'You stupid, stupid child!'

We all jumped; we'd forgotten she was there and that this wasn't a private conversation.

'My little girl's daddy has just died!' she screamed. 'And you're filling her mind with your stupid, stupid ideas! They say you're clever at school? You haven't a brain in your head! You're mental, that's what you are! Stupid, stupid child!'

I was used to rage, but there was something else in her eyes that was more horrifying. I felt I was looking over the jagged edge of a deep dark pit. I had never before seen despair. My mouth had gone dry and my heart pounded.

'I didn't think,' I said.

She gripped my shoulders even harder and spat, 'Didn't think? You can't think! You're not capable of thinking! You stupid, evil child!'

She let go, and went on walking. Stunned, we all walked along – separately. No one spoke. All I could hear was a voice in my head, 'My God, what have I done to her?' Finally, we saw the beach hut ahead, with my mother and Uncle sitting outside. I broke into a run and began to cry at the same time.

'Oh, go on,' said the woman bitterly. 'Run to Mummy!'

And run to Mummy I did, screaming my head off. My mother jumped up, horrified. 'What on earth's happened?'

'Skeletons,' I screamed. 'I didn't think!'

My mother hugged me. 'Calm down,' she said. 'I can't make out what you're saying.'

I thought Uncle would stay uncommitted, apart from expecting my mother to make the noise stop as soon as possible, but he was concerned. 'It's that woman,' he said. 'What's she done to upset the child like this?'

'It was me!' I roared. 'I didn't think!'

'We'll sort it out with her,' said my mother, but I could see the woman coming down the beach and screamed with real terror as she came nearer, so my mother said to Uncle, 'I'll take her back to the guesthouse.'

He nodded. 'Blasted woman,' he said.

I was comforted by his reaction. My mother took me for a walk till I calmed down enough to explain what had happened.

'It was my fault,' I said. 'I forgot about her husband. She said he'd only just died, but I thought it was ages ago.'

'It was ages ago,' said my mother, 'to a child. But for her it doesn't seem long at all, because she's so sad about it.'

'I made her worse,' I said.

'You weren't to know. Children joke about. She took it all wrong, that's all, because she's upset. But she shouldn't have taken it out on a child. Do you want to go back to the guesthouse by yourself and we'll see you later?'

'Is she going to be on the beach later as well?'

'I expect so, yes.'

'And for the rest of the holiday?'

'Yes.'

I decided, if I had to face her sooner or later, it might as well be now, so I went back to the beach with my mother. The other children, playing very quietly now, moved over when I arrived and silently included me in their game. Uncle smiled at me. The woman ignored me for the rest of the holiday. The next summer,

Uncle retired and we never went on holiday again. I still can't look at the photos of that time, of happy children playing on the beach, watched over by smiling adults, without remembering that scarlet, spitting face screaming into mine.

Thinking about the incident, even years later, made me cringe. But as well as the fear and guilt and shame came a memory of the reassurance as well. I prayed I would never hurt somebody like that again, but I also felt my responsibility was limited, and that even someone whose feelings are sore has a choice of how to respond – to make allowances for the offender's apparent hard-heartedness or to become hard yourself and inflict pain in return.

Later on, I'd like you to meet Paul, who became hardened to belief in Christ and experienced Jesus intervening personally to deal with that hardness – gently. But first, I'd like to introduce someone who feels he hasn't met Jesus, even though he's committed himself to overcoming hard-heartedness, has invested a lot of his time in learning about who Jesus is, and has sacrificed a close relationship in order to follow Jesus' way of life.

Dean is forty-six, has a full-time career in interior design, and for the last fourteen years has been a member of a movement within the Catholic Church called the neo-catechumenate way – local parish-based groups which aim to reproduce the pattern of life adopted by the earliest Christians. Membership involves sharing time together for eucharists, prayer meetings and retreats, sharing talents – letting them be used as a resource for the group – and being of service to the parish.

Dean is firmly committed to doing what's right, has a clear awareness of his own needs and weaknesses, and has made some difficult changes to his way of life. Yet in all honesty he believes he hasn't really met the person he's following, Jesus Christ.

7

....

Dean

I come from the outskirts of the Catholic Church. My belief was very naïve. I had a notion about God, no real idea of Jesus Christ, and my attitude was to ask God for things: that was my prayer. I wasn't looking for Jesus Christ; I was looking for something but I don't know what.

I had this instinctive need and guilt and I was trying to live as a perfect person with perfect morals but none of my friends were trying to live as Christians and it was really hard.

When I was at college I'd read an article on homosexuality and from then I became more and more aware that's what I was, but I believed that my sexuality wasn't compatible with being a Christian and although I was still going to church I was on the point of giving up. I'd joined an 18–30s group at the church but it was just about being sociable and doing things in a group; I don't like groups and it seemed too much of an effort.

At the same time, I was having problems at work: my boss was being unjust and accusing and I wasn't assertive enough to cope with it. Then I saw this poster in the church: it said, 'Do you hate someone?' That struck me as a very unreligious thing to say! There was a date for a meeting, which I thought would be just a one-off talk. If I'd known it was about joining a community I'd have run a mile. But I went along, because I did hate my boss at that time.

The very first thing the people who spoke at this meeting said was, 'The reason why you're suffering is that you need to love and to be loved, and you can't. There's a wall that's been built up because someone has hurt you. The only person who can break down this barrier to love is Jesus Christ.'

As soon as they said that, I started to listen. That was my first encounter with Jesus Christ, as a name; I had only talked to God. I'd always tried to put things right by my own effort but they said all my struggling to be perfect was making me suffer and I couldn't do it on my own and God loved me as I was – a sinner.

They talked about Jesus as a bridge between God and us – the one who came for sinners, not for the virtuous; the one who would take on all this sin that I carried around with me. It was a relief to be told that, because if God loved me as a sinner, there was no need for me to judge anyone else, like the boss – I could accept other people, faults and all. I used to expect perfection from other people as well as from myself, and I thought God did.

We were told that the opposite of love isn't hate but fear, and fear comes because we're expecting to be punished. I expected punishment for homosexuality, and also for making mistakes; if someone was angry with me I immediately assumed I was doing something wrong. But the antidote is love; it frees you from the fear.

If I let Jesus Christ be involved in my relationships I was able to accept people as other sinners loved by God as well, because this Jesus Christ would accept people as they were – and all my friends were, and most still are, total unbelievers. I talked to them about it a lot: I must have bored them to tears but I had to talk about it because it affected me so much.

My life began to change. One thing that happened to me, strangely enough, was that after I joined the catechumenate I felt free to sin. I'd never had a homosexual relationship before, but then I did. I just wanted to feel the freedom of not having to change, by my own effort, to make God love me. But I didn't know what I was or how I really felt, and I did experience the consequences; I found out for myself that sin causes suffering.

In the catechumenate we have a time for reconciliation – confession – and I knew what I was doing was sinful, but the possibility of forgiveness was there. We were told that everyone can fall but a Christian can be raised up again. It's not superficial: you have to identify your sin first, admit to it all, not hiding anything, and let God work on it – then you discover the mercy.

You do keep doing the same things again but you become more aware of what you're doing and then eventually you're freed from it. Some sins take more time to be freed from than others; they may be more deep-rooted, but each time you confess, you're getting deeper and deeper into the roots of it.

The catechumenate isn't group therapy: it's a community of people with different problems, searching for their life to be fulfilled. Everyone needs that; and I've looked for fulfilment in other ways: some of them were quite fun, but they end; they don't fulfil you.

Being in a community is stopping me having warped ideas about Christianity. You learn from other people. While you're by yourself you can convince yourself of anything but, with other people, your arguments stand or fall by them.

You don't have to do anything yourself but you do have to be open to Jesus Christ. I always want to do my own will and have my own plans and they're not always in accordance with the will of Jesus Christ. For example, I didn't want to break off the relationship I was in, but I became aware that Jesus wanted me to. I heard a lot of the teaching in Genesis, and Paul in the New Testament, about human beings being created male and female and how husband and wife should be, and I became aware that a homosexual relationship was going to stop me progressing with my life and going forward. It wasn't something I wanted to know. A lot of my friends were, and are, gay, and I started to separate from that lifestyle. I felt a bit marooned, neither one thing nor the other.

Saturday night is important in my friends' social life, but that's when we have the eucharist, in the community. I don't have anything particular in common with the people in the community, except Jesus, and I still don't like groups, and if I go out with my friends instead of going to the eucharist I don't feel I've done anything morally wrong, but I do feel I've missed out. What keeps me going is this instinctive knowledge that this is where I'm meant to be and this is what I'm looking for.

I don't know if Jesus Christ makes you a better person. Lots of people get wiser anyway, just through getting older. A lot of my friends are more generous and hospitable than me, yet they don't have a faith. I suppose it must be the spirit of Jesus Christ in them already – I don't know. I'm constantly amazed by people, their goodness; it comes about through their own experience of suffering, I think.

I thought my friends would pooh-pooh it all. A few were completely anti, so we remain friends but agree to disagree; most did listen but found it put a big question mark over why I was prepared to follow this route, which seemed dismal and lonely. It was the celibacy; they didn't see that as a way of life at all. People at work saw me as a curiosity, and a lot of people's first reaction was, 'Why don't you become a priest, then?' I couldn't be like a loose cannon flying around; they had to put me in a pigeonhole – which I didn't like.

The Church teaches that the act of sex is only right within marriage. It is hard for homosexuals, but no harder than it is for anyone else. I don't feel any guilt about being a homosexual in the Church, whereas I did before. Everybody has their own cross to carry. It's hard for anyone to live the teaching of the Church by their own effort, whether they're people who've got stuck with drugs, people in adulterous relationships, paedophiles… The people involved aren't condemned, but the Church does point out that it's not the way to find life as you really need it.

I know a lot of people whose marriages are breaking up and they're looking for new things, new lifestyles or new partners, but I know it takes another power to keep you away from sin and to help you keep the marriage together.

I still sometimes have a panic attack, thinking, 'If there's nothing in it, what have I given up?' But I remember the milestones and see it is the spirit of Jesus Christ that has caused these changes in my life. There have been some major changes. One was being freed from masturbation, which was a big problem for me at the time. I didn't ever think of it as a sin and I made no effort to stop, but it just stopped: the need for it just went away. That was a big sign to me, because no effort was required.

The second change was the release of the weight on my shoulders of my own efforts to be perfect. I'm still a neurotic, though – building up resentments and judging people and trying to be perfect and getting anxious – and I have to keep going back to the beginning and asking, 'Why am I fearful? Why am I expecting to be punished?' and discovering again that I need to love and be loved. Also, I never had opinions; I always saw both sides of arguments and was easily swayed, and I couldn't make decisions, but now I have a yardstick to measure everything by and I can see if something's wrong or right.

The third change was my attitude to relationships generally. And the fourth has been my attitude to my career and possessions. I don't see them as security any more. The anxiety about possessions is still there but my priority has changed.

A lot of people think you are what your job is; then when they lose their job they've lost everything. I'm not saying jobs aren't important, because they are but if I lost my job now I'd hope to see it as God changing my direction because he has a plan.

The sort of relationship I'd like to have with Christ, I'm still a long way from. I often wonder what it would have been like to be one of the disciples. You can't really know someone till you know what their sense of humour is like, and I can't work out his. He would have to have a sense of humour to be fully human.

Intellectually, I understand what Jesus is about; I believe what he's saying is right and I know now he's not a moralizer; he definitely has authority, but he's not austere, not like the kind of priests who lecture people and have an air of morality that makes you uneasy so you don't feel free to be yourself. He didn't condemn the adulterous woman, but what he said was wonderful: 'Let anyone without sin cast the first stone.'

But I don't think I'm near to him as some people are and I don't feel I trust him enough to confide in him yet. I've trusted people in the past and been hurt and there's a lot of healing that needs to be done, and perhaps it's partly why I'm homosexual. I can't say I've met Jesus Christ and I can't even say I'd like to. I'm not even looking for him; I'm learning about who I am, and it's always him that finds me. All I think is, I am going to meet him, and I can't tell you what it'll be like. But I have had experiences of him, put it that way.

I remember when I discovered that my landlady and her family had been forging my signature on cheques and cashing them; the police arrested them, but because they couldn't keep them long at the station they told me to leave before they came home, and I had nowhere to go. I went from one person's house to another and finally ended up staying in an area I didn't know. I see it now as a series of events bringing me to that place where I started going to the church and heard about the meeting – events leading me towards an eventual meeting with Jesus Christ.

I think the meeting will be a frank, straightforward confrontation about my life and the way it's going and what's to be done, in a very sympathetic and understanding way. I don't know what will come of it, but it will include the cross because if you avoid the suffering in your life you're not really living; you wouldn't experience Jesus Christ, so you wouldn't be happy.

Avoiding the cross is like living in a caravan – in the sense of confining your life to a self-contained space: you've got your four walls and your little telly and all mod cons, but it's not a full life; it's too small and safe.

I don't want a caravan life.

8

. . . .

It's clear by now that when anyone describes their relationship with Jesus, they're describing something different from anyone else's relationship with him, though there do seem to be certain elements in common.

Vulnerability, for example, seems to be a starting point either for an initial awareness of God or for a new stage in a personal relationship with Jesus – though it isn't really obvious which comes first: whether a period of loss or hurt in someone's life leads them to look for consolation to God, or whether a growing awareness of God makes a person become more open and vulnerable to the God who is there for everyone and in everyone.

The same experiences can have different effects too. Tragedy leads some people to reject God bitterly, even if they've previously counted themselves as a believer, whereas the same events – such as Mark's experience of having cancer – lead other people into a greater love for God.

Just as the children in the RE class at school absorbed different messages from the same teaching, so adults choose different reactions to the same lessons offered by life. Mark's point: 'When God seems distant, are we making him distant by emphasizing his mightiness at the expense of his intimacy? Am I moving away from God, or has he moved away from me?' provokes the question, 'Does God ever move away from me?'

Some would say that he does, that sometimes he may take a step away from me, not as a rejection but as an encouragement to me to take a new step in his direction and discover more of his territory and who he is.

Dean makes the point as well, though, that if the relationship doesn't seem as close as it could be, that could be by choice. Just as I can choose to hold a friend at arm's length, I can decide not to confide in Jesus Christ yet. I may want to find out more about him first, or I may need to feel more at home with myself before I ask him to move in with me. Perhaps even in a close relationship with him, I may want to ask him to move out, like Ann asking Peter to give her more space, so I can stand back and look at what this relationship consists of, whether it's a real closeness at every level or whether I've rushed into an appearance of intimacy that I'm not really ready for or sure that I want.

I may want to test Jesus out. What happens if I ask him to stand back for a while and give me time to think about what I want? Will he say, as Peter told Ann, 'I've warned you before, if you don't let me be the centre of your life, it's the beginning of the end for us'? Or what will he say? Maybe I'm too afraid of what he might say to even ask him the question at all, so I pack my bags and sneak away in the night and hope by the time he notices I'll be out of his sight.

Another of Dean's points was that the reaction to the prospect of a relationship with Jesus Christ might be the product of my experience in other relationships. If I've trusted someone I love and been hurt, will that make it harder for me to trust God? Is my distance from God a reflection of my distance from everybody who might get too close to me? Do I have a problem with trusting anyone and would I need to get to the roots of it – which could be painful and embarrassing – in order to understand why I don't trust the Jesus who says, 'Come to me when you're weary, overloaded and can't go on any longer – and you'll find I give your soul a rest'?

I'd like now to bring in Alan. He's twenty-nine, an assistant racehorse trainer who's also involved in voluntary work with homeless people. His childhood faith grew up and changed as a result of his close relationship with a girlfriend and of his courage in going to a psychologist and re-examining his relationship with his father and his evaluation of himself. Like many others, he found that self-knowledge and knowledge of God went hand in hand.

Here he is now – Alan.

Alan

I fell in love for the first time when I was twenty-four. I was trying to be a Christian but at the same time I was living with my girlfriend, so there was a big battle going on in my life. I knew you either loved God or you didn't; it was either all or nothing. So after a few months I found the strength and finished it, but she was always on my mind. For a good four months after we broke up, she was all I thought about all day.

I found a job back in Ireland for a few months, working with horses, and lived at home; my home had been with Anna, so it helped to have another home, and while I was there I was seeing a priest once a week and talking things over. After that, I took another job, away from home, and I started thinking about God more and it was then that he started filling the gap where Anna had been.

I started reading a book my mother had, called, 'The Way of Divine Love' by Sister Josefa, a nun who used to have visions of God and had heard him tell her things about Jesus' early life, about Joseph's work as a carpenter, and so on. God was becoming more real. I was sent to help out at another stables for a while; it was out in the country, very quiet, and there were only four of us working there so I had a lot of time on my own and I used to go for long walks.

Instead of thinking about Anna all day I was thinking about God all day, and because I'd fallen in love, it totally changed my relationship with God. It was like falling in love again but this time I was falling in love with God. He was no longer just in the church, but there all the time. One day while I was thinking about him at work, I even got a smell of roses; it was lovely – and that was while I was mucking out the stables, so it must have been from God!

I've had a lot of jobs – twenty-eight by now, I think, at the age of twenty-nine! They've mostly been working with horses, stud work or else racing, which I prefer. My main love was always riding but in recent years my love for the horses themselves has really opened up. Before that, I was getting cold and hard; I didn't really care for the animals themselves, but now I've come back to the love for them I had as a child. I have more respect for their feelings and their needs; I don't just see them as objects at work.

Even though I was building up a relationship with God, I still had all the hang-ups: I felt a failure because I'd failed at school, and then I'd kept moving around and hadn't stayed long in a job, and I hadn't been able to keep out of trouble with Anna.

By the time I was twenty-five I realized my chance of being a jockey was gone; I was too old. I was working as a stable lad and I was bored so I went back to a nursing home where I'd worked for a few months three years ago. I'd done it as a challenge; I didn't like being with sick people. My father had been ill ever since I'd known him. He'd had half his leg amputated, before I was born, and he kept going back into hospital and having more operations, and finally had to have the whole leg amputated. He was always in pain, and he died when I was nine.

But I found I liked the work. I even thought about becoming a nurse, but the desire wasn't strong enough to get through the three years of study. While I was back working there I started going to see a psychologist and went through all the thoughts about my father's death and being a failure to my dad. School, from the beginning, I was no good at; then I was never good enough at anything. Even swimming, which I liked, I never won – or boxing, hurling, football. I felt I'd let my father down because I had no interest in the things he was interested in.

I had no real love for myself at all. By seeing the psychologist, I saw that school was the teachers' problem, not mine. I was just different; I had dyslexia but it wasn't my problem; their problem was that they couldn't teach me. And I realized, through the therapy, that my father loved me as I was; he just hadn't that much time to give me. And I was always on my own; no one got close to me.

In the therapy, I had to find an image of myself, and I saw myself as an old unique book, turning page after page, and all this knowledge kept coming out of it, and I realized I was something special, unique and loving. I saw myself as a nice person. I saw myself saying, 'Look at me now, Dad; do you love me now?' and I could see him smiling at me.

I realized that some of the moving about from job to job was about not having confidence, but some of it was a desire for knowledge; I wanted to learn more and more. And the problem with not being able to behave myself with girls was that my self-esteem was so low, and that spiritually I wasn't getting fed enough. Although I had belief in God, and I did pray, it was on the surface. But later I had a real desire to go to church and to pray and to read the Bible.

You have your three desires: spiritual, physical and emotional, and the spiritual need is the strongest, so if that isn't fed, the other needs become stronger. By feeding your spiritual desire, you can cope with the physical and emotional desires.

Up till then, I didn't see Jesus as a father; my relationship with my own father wasn't good. But once I saw my real dad as loving me, I could see Jesus as a father – father, friend, and lover as well, because my feelings for him were the same as I'd had for Anna.

When I was obsessed with being a jockey, or there was a race, I'd get excited, and with Anna I'd got excited, but with Jesus I was even more excited, and what excited me was the love. The more I talked about him, the more I realized his love – when I put my feelings into words. And the more good I saw in myself, the more I saw in Jesus.

If I went through a patch where I was struggling, when I came out of those periods the relationship with him would be even stronger again.

To get through the bad times, I felt I had to leave more of the past behind – some hang-up about myself or some problem. When I let go of that, there was room for God to come in more, and then he grew. I was getting smaller and he was getting greater. I wasn't getting rid of myself, only of things that were actually restricting me and making me smaller – so really I wasn't getting smaller, I was getting bigger.

I was getting rid of these narrow ideas I had – like about other religions; I saw they all had something to offer. And that opened up my relationship with God.

After a year and three months at the nursing home, I felt I had to get back to working with horses, because if I was ever going to get married and have a family it was the only job I could make a living at, and I heard of a job I really wanted. I was a bit concerned about going there, though, because I knew I'd really changed. I'd been going to church every day and I wouldn't have time to do that there, and I'd become used to being around people who had a relationship with Christ.

I made sure that I had at least a half-hour every day of quiet time when I read something spiritual or said the rosary or something, and I went to church every weekend. I could still listen to God; he spoke to me through the books I read and through other people too: non-Christians who told me about their lives and their upbringing.

Most of them came from broken families and you could see how much they'd missed out on, how important family life is. If they'd wanted anything, they'd use the parents against one another, so one partner would give the child something just to get back at the other partner. A lot of people were very, very hurt by marriage break-ups.

I felt God was letting me know what they'd missed out on – loving parents at home – and now these desires that weren't fulfilled as a child, they were still looking for, in drink and sexual relationships. They were looking for a buzz the whole time but basically they wanted to be loved. One girl, especially, was from a very well-off family but she kept attempting suicide; then she picked a lad to go out with who was damaged nearly as badly as she was and they ended up half killing each other.

I tried to be as much like Christ as I could because that was the only way they were going to see any of God's love. 'Strange, weird and sad,' a thirteen-year-old girl called me. I asked why, and she said, 'You don't shout and swear; you're different.' I was, because I loved myself and I'd started to get to know God.

There was a fear that I'd go back to my old ways, but there was an even stronger desire to keep going. There were plenty of times when I failed as a Christian because I really wanted to get on with everyone and fit in, so I said some things that weren't really true and got into conversations that I shouldn't have, and I felt bad about it afterwards because I wanted to help these people and by being hypocritical I was doing a lot of damage.

Before Jesus became a person for me, I tried to keep away from people who had non-Christian ideas, because I was shy and didn't know how to handle them when they'd use me as part of their entertainment. They'd rip me to shreds because I couldn't say why I believed something. I was just saying what I'd been taught. They weren't my own ideas so I couldn't defend them. Now when I say something it's because I believe in it, so it doesn't bother me if they make fun of me.

I try not to talk about God unless the other person brings the subject up and even then I say as little as possible, unless I feel they really want to know; otherwise it does more harm than good.

I can see it going on and on till I die – trying to be more like Jesus. I was created in God's image and likeness and so was everyone else, so the best I can do for people is to help them become more like Jesus, by becoming more like him myself.

9

....

Everyone said how quiet and peaceful Uncle's house was, especially when you considered there were children living in it and it was in the city. Only his brother, on a visit from the States, said, 'There should be noise in a house with children in it. It's not peace, it's death – the silence of the tomb.' He christened the house 'the House of Death'.

It's hard to describe an atmosphere of gloom; easier to describe some of the things that Uncle said and did. Some of his sayings were, 'There's a right way and a wrong way of doing everything'; 'I'm not a pessimist, I'm a realist'; 'Expect the worst and you'll never be disappointed'; 'I don't suffer fools gladly and most people are fools'; 'Children should be *not* seen and not heard'; 'If you want to get a child under control you have to break its spirit first'; 'Spare the rod and spoil the child'; 'We had to make our own amusement; we never had toys'; 'You should always get up from the table feeling hungry,' and 'The world is full of damned fools.'

Every night, two bottles of milk had to be left in the fridge ready for his breakfast in the morning. One had to have half an inch of milk remaining at the bottom, because he didn't like the top of the milk in his tea, and the other had to be full and untouched, because he did like the top of the milk on his cereal.

If he came home and found my sister or me eating cake or sweets he would glare at my mother and say, 'Where's mine, then?' If she hadn't got some for him, he would take what was left of ours.

At mealtimes, the dinner was not served out on plates but left in the centre of the table in dishes. He would serve himself first and what he left in the dishes would be divided between the three of us. If he was annoyed with any of us, he would take all the food, or leave only very little. My mother would pretend she wasn't hungry that day, and wouldn't allow us to say a word, telling us to have bread and cheese afterwards. But he would hang around after the meal, on those days, and if we opened the fridge he'd say, 'You eating again? Sheer greed!' Lunch at weekends was served at one o'clock – not at five to or five past – and his tea had to be five-minutes brewed by four o'clock, with a second cup ready at half-past. There had to be pudding with lunch, and cake with the first cup of tea, with a second slice available in case he wanted it with his second cup.

When he was at work, my sister and I had to be upstairs in our bedroom by the time he came home, and not come down again till the next morning. We were allowed in the sitting room while he was in there but would be banished as soon as we dropped a crumb, curled up with our feet on the chair or rustled the pages of a book.

Board games took place at weekends when he suggested it, but he had to not only be allowed to win but to be allowed subtly, so it wasn't too obvious. When he won we had to cheer, to show we were prepared to be good losers.

There were moments when I felt I had begun to get close to him, such as the time he lay in bed for weeks with bronchitis and would call me in to keep him company. I wrote a story and read it to him in instalments, and he laughed and wheezed and asked when the next episode would be ready.

Sometimes I'd watch him gardening and ask him why he was doing something, and he'd stop work to teach me; or he'd be painting – superb watercolour sketches that revealed a real sensitivity – and I'd watch him bring a landscape to life out of a swoosh of colour-wash; or he'd sit and talk about his childhood, the mother who never had time for him and the governess whom he loved more than his mother, till she was dismissed because he was too old to need a governess; or he'd listen to music on the radio and I'd dance round the room to it, while he covered his eyes and promised he wasn't watching.

At those times, I caught a glimpse of the person he was and could be, and every time I felt that the relationship was now on a more human footing and life would be easier now, he would erupt suddenly into that other person, the one with the hard black eyes and bulging, purplish face, who lunged at me with cruelly gripping hands – the same hands that had held the paintbrush or gently separated the roots of an overgrown perennial. The demon in him would triumph over the human being, without warning and without pity either for him or his victim.

He had a reputation for being good with children, and he could be – as long as they were neat and clean, obedient and smiling, and as long as they went home at the end of an afternoon at his house.

I believe, in all our time of living with him, we did as much harm as good. If we'd lived somewhere close and gone to tea with him from time to time and he'd taken us out for occasional treats, it might have softened him and helped him let go of his bitterness and the sense of rejection he felt from his own childhood, and for us he would probably have been the perfect relative.

But having people with him all the time, even children upstairs and silent in the same house, was too much for him; it unleashed something in him beyond his control. He went far beyond being the irritable eccentric the family judged him, and stepped over the boundary into a tormented destructiveness that never showed in public, and was all the more frightening for being a side of him no one suspected.

When I was ten and my sister was eleven, Uncle retired from work and announced his plan to sell his house in London and move to the country. We weren't sure if we were included in the plan, especially as he did his house-hunting voyages without inviting my mother. She thought about leaving, but six years of 'keeping the peace' by giving way to Uncle's moods and whims had drained her of resilience and made her more and more like him, and I wasn't sure how she would cope without him now. She decided to leave the decision to him, and one day he came home and said he'd bought a house and was taking us all to see it. My mother told us not to question him and to wait and see how many bedrooms it had.

It was a bungalow in a row of six, overlooking a field, and it had four bedrooms, one for each of us. We were all going into retirement, as a family. I don't know why, but as soon as I saw the house, I felt God had listened to me. All right, for reasons of his own, he'd decided not to get me away from Uncle, which was what I'd really prayed for – but there was no possibility that, even with Uncle at home full-time and all of us living under this one much smaller roof, this house could become another 'House of Death'. It looked too reassuring. So I thanked God that day, and I thanked him later on more fervently.

There was a lot about living there that wasn't ideal. The house backed on to a railway line and was downwind from a sewage works; the neighbours and Uncle had constant rows; he had a running battle with the local farmer whom he threatened to sue because the cows sometimes strayed into our garden; my mother was becoming more unwell; I found it hard to settle into the school, and everyone seemed to come from the same kind of background: there was none of the cultural mix of our last school and neighbourhood, and our poverty seemed less acceptable. We lived in a decent house, furnished with the expensive antiques Uncle cherished, and went to a private school – accepted by the nuns without paying fees. Uncle contributed the roof over our heads and the food we ate, but not clothes or shoes or money for school dinners or anything else, so we looked well-off but weren't, and it was difficult to explain to friends, or to teachers at school, that we weren't being unfriendly in refusing invitations to go swimming, or unco-operative in not having the correct uniform or stationery when told to bring it – without fail – by Monday.

But there were ample compensations. Uncle bought us bikes, so that petrol wasn't wasted on taking us the three miles to school, and my sister and I cycled round the countryside and went for long walks, and the farmer – in spite of Uncle's threats of suing him – welcomed us and allowed us to 'help' as often as we liked, which we soon interpreted as every moment of our spare time.

By the time we were in our teens we'd learnt a lot and our 'helping' had ceased to be a kind name for the farmer's tolerance. The farm was small and money was short and we often worked harder and faster than some of the casual workers the farmer took on in the summer, and we were proud of being able to do something to repay the kindness of this man and his family.

One day when I was working there I suddenly felt the presence of God, unexpectedly and unmistakably; it doesn't sound particularly other-worldly but it went beyond my normal feeling of contentment when I was at the farm. I was fourteen or fifteen and it was summer. A change in the weather was forecast and the rest of the harvest had to be brought in quickly. Bales of hay lay on the ground in two fields, far apart, and there were two trailers but not enough pairs of hands.

The farmer's twelve-year-old son, who was small and thin but always begged to be allowed to help his dad with everything, even when it was way beyond his strength, volunteered the two of us to clear the smaller field. His father said no at first; it was too much for us. Then he gave in, drove the tractor to the field and left us to work.

We were making real progress: Jimmy was pitching the bales up to me, red in the face, sweating and staggering under the pitchfork, and I was up on the trailer, heaving, shoving and stamping the bales into their tightly-packed pattern. I don't know whether it was the heat haze or sheer exhaustion that set the scenery shimmering! We were both extremely happy, imagining his dad coming back and finding we'd completed this man-sized job for him.

Suddenly I felt the sun pouring into me – not just warming my skin, but like a liquid ointment pouring right into my bones, even into my soul, and I started thanking God. All I could think was, 'Thank you! Thank you!' I felt that God was a real father who knew who I was, where I was, and how much I wanted to work for him, and that he had known this was just what I needed. He'd rescued my soul from distress, as the psalm says, and brought me out of the House of Death and into the sunshine, given me the freedom to move and develop my strength in this lovely place, among the fresh smell of the hayfield and the warm welcome of this cheerful and uncomplicated family.

The farmer's delight, when he returned and found he only had to help us with the last few bales, was just the icing on the cake. I carried the memory around with me for ages, and I'm sure it helped me through the next crisis, which was my great-uncle's worst and most unexpected fit of rage.

His retirement wasn't as difficult as expected; he liked to walk into town or around the country lanes and would be out for the whole morning; he'd lost the stress of commuting to work every day and seemed more relaxed; he joined a painting class and was one of the best there; he went visiting his cousin who lived a few miles away, and he had more time for his gardening.

He continued to play the old games of taking all the food or barking out insults, but as my sister and I had more life of our own now it generally affected us less. Only my mother seemed more stressed; they had a few violent arguments, and several times he hit her. When we went to stop him, she shouted at us to leave her alone and get out of the way and let her deal with this, but she'd carry on arguing with him even while he was hitting her. My sister and I shut ourselves in the bathroom and cried.

We suspected she might be nearing a nervous breakdown but when we suggested she might go to the doctor for help, she took it as criticism and said there was nothing wrong with her; the problem was that she was 'the jam in the sandwich' between us and Uncle, trying to keep everyone happy and getting no thanks for it. Our suggestion of leaving Uncle and living on our own, the three of us, was seen as rebellion. Her solution to the tensions was for us to 'keep out of his way and don't annoy him'. He was still coming into my bedroom while I was undressing. My mother remonstrated with him once or twice. He'd say, 'This is my house; I can go where I like in it.'

My mother said he was an old man, an innocent, born and brought up in the Victorian era, who didn't know what he was doing; there was no question of any sexual motive. But the Victorians knew better than anybody the difference between decent and indecent and it wasn't innocence that made him wait till my mother was in her room or the bathroom before bursting into my room to deliver a rebuke about leaving my book in the sitting room, or some similar offence, while his eyes roamed over me. 'I'm not interested in you!' he would sneer, when I snatched up my clothes from the bed and held them in front of me, but he would still tear them out of my hands, 'to make sure you're listening to what I tell you'.

Once I heard him hanging around, breathing heavily, in the kitchen, which in the bungalow was next to my room, and I dragged the chest of drawers in front of the door so when he tried to open it he couldn't get in. Thinking I was safe, I started undressing, but he simply went round through the sitting room and came through the other door. That evening there was extra 'punishment' for trying to keep him out of a room in his own house.

It somehow never occurred to me that he didn't have the right to do whatever he liked in his own house. I simply thought that we shouldn't have been living in his house, so he couldn't exercise these rights. He used to time us in the bathroom and complain if anyone occupied it for too long, so mostly I kept on undressing in my room, but I developed the knack of changing very quickly and trying to stay decent at every stage, listening out all the time for sounds from the two adjoining rooms so that I might have some warning that he was about to open the door. It was a tiring way to prepare for a restful night's sleep. It was a tiring way to live.

I have since met many other adults who were abused in childhood, and it seems to be a common part of the experience, this tiredness. To have to be constantly wary, on the alert, ready to be defensive, expecting the unexpected at all times, is not a natural way to live. There is a tiring factor as well in being regarded as a sexual object from the age of three or four. Even those children whose abuse was limited to remarks or glances – sexual innuendo or lust that was never acted out physically – report the same effects: self-consciousness, defensiveness and constant weariness.

By early teenage years, when children raised in safe families are beginning to feel an interest in sex, the abused child is sick of the subject. The double meanings seem sinister, the jokes are not funny, the factual information is unwelcome; all of it seems to infer that the abuser is right – that nothing wrong is happening and that to object to anyone leering or lusting is making a fuss about nothing and being humourless about something that is, after all, just a harmless joke.

Another effect of being the focus of someone's perversions is that the child's sense of its own sexuality is awakened far too early.

Like someone woken up at dawn because the alarm clock goes off at four in the morning instead of at seven, it may be impossible, once awake, to get back to sleep again. That means that the abused child struggles to deal with feelings and images which would not normally trouble him or her until the onset of adolescence. That too is tiring. Some children react to this, when they reach adolescence, by shutting off from relationships and shunning even the slightest mention of sex. Others become addicted to sex, accepting the most excessive or dangerous situations as if trying to prove to themselves they can cope with anything; they will never again be forced into sex because they themselves initiate it, even before the other person has made any suggestion. Both kinds of behaviour are attempts to escape the reality of what has been done to them and to avoid being overwhelmed by the fear and sadness, hurt and anger that abuse inevitably brings.

It's easier to keep on pretending that everything is fine, or that life is just generally miserable, than to begin to identify the source of such painful feelings. Sometimes it takes a more obvious assault, or a change from the normal pattern, to enable the child to begin to identify the source of her general tiredness with life or state of inner turmoil.

One Saturday when I was fifteen, my mother and sister went into town shopping. I would normally have gone with them but I had bad period pain and stayed home. Uncle was working in the garden and my mother said, 'He won't be in till lunchtime, so stay out of his way and he won't bother you.'

To ease the stomach ache, I ran a deep hot bath and was soaking in it when Uncle's shadow appeared outside the frosted glass window of the bungalow and he shouted, 'What are you doing in there?' I said I was having a bath, and he said water was coming out of the overflow pipe and on to the concrete path. I called back that it was all right; there was nothing wrong, just that

I had the water deep; it was only water. I thought he was afraid there was some blockage in the plumbing or a leak.

He shouted at me to come out immediately or let him in. I leaned forward, but gingerly, because I was embarrassed; I wasn't sure how much could be seen through frosted glass at close range – his face was pressed against the window.

'I'm letting the water out now,' I called. But he started to bang on the glass and shout, 'Let me in, this minute!'

'I can't let you in,' I said, 'I'm having a bath!' I was sweeping the water with my hands, trying to force it down the plughole faster. My mother and sister hadn't been gone for long; they might not be back for an hour or more yet. He continued banging and shouting, pounding on the glass with both fists and roaring, 'Let me in! Let me in, you damned insolent girl!'

I don't know how long it went on – maybe ten minutes or maybe even less, but it seemed a long time. I thought the window would break under the impact of his fists and then he'd blame me for it and that would be an excuse to do God-knows-what to me in the name of punishment.

I tried to lie still and prayed for him to calm down. My usual response when he became violent was to go motionless and silent, even to the point of not having any thoughts, so his rage would fall into a vacuum and have no reaction to feed on. Even blinking when he threatened me with his fist in my face, he could interpret as insolence. I realized it was no good answering him. The plug had wedged in the plughole again, so the water wasn't running out any more, but it was obvious that it was no longer reaching the overflow, and I didn't want to move. I could see his mouth opening and closing against the glass as he shouted, and he was twisting his head around, trying to see in.

Suddenly he stopped and I heard him stomping down the path. I was shaking from head to foot, not knowing if he'd given up or whether he was coming in through the kitchen door. I was sure I'd locked the door of the bathroom, because I always did – but then I wasn't sure. I was too frozen with fear by then even to turn my head and look.

There was silence; I couldn't hear anything either from inside the house or from outside in the garden. Before, I'd heard him digging and stamping the earth off the spade, but now there was nothing to be heard.

I lay there for an hour, despising myself for my fear but afraid to move. The water was stone cold by now and, because I had my period, stained with blood. This upset me more than anything; there was something gruesome about experiencing his violent reactions and then finding myself lying in blood. By the time I heard my mother come home, I was shivering and crying and 'in a state', as she put it. When I told her what had happened, she said, 'I told you not to annoy him. There was no need to stay in the bath getting frozen; he's gone out, anyway.'

The following Saturday I woke up late and heard the car start up outside, so I quickly dressed and ran out and saw my mother about to leave to go shopping. I asked her to take me with her and she said no, she didn't want to hang around. I said I was ready to leave straightaway and I wouldn't slow her down; I wouldn't stop and talk to any friends we met in town; I just didn't want to be left alone with Uncle again. She said no, she wanted to go on her own. I started crying and pleaded, trying to open the passenger door, but she locked it from the inside and stared straight ahead, revving the engine. I stood in front of the car and shouted at her not to leave me at home. She released the handbrake and rolled the car forward, driving it into my legs. I jumped aside, and she drove off at speed.

I found her reaction more frightening than Uncle had been. It may be that she simply saw my behaviour as an adolescent tantrum, not connecting it with what I'd told her the week before, or she may have believed it impossible that he'd ever do any real harm. But to me, at that time, it seemed that she didn't want to know what Uncle did when she wasn't around. A few weeks later, the cat brought in a live rat and left it in the bathroom, and Uncle beat it to death in the bath. The bath was full of blood, and I thought, 'That could have been me.'

In those days, the minimum school-leaving age was fifteen, and although I was due to stay on at school for two more years and try for university, I decided to leave home, get a job in a shop and find a bed-sit.

I was too ashamed to tell my friends what was going on at home, so the only person I told of my plan to leave was my sister. She was sympathetic, but talked me out of it. She said, 'I've thought of leaving too but I've worked it out; you wouldn't get paid enough to live on yet and you might have to come back home, which would be worse. You're a year ahead of your age, so if you stay on for A levels you can leave home and go to college at seventeen and never come back again except to visit; it's what I'm doing.'

It made sense, and I stayed. There were several more times when I nearly left, then something happened that helped me to know that God was still with me.

A nun arranged a few days' retreat for the fifteen- and sixteen-year-olds at our school and a neighbouring school, and promised that anyone who wanted to could go, even if they couldn't pay for it. We stayed in a modern annexe to an old convent and spent most of the daytimes going on outings, but with some prayer time at the beginning and end of the day. It was relaxing and fun: a holiday. The only part I found difficult was that a discussion was planned one afternoon; it was about sex and relationships. As soon as it began I was afflicted by nausea and stomach pains and had to be taken out and left to rest in another room till the end of the discussion which was, the others said, open and frank and relaxed and 'really good'.

On the last afternoon, we were given time to go away on our own and pray in a different way: by asking Jesus to speak to us and then sitting listening and seeing what thoughts came into our minds in the quietness. I'd never heard of listening to Jesus before, or thought that he might want to talk to me personally. I was willing to try it, though doubtful that he'd have anything to say to me. But as I sat there, I seemed to see Uncle's face, and the thought came to me – not as a stern instruction but a gentle suggestion of help – that I could try living with him.

The inference was that it wasn't any good being in the same house and trying constantly to avoid him and not make him angry; that wasn't living. I had to try to find a way of forming a real relationship with him, something worthy of human beings. My mother's way of dealing with him by humouring him and keeping out of the way when he was aggressive hadn't worked and didn't suit me – but now I was a young adult, no longer a child, I could try it my way.

It sounded right, but I didn't know what my way was. But I felt if I kept in mind that I wasn't a child now, and if I could control the outward signs of my fear of him and speak to him as an adult, perhaps it would change the way he treated me. A tyrant needs a victim who can be humiliated – not a confident young adult who remembers she's loved and valued by God and retains a sense of her dignity, even in circumstances designed to humiliate.

I felt happy after this session of listening to God, and even keen to go home and try out my new adult courage. But before the time came to go back, something happened that tested my courage to its limit and sent me crying to God for help.

There was a party, that last evening of the retreat – without drink, but with music and dancing and a lot of laughing – and we went to bed late and happy. Everyone went to their rooms, two to a room, and gradually the talking died down and the place became silent. My room-mate was asleep.

I heard the doors down the corridor opening and closing and thought maybe Sister was coming round checking we were all in bed, though she hadn't done that the previous nights, and it seemed a bit late; it must have been an hour since we'd gone to bed.

The door of our room opened, then closed again. No one put their head round and looked in, which seemed a bit strange. I heard the next door opening, then the next one, then the doors down the other side of the corridor, the one opposite ours, and all the doors beyond it, back to the beginning of the corridor.

Then it started again. I leaned forward this time when our door opened, to see who was opening it, but I couldn't see anyone. It closed. I heard the door of the next room open and close, the same way, then all down the corridor and back again. Then it started again – only slightly faster this time.

I was starting to feel uneasy, so as soon as our door closed the second time, I hissed at my room-mate to wake up, then hissed louder, then shouted, and finally got out of bed, went across the room and shook her. She muttered in her sleep but wouldn't wake. Meantime, the doors on our side of the corridor had started opening again – and again, slightly faster. I couldn't hear any footsteps, and by the fourth or fifth round, the doors were opening and closing faster than anyone could have gone, even running, from one door to the next.

It went on all night, from shortly after midnight till six in the morning. By that time, I was not only gripping the sheet but chewing it up! My prayers had changed from requests for help and protection, which sounded like panic and were only making me feel more vulnerable, to merely repeating the 'Glory be to the Father', hour after hour: 'Glory be to the Father and to the Son and to the Holy Spirit, as it was in the beginning, is now, and ever shall be, world without end, Amen. Glory be to the Father…'

When it was starting to get light, something else happened. The door before ours opened and closed as before, and I waited for our turn, but there was a delay. I was even more scared by this break in the pattern. 'Oh God,' I prayed, 'whatever it is, don't let it get me!' I heard a sound in the corridor outside; it sounded like someone falling heavily against the wall then sliding down it, groaning.

In the morning, one of the girls said, 'Why didn't you go out and look?' but there was no way I was going to do that; whatever it was, if it was visible it wasn't something or someone I wanted to meet, and if there was nothing to see at all, that would have been even more frightening!

Whatever it was, it certainly got me praying, and maybe it served as a reminder that if I was going to go home and start trying to create a new relationship with the great-uncle I'd always been afraid of, it would be no good relying on my own very limited understanding and courage. My only hope and safety lay in throwing myself on the mercy of the God who appeared to be offering me help to live the life I had, rather than rescuing me from it.

10

....

One of the benefits that many people quote as going hand in hand with an awareness of the present reality of Jesus Christ is a growth in self-respect and a change from seeing themselves as a victim – whether of sickness or poverty or violence. In giving God control of their lives, they find they regain their own confidence and power of choice, as though whatever is given to God, he returns to the giver with interest.

Someone who's had more cause than most to feel like a victim is Kiran. Since coming to England from India as a child, she has been subjected to racial hatred and bullying at school, and malice and gossip at work. Her one defence, she says, was her anger – but her cost, in discovering Jesus, was to give up even that and let him be the only defence she had.

Now twenty-nine, she looks back at her move from victimization, through anger, to the freedom of allowing Jesus to bring to life her confidence and develop her talents.

Kiran

When I was younger, Jesus was thought of as a very holy person. I thought I was bad and that you had to be a nun or a saint before you had a relationship with him. A lot of the religious people I knew did things that didn't seem good. In school, the ones who thought the world of themselves and were horrible about the other children would go to church and pray before their exams, and they'd sail through them, so I thought they must be chosen.

At church, some of the people there wouldn't shake hands with each other, till a group of West Indian women went to the priest and complained and he told the parishioners off. The people at church who were well-dressed looked down on poor people like alcoholics.

I did RE at school so I could see Jesus came as a poor person, and he was Jewish, and he healed everyone – yet all the people who prayed and went to church acted differently. I could see there was a contradiction, but nobody did anything against it or said, 'That's not what Jesus told us', so in my mind there was a conflict. It seemed that if you were pretty, clever, rich – and of course, white – then you got all the success, and if not, then Jesus wasn't with you. They all said that youth and brains and prettiness were gifts from God – but he didn't seem to give them to everyone. I was at a religious school, but the pupils looked down on anyone who had a menial job, and the staff did as well.

I saw Jesus as a tall, strong person who could take anything – even being crucified: I didn't think of him as a man in pain. I saw him as always very strict and telling you off – like the nuns. He wouldn't appear to anybody or talk to anybody like me; I never thought he came for sinners, only for the good.

I used to go to church but I couldn't really listen to the scripture readings because they were so different from the people's actions and you couldn't listen to both.

My mother brought me to a prayer group: she'd seen this man healing people, and the priest had explained that Jesus would intervene through the healing prayers. When the man prayed with me, he said nothing happens to you that God doesn't know about, and not to be afraid to talk to Jesus. At this time, I was afraid to go to church and I used to run out. I felt really bad, like a sinner who shouldn't be there.

I came from an environment where if you weren't perfect, you were bad. We were very poor at the time and being the eldest I had a lot of responsibility and couldn't seem to live up to what my parents wanted. My family thought I was bright and I wanted to be a doctor or a lawyer, but the school said I couldn't be because I was in the B stream. Once you were graded at school, you stayed in that grade for life.

I was six when I came to this country from India. It was a friendly culture there – people talk to each other in the street – and this culture is much less so. At school, you couldn't talk to people in a different class or even a different stream. All the low-streamers had such a low image of themselves that they had to find someone to take it out on – so they picked on people of a different culture. As college students too, you couldn't just talk to anyone. No one accepted you for what you were; you couldn't be different in any way.

There was a lot of racism from the neighbours and at school. I felt that the world was so awful that I was scared of growing up and I wanted my parents to protect me, which of course they couldn't.

As an adult, I was going to join the anti-bullying campaign for schoolchildren but the man who prayed with me was afraid it would inflame my anger, because when you join groups like that you can pick up other people's anger as well as your own. He said I should give it to God instead. You can't work for justice while you're looking for revenge. Mahatma Gandhi said, 'An eye for an eye makes the whole world blind.'

My anger was so uncontrollable that I didn't know where to put it; I wanted to help people but I had so much anger, I knew I had to give it to God. I tried to pray but I had very bad concentration, and at first I was trying to hang on to the anger because it was the only protection I had.

My only value was money; that was all I'd been taught. I came from a society where money was held in respect, so I was trying to get money and buy things, to get respect for myself. I had a job but there was no choice: I couldn't leave that job because no one else would employ me.

But then I met other people, who explained that suffering can bring you closer to Jesus, because there's nothing God expects us to take that Jesus hasn't taken before, and I began to feel better about myself then; I'd felt ugly and rejected before. People had told me I was pretty but I was so negative I thought they were mocking me and I never took it seriously.

I'd been going to leave the Catholic Church and become a Hindu, but then I saw there was a difference between Catholics who practised and those who were just Catholics in name. I felt that God started helping me and saying, 'Look, these things you've been hearing about me and my son are wrong.' And I could hear him telling me to leave the job and try for an access course, to qualify for university.

I was considered mad for giving up my job. I was called a religious maniac – because people who are going off their rocker always seem to talk about religion – but when I saw these groups of Catholics really acting as Catholics, sharing and being friendly and praying for others, I saw it was how God expected people to live their lives; they weren't mad at all.

This man who prayed with me at the healing group said once, 'If you wonder why your neighbour has the biggest car or the best job, it may not be because God likes him more but because the devil already has him! If you're suffering, you're doing all right!'

It made sense to me that people who cling to their prettiness or brains or materialism or having the best job will see at the end of the day that without God it will mean nothing to them.

God has really sent me a lot of people now, friends and also people in need that I can help. Before, I was too busy worrying about myself. When I was asking God for money, he didn't give it to me, but when I started asking God for his will, then he gave me the good things – and the money I needed to live on as well.

When I found my own flat, I knelt down and offered it to God and asked him to employ me in some way. Before, I had nothing to give, so I'd just take. Now, if I have any problem I give it to Jesus and he helps, so I spend less time worrying and have more for other people.

People said I was nothing, but I wasn't to God. Jesus called fishermen – not the Pharisees and the well-educated, but the poor. It has nothing to do with being educated: that doesn't make you closer to God. And through my studying and passing the access course and getting on to a law course at university, God is changing the world a little – making it more difficult for people to label other people.

With Jesus, I feel that we're friends now, like brother and sister. When I first started hearing him talk to me, I was worried, thinking it couldn't really be him because he had faith in me and was telling me to risk taking the access course and so on, and I thought that couldn't be right. But Jesus isn't like other people; he doesn't manipulate you, because he has nothing to gain from making your life a misery.

I know we all have the ability to hear God clearly if we want to. When the teacher at school used to talk about who comes from God, who is the Good Samaritan and so on, I had the impression I wasn't. But if God chooses to speak to me and chooses to employ me, that's his choice.

To go to college, I had to give up my job and my flat, but I did trust God and he supplied me with everything. He's not like a teacher who says, 'You can't do it'; he'll help you. He's not someone who tells you to mow the garden and doesn't give you the tools to do the job.

When I was finding it difficult to pray, someone suggested that I write to God, write down how I felt and then write down what I heard him answer, and at first I felt, 'Is this right? Am I hearing him right?' But I knew if I got it wrong, he'd still help, and if I went on this college course and failed, he'd still bail me out. I asked him to give me a reason to live, and I asked if he needed me, to help people, and he did. I prayed for my family as well, when they were going through problems, and God really helped them.

I became more confident, about my ability and about my looks. People tend to judge prettiness on whether you could become a model or have a lot of boyfriends, but God showed me that his ways of using gifts like prettiness and brains aren't the same as our ways; politicians have brains, but they don't necessarily have wisdom!

I thank God now for my looks, because I don't want to say something's yuck if he created it, but I realize that the looks aren't really for me; they're for other people to look at and see God's creation, not for me to stand looking in the mirror all day!

Any negative ideas I had from the past don't really wash any more. I know God sees me as one of his children and that even if I was on Death Row for murder, he'd still forgive me. So I'm able to forgive other people too, because their violence and calling people names is just weakness, basically.

I changed my ideas about Mary, Jesus' mother, as well. As a child I saw her as very beautiful and very good, someone who was chosen – but I didn't see her as someone who suffered or someone who told the truth. I think I was jealous of her. I didn't really know her.

When I started praying the rosary, I was able to put myself into her shoes: she was scared when she was going to have a baby; being the mother of God didn't make her boastful, and her poverty made her stronger. The beauty she had wasn't about looks but something deeper that radiated from her and made people want to be closer to her, the kind of beauty only God can give you, whereas some beautiful people are really cold.

It's like the story of the king's new clothes that everyone admired, even though no one could see this marvellous invisible suit, and only one small boy pointed out that he was naked: if everyone says about somebody, 'Isn't she pretty?' you say yes, because you'll be accused of being jealous if you don't agree. But it's the personality of the person that makes them attractive, and I'm sure that's how God sees beauty. At the emotional and intellectual levels as well, what he's looking for is spiritual intellect and spiritual wholeness.

What God made me see, through all his family but especially through Mary, was that real strength comes from God, whether you're male or female. It does away with all the gender stereotypes. Everyone tells you,

'Be feminine; dress like this and behave like that...' but femininity and masculinity aren't that straightforward and aren't stronger than one another. That image of Mary holding the body of Jesus after he was taken down from the cross is a reminder of what real strength is, and real femininity.

When Jesus came to life for me, he also made Mary real for me and it's helped me a lot, getting to know who she is.

11

Doubts are something that no one who believes in Jesus – or in anything – wants to admit to, but the struggle with doubt and cynicism seems to be an essential ingredient in the progress towards a faith that becomes the whole bedrock of someone's life, not just a tacked-on philosophy that never challenges their plans or threatens their life.

John the Baptist had a bad attack of the doubts when he was in prison prior to being beheaded by King Herod, and who could blame him? His adult lifetime had been spent in a desert known for its harsh extremes of climate, existing on the most meagre subsistence diet, and his mission consisted of preaching to the crowds who trailed after him, either looking for help with their lives or just out of curiosity, like people who go to tarot readers or spiritualist mediums now. Maybe for some he was no more than the current attraction – a 'prophet' with a shaven head and ragged clothes, who claimed to have a message from God.

If they were expecting words of comfort, though, or a feel-good experience, they would have been disappointed. He had the same uncompromising message for all of them. The first point he made was, 'Repent': that is, have a rethink about your life and make the appropriate changes; and the second was, 'Believe the good news': forgiveness is available from God, and he's about to send someone who'll set you on the path to a life of goodness. But before you can start the new life, first you have to clear out the rubbish!

To people who denied there was any rubbish in their life that needed clearing, this wasn't a welcome message, and John's approach was hardly a recipe for popularity. It would have come as no surprise to anyone, least of all John himself, when he was thrown into prison for refusing to condone Herod's affair with his sister-in-law. In the meantime, though, John's mission had been accomplished. He was there to clear the way for the expected Christ, and he'd been given a sign to recognize him by. When he baptized people in the River Jordan, immersing them in water as confirmation of their desire for a cleaner life, he was told that he'd see the Holy Spirit – the spirit of holiness, the spirit of God himself – come down on one person and stay there. This person would not just experience a fleeting touch of God, or reflect his personality for a brief episode, but God would stay joined to this person. John wasn't told in advance who this person would be, but he was in no doubt that he'd know this sign when it happened.

When he did see the phenomenon occur, he lost no time in telling everyone: 'That's the person you should be following; up till now you've been following me, but I was only the pathfinder for the real one.'

Some of John's followers seemed to resent this on his behalf. 'You're the one who introduced this baptism idea,' they said, 'and now this guy comes along and takes all your followers away, because his friends have started copying you; they've set up on the other side of the river, baptizing people, and everyone's going to him now instead of coming to us.'

John's reply was quite revealing: 'I'm not the bridegroom, I'm only the best man. The bridegroom is the one who gets the bride, but the best man is happy for him because that's his role: to stand by the bridegroom. But once the bride comes along, the best man's role diminishes; he stands back now and leaves the bride to the bridegroom.'

Later, the community of followers inspired by Christ – called 'the gathering' or 'the church' – was to be described as the bride of Christ. So John knew, as soon as Jesus came on the scene, that his own role now consisted of fading out.

But it must have been terribly hard for him, still only a young man – only six months older than Jesus – to be thrown into the palace dungeon and left there, hearing secondhand reports of miracles and the crowds of people following Jesus, and realizing that Jesus wasn't going to come and do a miracle for him – get him out of prison before the king made a hot-headed decision to execute him to amuse the latest girlfriend.

He wasn't to know, at that stage, that Jesus was later going to refuse to rescue himself in similar circumstances – stepping forward and saying, 'I'm the one you're looking for,' when the guards came to arrest him in Gethsemane, and explaining, 'My kingdom isn't of this world,' when asked why he didn't use his influence with God to save himself from a bloody death. All John knew was that Jesus was out there drawing the crowds by curing all kinds of illnesses, and John was in prison, alone and apparently forgotten.

So he called on the help of a couple of friends to carry a message from him to Jesus, 'Is it really true, after all, that you're the one I was told by God to prophesy about, and the one all the prophets of previous generations were announcing – the Messiah, the Christ, the Chosen One, the Just One, the Suffering Servant? Or are you just another holy man and we've still got to wait for someone else to save the world?'

It was a fair question. All right, he'd been convinced in the early days of meeting Christ. He'd never before seen someone so in tune with God's spirit, someone who didn't show signs of integrity then blow it with some display of self-centredness or lack of compassion. But now poor John – not only Jesus' 'best man' and the prophet who'd paved the way for him, but also a blood relation, his cousin on his mother's side of the family – was languishing in prison, possibly never to get out again, and Jesus was getting on with his own life as though John had never done anything for him.

But he didn't get a straight yes or no answer to his question. The message Jesus sent in reply was to remind John of what he knew already: 'Look at what's happening; look at the signs, and judge for yourself.' The people who were most in need were getting their needs catered for perfectly and in very obvious ways: blind people were finding they could suddenly see; people whose bodies were rotting with leprosy were suddenly restored, clean as new.

And perhaps even more important – people whose lives had seemed hopeless were hearing the 'good news', and it really did strike them as good news. The most marginalized and powerless members of society were being told what they'd always suspected: that the real power belongs to the people who love, not to the people who exploit, and that this power doesn't just take effect in some future heavenly realm but is real and effective in this life, working away unnoticed by the exploiters and the power-crazy but having a solid effect on the fabric of life.

John was reminded, very gently, that the bridegroom must go ahead now with the marriage. Be happy, Jesus told him, and don't lose faith. Then he went on to tell the crowd who'd been listening while John's friends reported his doubts, that John was a great man.

He reminded them of what had made them go looking for John in the first place – not because he was a person with sensational powers, or a 'child of nature' living in the wilderness, or an example of changeable fashion for minimalism or austerity – but because, deep down, they sensed who John really was, a person sent by God to prepare them to meet the real thing.

And perhaps there's a John the Baptist in all of us, a voice crying in the wilderness of every person's heart, prompting us to get ready to meet our God. And that voice isn't always the voice of faith or our innate instinct for God; it may also be the voice of our doubts, the niggling thought in the middle of the night which suggests, to agnostics and to committed Christians alike: 'Is this really what it's all about? If Jesus is really sent from God to show the world we're safe, how come I'm left alone in the dark with no apparent way out?'

Jesus talked frankly about the cost of being a follower of his way of life and said we'd be well advised to work it out in advance. It's not a good idea to start building a multi-storey office complex then find you've run out of funds when you've only got as far as the first floor. Or to walk down the street in a war zone then be hurt and surprised when a sniper lines up his sights on you.

One common factor in all these different accounts of people who've met Jesus Christ, and people who feel that they haven't, is that they all seemed aware there was a cost. When I was at university, none of my friends were practising, churchgoing Christians. No one ever expressed a conscious ambition to be like Jesus Christ. But the highest form of praise for someone was that they were 'a real human being'. If a driver slowed to a halt to let an old lady cross the road, or a student allowed another student in a hurry to jump the queue in front of him, someone would exclaim, 'Oh, great – a human being!'

A human being was someone who, in either a small or a major way, cost themselves some trouble and sacrificed their own convenience in favour of someone else – probably a stranger who hadn't done anything to deserve special treatment but seemed that they might benefit from a lift.

It strikes me that maybe Jesus becomes real to people who are being real with him, or with themselves. At the point in a person's life when they're being 'a real human being' – either in the sense of putting someone else first, or perhaps by being honest with themselves about the mess in their own life – maybe then the door opens to that spirit of Jesus Christ, the one who paid the ultimate cost of being 'the son of man' – the human being – and was crucified for nothing more than knowing and being who he was.

I'm certain that there is a cost and I do have to do something to invite him, consciously or unconsciously, if I want Jesus to come alive in my own life. He did promise, 'If you're looking for me, you'll find me.' But he also described himself as, 'the way, the truth and the life'. Does that mean, 'If you're looking for a way of life based on truth, you'll wind up coming face to face with Jesus Christ?'

It's noticeable that he didn't say, 'If you're looking for enlightenment, you'll find me,' or 'If you're looking for supernatural powers or spiritual experiences or a philosophy of life that suits you as an individual...'

People who are looking for these things generally seem to evade encounters with Christ. They don't seem to follow the John the Baptist route, moving from a way of life built on truth without compromise, to a discovery of the cost of that way of life, through a lonely and agonizing confrontation with their doubts, then resorting to some human intermediaries to present their painful conflict to Jesus Christ, and finally receiving affirmation from Christ: 'You've done as much as you were told to do; now let me take over my role, and stop trying to make sense of it all yourself.'

12

....

Some people believe the power of prayer is nothing more than the power of positive thinking.

I'm sure it must be more constructive in anyone's life to think positively rather than negatively. One of Jesus' early followers, Paul, in a letter to one of the distant churches, advised the people not to use harmful words in talking, but only to use the kind of words that build people up and give them encouragement. In the same way, by using harmful words even in our private thinking we can only discourage ourselves and drag down our confidence level.

But prayer has to be more than just psyching ourselves up to expect the best and subconsciously making it happen. If that were the case, everyone would get exactly what they wanted, just by thinking about it in a determined way. It's an attractive idea – if only life were that simple!

There are many instances of a person suddenly experiencing the presence and closeness of Jesus at a time when they're very far from thinking positively or summoning up a comforting image by willpower.

One woman told me about the time she was raped. Confused and angry and ashamed, she told no one about it for years, but sank into deep depression. One evening she was lying on her bed, feeling such despair that it became really oppressive and she was in a state of torpor – an apathy so deep it was almost like sleep, but there wasn't any restfulness about it. Her body felt so heavy she couldn't move it. Suddenly she felt her hand being lifted up and held, and heard a voice calling her by name and saying, 'I love you.'

This woman was a musician, and in one corner of her rented bed-sit was a small harp that she'd been too depressed to play for a very long time. But, on another occasion when she was alone in her room, she heard the sound of a hand brushing gently across the strings, and the words came into her mind, 'You're not alone.' She wasn't, at that time, capable of positive thought – or even coherent thoughts. She says Jesus came to her when she needed comforting and hadn't an ounce of comfort in herself.

Being complex creatures who function on many levels, sometimes we have conflict in what we want. The conscious mind, for example, might want power and wealth and success, while the emotions want to slow down and find peace and be loved and the body needs rest and freedom from tension and strain. And the soul, deep down, might long to return to its roots and surrender itself to God. All these levels, then, pray for what they want most – so which of these jumbled and contradictory prayers will be met by God: the instincts of the body, or the mind, or the emotions, or the soul?

I believe he listens to us at the deepest level, even when our self-knowledge doesn't take us that far ourselves and we may have no conscious realization of what our own spirit is pleading for.

That's why asking to know God's will and praying for that to be done in our life is not an evasion of responsibility but an acceptance of the truth about ourselves that only God is aware of, and a remedy for the conflict in ourselves.

Several of the people in this book have mentioned how essential they've found it to try to discover what God wants, through the scriptures or through people who already have a relationship with Christ, or through listening and asking Jesus himself to make it clear to them.

For many people, their childhood teaching about God has lacked conviction, and their experience of churchgoing people has lacked sincerity – but as adults they still accept these impressions as the final word on him, and reject belief in God, not just belief in the faith and authority of their teachers.

In human terms, I'd never claim to have a relationship with someone I'd only heard about through a third person – especially if that person made them sound so boring! A good historian never relies on other historians' theories and interpretations of historical facts, without searching out the primary source material – contemporary records and eye-witness accounts of the events. A good employer never employs someone on the basis of a third party's reference, without interviewing them in person.

Yet a lot of people either call themselves Christian or reject Christianity, on the basis of their school-day experience of church services and religious education, even when it was obviously lacking in something. The 'Christianity' they're either accepting or rejecting is a concept formed from half-remembered texts, second-hand theories and inadequate personal example. The written records of events as recalled and passed down the generations by Matthew, Mark, Luke and John – and the letters of Peter, James, John and Paul – are not consulted, except to prove or disprove their preformed personal theories.

We take more care in choosing a dinner from a menu than we do in choosing our relationship with the person of Jesus who claims to come straight from our creator! At least before we order food we want to know what's in it!

One of the few scraps of information handed down by Jesus' contemporaries about his mother Mary is that she 'pondered things in her heart'. She usually had trouble understanding the things that happened to her at the time: she was 'deeply disturbed' by the angel's announcement of her imminent conception and asked, 'How can this come about?' She was 'astonished' by the shepherds' report of how they'd known about her newborn baby, 'wondering' about Simeon's recognition of his Messiah in the baby in the Temple, and 'worried' by the twelve-year-old Jesus' three-day disappearance. She let herself be talked into going in search of the adult Jesus, by relatives who told her he wasn't making time to eat or sleep, and heard that he refused to come out and speak to them.

She must have had more trouble trying to understand God's ways and make sense of what was happening to her than the rest of us do. We're not told she was highly educated or unusually intelligent. But her response to all her bewilderment was to 'ponder' and to 'store all these things up in her heart'.

It was a system that seemed to work, because she was able to stand at the foot of the cross, as a mother, and not run away or try to stop the events – as Peter had done and been rebuked by Jesus for not understanding. And she was there at Pentecost, when the Holy Spirit came, giving her support to the men who'd called themselves disciples of her son and then run away and left him. That must have taken more than human strength and forgiveness.

Another common element among the personal histories in this book is a tendency to remember and think about the signs of Jesus' reality and to allow them to make an impression. Some people were quick to act on the experience and some were reluctant to allow it to change them, but none of them dismissed it. All of them 'pondered these things in their heart'.

If God has no favourites, as the prophets and psalms in the Bible would claim, then if he has given signs of his son's existence to even one person in our universe, then surely he's given them to everyone, in some way? But what do we do with them, even if and when we recognize them as signs of something beyond our current concept of reality?

If one person says God has done so much for him, and another says God has done nothing for her, can both of those statements be truthful, if it's true that God created both people and has no favourites? Or are they both talking about the same reality from a different perspective or mental attitude, in the way that an optimist and a pessimist do when one says the glass is half full and the other says it's half empty?

Although positive thinking doesn't explain the apparent power of prayer, I believe it does have some part to play in inviting God to work in a person's life.

Jesus said, 'To anyone who has, more will be given.' The people in this book who believe he has given them everything, even himself, do expect more. They keep in mind and ponder on the favours he's given them, whether big or small, and some emphasize the importance of thanking him or thanking the people he sends them. Their way of thinking about him, then, is positive, and leads to more positive expectations of his readiness to help.

Let's listen now to an account of a different relationship with Jesus, from someone who feels that Jesus hasn't done anything for him personally and that God takes no interest in his individual life.

Cyril's perspective on life seems mainly political – perhaps a result of his work as a historian, or perhaps a cause of his choice of that career. Ask him about his personal relationship with Jesus Christ and he talks about the institutional Church as an instrument of social change or moral or temporal power.

Cyril

I know I went to Sunday School but I can't remember anything about it except being given little pictures. I remember not liking it and being relieved when it was over. I don't know why my parents sent me. My mother did the flowers in the church. I don't know if they really believed; I think they must have done because they used to go to church when we were on holiday. But I don't remember ever talking to them about it. I think they stopped going to church when I was fourteen.

I don't believe anyone ever mentioned Jesus as a person to me. At prep school, we had chapel every morning before breakfast, and two services on Sunday; I played the organ. At boarding school we had chapel every evening and three services on Sunday. Sung Eucharist used to go on for one and a half hours at least. The public school I went to was actually originally founded for the sons of Anglican clergy. My family was Church of England, but the only reason I was sent to that school was because it was where my father had been to school.

We must have had RE lessons but I can't remember anything about them at all. The only divinity lesson I remember was when the housemaster read out the marks, with funny comments. The housemaster was ordained but had decided to become a teacher, and was also a country landowner who spent the holidays at his country residence. In divinity, we read the Old Testament and that was it: we never got as far as the New Testament.

The only impression of God I had was that all the school were herded into the chapel just to fill it, because it was the biggest chapel in Europe and it had cost so much time and money to build.

We were just at the school to do our lessons and get qualifications. My parents never asked what we learned about God. I suppose I believe in God, and in Jesus. My image of God was an old man with a beard. I still have that mental image really. I see God as avuncular, a benevolent despot, and Jesus as self-sacrificial.

My view of organized religion has been tarnished by my study of religion, which has caused more wars than anything else in the history of mankind and still does, whether Christian or Muslim, or sects within those religions. They largely derive from the authoritarian nature of the religions. People use the Church as a lever to gain power. In medieval times the bishops were the most powerful people in the State. That situation doesn't come from the doctrine, it's an abuse, but it seems to be where organized religion leads. It's people manipulating the Church to get personal power. I don't know much about the organized Church now. But people still use religion as a cause, as an excuse to serve their own interests.

There are some very good people in the Church, who use the Church for good, but some tend to be suffocatingly evangelistic: they're probably so convinced in their own mind of the righteousness of their cause that they believe the end justifies the means – the means ranging from insistence to mental torture, propaganda and indoctrination.

Within Christianity, I think it depends whether it's a parochial or national level. If a small community, through the church, uses the parochial organization to serve the interests of the disadvantaged in the community, that can only be a good thing. For many people, it's primarily a social organization, but I don't think that matters too much if good is done by it.

I don't think a great deal about personal faith. I expect I have some personal faith, but it's not particularly strong. I have faith in a supernatural being that's mysterious and not interested. I don't think it's possible to get to know him. I don't see him as someone who's personally involved in people's individual lives, unless individuals have great faith and perceive it that way; it's real to them, and I'm prepared to accept it could be, but I don't know.

If people have faith, they do have a personal relationship with Christ, and it's something I admire but whether it's something I'd like myself, I don't know. I don't call myself a practising Christian, but it depends what you mean by it. The sacrifice of Jesus and his life must have achieved something because a religion grew up based on his life. I can't say in practice how it's made any difference to my life or if his life has had any influence on mine; the moral code that Christianity espouses is something that I think is good and that one should strive to emulate.

The kind of life Christ lived was simple, caring for others, justice. I hope it's affected the way I treat other people. I don't follow the example of Christ; I follow the teachings. He lived in a different society. I follow the main principles. The world has changed.

For example, I follow the teachings as they are interpreted by men, because they've been interpreted quite differently, so one chooses the *interpretation one thinks best, based partly on convenience, one's personal situation, and partly on one's own opinion.*

I'm sure the person of Jesus has some reality now for some people, but I don't think in those terms. I see him as a historical figure, but also someone who created a code of morality. That was his purpose in coming. I see him as the son of God, who founded a church, or a church was founded in his name. His purpose was to create a code of morality, and probably founding a church was the way of spreading it. The Jewish faith was a code of morality but it was one that was practised only by a small group of people.

I don't know if I believe in life after death. I believe Jesus was raised to life after he died, physically. I suppose he's still alive in a spiritual sense but not in a physical one. I don't pray very often; I do occasionally. I don't really make any distinction between praying to God or to Jesus. It takes the form of asking for better health. I haven't had any example of prayer being answered personally. I've never felt the presence of God; I don't get any sense of his presence. I'm living by myself.

13

· · · · · · · · · · · · ·

Marianna's story has several of the elements that are beginning to be familiar in these accounts of people who unexpectedly encounter Jesus as a real person present in their lives.

She was in a vulnerable situation, had been a victim of violence, and was in great need of help. She also wanted to know – and demanded to know – who God is.

Her reactions to the experiences she received as a result of her prayer are also familiar: she thanked God, remembering that what she'd asked him for had been given, and she went out of her way to thank the people who helped, seeing them as sent by God as well.

What she doesn't mention is the many times she was offered false sources of help and turned them down because they were wrong. When the family was going through its severest financial difficulties, one of Marianna's neighbours told her how to fiddle a social security claim, another offered to shoplift for her, and several times she was offered goods which she suspected were stolen.

It was after she'd said no to all of these options, because she believed the effect of dishonesty on her children's lives would be more damaging than the effects of poverty, that the real help started to arrive.

Marianna

I think I realized Jesus was real from a young age, because I used to have conversations and expect him to do things for me, like changing my life, but I didn't know he loved me.

One Good Friday, my dad tied me to the washing-line post as a punishment for crying during the church service. There was a thunderstorm and I asked Jesus not to let the lightning strike me.

When I was eleven, I asked him to get me away from my home, and the priest came and took me to the police and I was taken into care, into a convent, for protection from my father.

Suddenly, I started to live my life every day without fear of being punished by God, because the nuns were kind, in general. I saw priests and nuns as representing Jesus on earth, and they were the ones who'd rescued me from home, so I saw him in that answer to my prayer, and my idea of God began to change then.

When I used to go to Mass, I used to pray to the Sacred Heart and sit and listen and I heard him speaking to me; I was about thirteen then. What I heard was, 'Come to me.' I took it literally and climbed up on the altar and embraced the big statue of Jesus, the Sacred Heart – but I was dragged down by an elderly nun who came in! I was confused then about what Jesus wanted: this gentle voice, then this maniac nun shouting that I was being blasphemous!

The next thing that changed me was, when I was fifteen, being tricked into leaving the convent. I was called to the front door to find my bags packed ready to leave. I couldn't believe they were sending me back to live with my parents again, after all the violence. I remember hammering on the convent door to be let back in.

I got into my parents' car and thought, 'God just plays tricks on people, lets you feel safe for a while then blows it all up in your face.'

After that, I don't think I prayed for about fifteen years, or felt part of the Church. Then, when I was thirty, my brother died – the only one who'd ever stood up for me at home. He'd been living in Holland, and

I was alone at his funeral. I wasn't expecting to see his face, but there was a glass lid on the coffin, and his face was all twisted and contorted; he'd obviously died in pain, and I found myself screaming at God for letting this happen to him.

I screamed that I wanted to know if God was real; I didn't care if he was good or bad; I just wanted to know what he was like and what was the purpose to this life and why he gave us people to love and then took them from us.

There was nobody there to comfort me or calm me down, but it happened anyway; it was like a blanket of peace came down and two arms were holding me steady and keeping me still. I knelt down and started praying the 'Hail Mary'.

A couple of months after this I was still in grief because my brother's death made all the memories of my childhood come flooding back into my mind, as though they were happening all over again.

A friend asked me if I'd like to see a priest, to talk about things, and initially it was this priest giving up his time and listening to me that made me start to realize that God did care and that he had listened to me. I was quite frightened at first, though, because as a child I'd been told that priests were God taking different human forms, so when the priest touched my hand, to me it was like God reaching out and touching me.

Financially, things were very difficult at that time, and I had a large family. The priest told me, in my prayer time, to start asking God for the financial help we needed, which was something I'd never done before. I'd always been told God was only interested in my soul and not the details of my life.

I met some other Christians, and one night at a prayer meeting I heard someone read a passage of scripture that I'd heard before but had never really taken in. I believed I was basically evil, and this passage said, 'If you who are evil know how to give good things to your children, how much more will your heavenly Father give good things to you who ask.'

It seemed as though this was God's voice speaking to me, in the man who was reading, and it felt like he was saying it specially to me. So I asked God there and then to give me everything he wanted to give me, and I just opened up my heart to receive everything. My whole being was suddenly filled with an overflowing feeling of love that I'd never experienced in my life before.

From that point, I continued to ask for everything I needed for myself and my family and for others, and these prayers were being answered, on a daily basis.

One day, the cupboards and the fridge were empty, and all I had left was a one pound coin. I went to Mass with the children, which was still a new thing for us to do. On the way, I was trying to decide whether to get bread and milk or whether to put my faith in the words I'd heard. When we got to the church, I told the children we'd have to pray today for the food, and we held hands and said the Our Father. Then I put the money in the collection plate.

When we went home, we were invited to a birthday party, and there was food. I thought, 'This is great, but what about tomorrow?' One of the older children had stayed at home because he thought the party was too young for him. While we were out, someone knocked at our door and my son let them in: it was a couple I'd met but who didn't know anything about my circumstances. They had lots of food with them, and they filled up the cupboards and the fridge. When I arrived home, my son said, 'You'll never believe what happened while you were out!'

Through the parish, I found out where these people lived and I went to thank them. I asked the woman what made her call round with the food – if anybody had said anything to her – and she said no. She'd been at Mass, the one following the one I was at, and I came into her mind. She knew I had a large family, and she kept getting this idea coming back to her that there was nothing in the house to eat.

It made me realize more that Jesus was really living and very much present in others. It wasn't just a nice person using their intuition. That had been my prayer to Jesus; I'd asked him, not anyone else, and that was it. I wasn't just asking for things; I began to converse and to listen and to hear him, which, on a daily basis, changed my whole life. I wanted to know who Jesus really was and what he wanted me to do with my life. I felt that he wasn't asking anything of me, just for me to be confident in the knowledge that he loved me. It was very easy to be confident, once I heard his voice; it was so real, it eliminated all the doubt. It was real reassurance of how much he loved me, but also guidance in the way he wanted me to be.

I used to think that to be loved by anyone I had to give blood, really go over the top and do a lot for them, and Jesus was constantly telling me that he loved me just for being who I was and to stop wearing myself out with people, trying to make them love me and looking for approval.

I was just at the stage of learning to stop that, when suddenly things became really stressed again, financially, and I couldn't see where Jesus was in my life. We were about to be evicted and the children put into care. One night, I was determined to commit suicide rather than this happening.

I was in the bathroom, with a Stanley knife in my hands, determined to cut my wrists, but God wouldn't allow me to do it. It physically felt as though there was a person firmly holding my hand with the knife in, not allowing me to go ahead with it, until I broke down and cried and agreed to live.

It changed then; we were given the offer of a house, through opening up to people about the seriousness of the problem. It was hard, telling people, but I knew that God wanted me to be open, and through this, and others praying and listening to God, the situation totally changed and a house was provided, through some new people.

God was showing me that we are family and that he's very much present in other people. That meant a lot to me: it wasn't just our financial problems being solved; it was like God giving me back a family that I felt I'd lost – a large family, like the one I hadn't lived with since I was so young.

Now, on the surface, there is some panic as to where God is, because I've given up work through bad health, and there isn't enough money coming in, and I'm waiting. Inside, there's a peace because I know Jesus is here in this and I'm not alone, but on the surface I'm getting anxious because I'm not sure where he's leading me at the moment.

When I was first looking for Jesus, my husband was very angry, and jealous – because he knew this was a real search for love. He was very cynical about God, and he could see I was changing quickly: my need for my husband was decreasing, and it frightened him because he thought he was going to lose me. He spent a lot of time trying to stop me from having this relationship with God; he felt I was wasting my time.

The bottom line – the thing that really changed him – wasn't the things I was saying, but all the good things that were happening to us as a family; he himself had never experienced the love and the goodness from people that he was witnessing, and after a while he kept saying, 'This must be God's work.'

As the years have passed, he's come to depend on God more himself. He prays now, instead of asking me to ask for things that we need. He still feels that he himself is 'some way down on God's list of priorities'! But he hasn't given up talking to him and hoping, and he does admit to hearing God frequently, and he isn't ashamed to admit it to anyone now.

I'm not afraid of dying: I expect sheer joy! I was resting in my bed, not feeling well, the other day, and my daughter came in and said, 'Don't even think about it, Mum; you're hoping you're going to die today, aren't you?' I'm not sure if it's healthy really; it sounds almost cold but I find myself rejoicing inside when I hear someone's died, instead of grieving – I mean, not if someone's been murdered viciously, but normally I just feel happy for them. Or, I can grieve but I can get over it very quickly; I know it would never grip me, the way it did when my brother died; that could never happen again.

But there is a temptation to want Jesus to come and take me before

*my time, and I think he's still got more work for me to do –
unfortunately! Working for him is just continuing to witness to him in
my life and help others to come to the knowledge of his love. The
witnessing is both talking and continuing to live the way that we do,
trusting him for everything.*

14

· · · · · · · · · · · ·

Cyril's view of Christianity as a moral code is a widely held one. I've heard a lot of people profess that loving one's neighbour and doing no harm to anyone is a way of life based on Christian values. And many people who live according to that code see no need – unless you feel the need – for daily communication with God or belonging to a church or becoming familiar with the Christ of the gospels or trying to form a personal relationship with Jesus Christ, even if they think it's possible.

But in the experience of most of the people in this book who say Christ has come to life in their life, morality is not the main issue, nor even a very high priority. They stress the love of Jesus for them as sinners, his acceptance of them as they are. If they change their way of life, it's as a side-effect of becoming more aware of their own desires, or gaining the self-respect to refuse to be manipulated, or finding that certain behaviour no longer fulfils a need.

Ann found that Jesus didn't give up on her, even when it took her four years to obey his instruction to leave the man she was living with. And Dean actually *began* to sin, and to enjoy the freedom to make his own choices, when he realized Jesus was real and was willing to forgive him.

Even Marianna's refusal to use underhand means of getting money or goods for her family was motivated by more than adherence to the moral rule-book, because she also refused to accept some charity donations that came from perfectly legal sources, simply because once she realized that she and her family were valued by God, she was no longer willing to accept rubbish. So when well-off women from the parish offered to come and advise her on tasty ways of cooking cheap meals but didn't offer to provide the ingredients, at a time when the most the family could afford was beans on toast – without the beans – she politely forgot to set a date to invite them.

When a church welfare group delivered a sack of secondhand clothes and she found it contained shirts with the collars torn off, blouses with heavy sweat-stains under the armholes, filthy and torn net curtains, and stinking shoes, she put the whole lot out for the dustmen. When another person brought a 'charitable' donation of ten loaves of bread – all stale – she did the same.

She was heavily criticized for it. People said, 'Beggars can't be choosers,' and, 'Some people don't want to be helped,' but once Marianna had felt the love of God, she just couldn't feel like a beggar any more. She felt that Jesus was living in her life and in her house, and she didn't want rubbish brought into a house where he lived, or where her children lived – whether the rubbish was old net curtains or sin!

Another point that makes me doubt, personally, that Jesus was sent to establish a moral code is that he was a practising Jew, and he himself said the Jewish moral code is perfect: not a single dot or dash would disappear from that Law, until the end of time. And why should it? It had been handed down to Moses by God himself, as the infallible and unchangeable 'user manual' for all human beings, beginning with the people God chose to be his own – the Jews – and through their fidelity to God it was intended to spread to the other nations.

The Ten Commandments cover every aspect of human life and every human device for avoiding what's right. Even today, there's nothing to interpret or adapt, in them. They're perfectly clear:

worship God with your whole being and don't idolize or rely on any other resource; don't steal, don't kill, don't fornicate, don't slag off your neighbour.

We all *know* them. Even if we'd never heard them in our life, we'd know them in our bones. Thou shalt live like a human being, not like an animal... yes, we know that. God didn't need to send his son to tell us how to behave, nor to offer an alternative moral law.

The reasons Jesus gave for coming to earth were to do with sheep being harassed and dejected and needing a shepherd, and sick people needing a doctor – not a new set of guidelines for health.

We need a redeemer from our addiction to evil which, despite all our good intentions to keep the moral law, constantly distracts us from being the good people we'd like to be. 'You who are evil yet know how to give good things to your own children,' is one way Jesus described us.

I need someone to pay off my debts – the terrible times when I haven't done anyone any harm, because I never got close enough to them to do any good. I need someone who can and did keep the real spirit of the Law and who will stay with me in my daily doomed-to-fail efforts to do the same, giving me the power of his own success.

Jesus did give clear moral guidelines, but not to make a point of showing anyone how badly they'd failed to come up to scratch; only to ease the hopeless confusion they felt as a result of the self-righteous 'Pharisee' element (which exists in every religion and every non-religious field of life) turning the Father's simple recipe for happiness into a minefield where they were afraid to be human.

He did come to establish, or rather to restore, justice, but not the bureaucratic 'justice' of insisting that tired people kept every minor regulation with the same emphasis as the fundamentally vital commandments of love for God, neighbour and self.

And he didn't even insist on those vital commandments without first intervening personally to make each person's life less of a struggle so they at least had the energy to think about whether they'd prefer to be good rather than evil.

He didn't come as a lawgiver, because there already was one – the Father. And he didn't come as a law-enforcer, because everyone already had one – their conscience. He came as the embodiment of the law. God's law was his flesh and blood, ingrained in every cell of his body, accepted in his spirit, embedded even in his genes.

Jesus didn't die in order to create another religion. He died to crack the fear that prevents human beings from living real human lives. He accepted a death he could have escaped from, to rescue us from a spiritual death we'd proved we couldn't avoid, not even with the benefit of a perfect moral law as our guide.

The only requirement for being counted as one of Jesus' people is to be one of God's children – that is, a needy human being, a regretful sinner, a directionless sheep, or a sick patient – the ones Jesus came here for.

Conversely, the only way to write myself out of my inheritance of faith in God's love for me is by saying that Jesus bears no relation to me and I don't need his help. A way of wording that might be, 'I'm a good enough person already; God can't complain about me, so he ought to treat me decently and give me a reasonable life.' That should make it clear enough to God that I don't want the kind of love and compassion exemplified by his treatment of Jesus Christ.

But it's also clear then that I'm expecting God to conform to my own version of love and compassion and my own specifications of what God should be like, rather than trying to find out, in the light of the history of Jesus Christ, who he is.

15

. . . .

'How can I form a relationship with someone I see as a tyrant?' was the question that occupied me when I returned from the school retreat, at the age of fifteen. I accepted what my sister had said, that running away was not a solution. And I accepted what the priest had said, that Jesus might have something to say to me. And what I had heard did seem to come from him, partly because it struck me as the truth, and partly because it wasn't what I wanted to hear: 'Try living with him.'

I looked at what I knew of this great-uncle I lived with so reluctantly. He had done something good; he had taken into his home a family with no means of support. But then, no one else would housekeep for him, on the terms he offered. He had promised, in return for all three of us being his unpaid servants, an ultimate reward: my mother would inherit the house that belonged to him.

On the other hand, the house he lived in had just become very much smaller, and every time my mother had a row with him, he went to the solicitor next morning and changed his will! So there was no point in putting much faith in this promised inheritance. And in the meantime, he showed no concern when we had no money for shoes or for outings, and whatever he gave with one hand, he seemed to take back with the other.

He could be generous, amusing and sympathetic. His talents for art and gardening bore witness to a reverence for beauty. But he could also be abusive, contemptuous and violent – and I never knew which mood he would be in. How could I live with him?

If God told me to do it, it must be possible, and it must be worth doing. God had not chosen to rescue me from this tyrant; he had told me to live with him. And because God is love, that must mean that I had to find a way to love him – mustn't it? But if God is love, I reasoned, he can't be on the side of someone who's cruel to me – can he? So I wasn't being asked to love the cruelty in the man, but I was being asked to love the person who could be cruel as well as kind – even if he chose to be cruel far more often than he chose to be kind. But how to love someone who rejected all approaches?

I began to think about what kind of person Uncle was – apart from the way he related to me. After all, I'd only known him since I was four. He'd existed a long time before that. My mother spoke fondly of how good he had been to her and her family when she was a child. And she'd lived with him for a year as a young adult, not as his housekeeper but as a family member.

I began to ask him more about himself. There had always been times when he'd reminisced about his childhood and my sister and I had listened with interest, but now I began to piece together what he'd told us and asked him to fill in the gaps. Which brother was the eldest and which came next? Which member of the family did he feel closest to? Why did he say he never really knew his mother, when she lived in the same house? How did he feel when his governess was sent away? Why did his family all emigrate and why didn't he go with them?

He didn't seem to resent the questions, but occasionally he'd get angry at some memory, usually of something one of his brothers had done or said, and he'd get up abruptly and go out of the room, slamming the door, and my mother would say, 'I've told you not to upset him!' But later he'd often return to the subject himself, and bring up some good memories as well as the ones that had sent him into a black mood for hours or days.

Whereas before I'd avoided being alone with him, now I began to do so deliberately, though only in ways I felt safe – usually in public. I'd walk into town with him, or go to meet him on his way back from his daily walk.

The usual time for a verbal abuse session was after supper, over the washing up, with my mother out of the room. He would stand and watch, at close range, the way I either washed or dried the dishes and would make comments. 'Are you doing it that way because you're daft or because you're trying to annoy me?' was the common starting point.

I decided that living with him meant treating him as a human being, even when he was giving the impression of being a tyrant. And treating him as human included taking the risk of annoying him, rather than humouring him or behaving like a victim. So the first time, after the retreat, that he came out with this line, I handed him the tea-towel, smiled, and said, 'You're very welcome to show me the right way to do it!'

His face darkened, and he growled, '*I'm* not going to do it! Don't be so damned impertinent!'

I carried on drying up, and he left the room. My sister turned round from the sink and raised her eyebrows at me. My mother came into the kitchen. 'What have you done to upset him *now?*'

It didn't solve anything and life with him didn't get any easier, but over the weeks and months, something did change. I stayed polite, but I refused to play the frightened child ever again. I was an adult; he was an adult, and I was going to remember it even if he didn't. Often, after I'd refused to be intimidated, I went to my room shaking, but I found that if I could control the outward signs of being frightened, eventually the inward quaking subsided.

I really felt that God was helping me, but there was a lot of conflict, because I wasn't doing what my mother told me. For instance, if a friend wanted to call round to see me at the weekend, I was meant to ask my mother and she would tell me not to mention it to Uncle and she would wait for 'the right moment' when he was 'in the right mood' for this favour to be asked of him. Only, often enough, there wasn't a right moment or a good mood, in time for the weekend, and I'd be told to put the friend off till another time.

I decided it was no use trying to have a relationship with him if I asked all the difficult questions through an intermediary who was afraid of him. So the next time I wanted to ask if a friend could visit, I asked Uncle myself, in front of my mother, during supper, ignoring all her frantic signals to me to keep quiet. 'Can one of my friends call in on Saturday afternoon?'

He set his mouth grimly, put his head down and pretended he hadn't heard me. My mother glared at me. My sister became nervous.

'Have some potato, dear,' said my mother quickly, pushing the dish towards him. He took the spoon and scooped the lot, leaving none for anyone else.

I left it till after supper. He went into the sitting room and closed the door, which was a signal that no one else was welcome and we were expected to spend that evening in our separate bedrooms – or if my sister and I spent it in each other's, we had to talk in whispers because the sitting room was next door. I knocked on the sitting-room door and went in. He didn't look up from his book and pretended to be reading.

'Hello,' I said.

He didn't answer me.

'Hello,' I said. 'Can I have a word with you?'

He looked up, grudgingly. I had the feeling he didn't know how to deal with the situation, which was new to both of us.

'A friend of mine has said she'd like to call round and see me,' I said, 'on Saturday afternoon. If it bothers you, I can tell her not to come, or we can go out for a walk. But I've been to her house a few times and I'd like to ask her to stay for tea.'

'What are you asking me for?' he said. 'You do what you damn well like in this house. I hardly know I live here.'

'I won't invite her if it upsets you,' I said.

He rustled the pages of his book and pretended to read again. I nearly ran out of the room, but I stood my ground. There was a long silence, during which he didn't look up and I didn't go away. In the end he said gruffly, 'You do what you like. Doesn't bother me.'

'Thank you,' I said, and left.

It sounds silly to say that it took all evening for my heartbeat to settle down to its normal speed, and it was silly; it showed how we'd all allowed human relationships to degenerate into a caricature of how they should be.

We'd colluded with Uncle's elaborate rituals for expressing disapproval and resentment, instead of expressing our own desires and fears in plain words and asking for straight answers and statements. The result was a maze of hints and strategies and manipulations, instead of honest conversation, and it spilled over from the relationship the three of us had with Uncle till it contaminated the way we related to each other as well, and to other people.

Before the retreat I'd been in the habit, when I wanted to make some request of my mother, of making it sound as if I was pleading for favours: 'If I finish all my homework, and promise I'll help with the housework at the weekend, can I please go out tomorrow evening, even though I know it's a weekday and you usually say wait till the weekend?'

Now I began to say instead, 'I'm planning to finish my homework tonight and do tomorrow's by Wednesday, because it doesn't have to be handed in till then, because I've been asked out tomorrow and I'd like to go.'

Sometimes it worked, sometimes it didn't, but at least it left me with some self-respect. And an unexpected ally appeared: I'd started going out with a boy I'd met on the retreat, who came from a normal, cheerful family where everyone said what they thought. He wasn't afraid to come to the house, as some of my schoolfriends were, and refused to be bullied while he was there.

The first time he met Uncle, without waiting to be introduced, Uncle barked at him, 'Take your hands out of your pockets! Who are you?'

The startled sixteen-year-old took his hands out of his pockets, then drew himself up to full height – he was taller than Uncle – gave a broad smile, grasped Uncle's unwilling hand and shook it, introducing himself, then put both hands firmly back in his pockets. 'I thought about it,' he said benignly, 'but they're my hands and my pockets and they're used to each other by now!'

Uncle's face turned grim, then, to everyone's surprise, he laughed.

I was impressed by the boy's courage. 'I'm stupid,' I told him. 'I just lose my nerve with him.'

'You live with him; I don't,' my friend said. 'But there's one thing you're doing wrong – you're trying to keep him happy all the time. Why? If he wants to be miserable, let him; that's his look-out, not yours.'

I was learning, and one of the things I learned, through trying to do what I felt God had asked of me and live with Uncle instead of co-existing in the same house, was that being nice was not the same as being good. When Uncle came into my room, instead of nervously trying to cover myself up and dodge his greedy eyes and hands while he pretended to be telling me off for some offence, I began to shout as soon as the door began to open: 'Get out of my room!' And when he didn't, I'd raise my voice and shout, 'Get out of my room! Get away from me!'

At first the shouts came out as no more than a hoarse whisper, but I gained in courage and volume, till the day came when he looked anxiously over his shoulder and then backed out of the room, swearing at me under his breath.

We'd been studying the life of Jesus in the gospels, at school, and one thing that had struck me about Jesus was that he wasn't a nice person – not in the way I'd been taught, the way of never hurting anyone's feelings or doing anything that would upset anyone and never answering back when someone was abusive.

In fact, I felt nervous of Jesus, not sure if I'd like to meet him and if he'd like me, or whether he'd greet me like one of the scribes or the Pharisees: 'You whitewashed tombs! Clean and bright on the outside, putrid and rotting inside!'

Or would he say about me what he'd said of Judas: 'It would have been better for that person if he'd never been born'? It was something I often felt about myself and, of all the people who knew Jesus personally, Judas was the one I identified with the most.

I used to reason that if I had never been born, my father might not have left home, my parents might still be living together, for better or worse, or else my mother and sister would be living with Uncle, succeeding much better than I did in not annoying him, and everyone's life would be easier.

I agonized over whether things could happen that were not God's will – if he made his choice plain and yet people chose to ignore him. If it would have been better for Judas not to be born, why was he born? Because it was God's will or because Judas had somehow overridden God's will and, even before any sign of his being physically formed, had made a decision to come to earth, regardless of whether it might have been better not to?

And if that was the case, was I meant to have been born? Or was my arrival not only a supremely tactless act of mistiming but also a sin, a wilful rebellion against God's plan for me not to come?

And if my birth was a sin, did that mean that whatever I did with my life I couldn't make it a good one, since I was never meant to be here in the first place? Did it mean that everything I did, whether good or bad in itself, was a sin, because my whole presence on earth was against God's will?

I was beginning to learn who Jesus was, and that his idea of goodness did not mean being a victim or fulfilling other people's ideals, but I was still very far from seeing God the Father as someone who creates because he loves to, and who loves each one he creates, and that part of that love involves making the person's existence on earth not only valuable but necessary.

It was going to be years and years before he gave me a remarkable sign that every person's life has a purpose, and that Jesus' sadness over Judas was that Judas, whom Jesus had chosen as a disciple because he loved him and believed in his potential, had made a determined daily succession of choices to avoid love, and had ended his life more unloved and more unloving than when he began.

16

· · · · · · · · · · · · ·

The same difficulty I felt in beginning a relationship with the uncle I'd only experienced as a tyrant is felt by many people with regard to God. Even if you feel a desire for God, how do you begin to even want to get to know him if the people who have represented him in your life have been cruel or hypocritical, prejudiced or superstitious, and have given you the impression that God is on their side and is therefore like them?

Adulthood, life experience and common sense do a lot to sift out the truth from the rubbish. As we get older, we find less difficulty in seeing that a priest who abuses children, for example, is not a man who represents God but a paedophile, or that a nun who enjoys beating children and humiliating them is governed by sadistic, not religious, impulses.

Religious life too has changed, and it's no longer assumed that entrants into religious life have no personal problems or that their emotional damage will be automatically ironed out by pious practices. Clergy are no longer placed on a pedestal, like statues, or when they are, no one's surprised that they break when life knocks them off it. Our images of Christians and the Church, on the whole, become more realistic as we grow up and grow more aware of our own ideals and aspirations and weaknesses. People who quote the abuses of the Church as their reason for avoiding God are using the Church for their own self-interested purposes, just as callously as those who hold authority within the Church and abuse it.

But perhaps the first step towards growing out of our tyrant-image of God is to become aware of him as a person in his own right, quite apart from our bias on how he's treated us or the people we love. And for many people, the change comes when they start to glimpse not just the power but the vulnerability of God.

It's there throughout the Old Testament, in his grief over his people's rebellion, but it's not always easy to see and we are frightened off because, alongside his promises to restore and console his creatures, there are promises to destroy those who insist on persevering with evil when offered the chance to do good.

It's easier to see the Father who is vulnerable to his children in the New Testament accounts, in Jesus and in his followers – like Paul, who agonizes in prison not over his own injuries and restrictions, but over the self-inflicted damage of some members of the early churches, who are turning away from the simple goodness of the gospel message and distorting it into something self-indulgent or irreligious.

The gospels don't distort God, but when we've been taught them by people who lack conviction, we receive their message through a filter of cynicism or lukewarm belief, and develop a jaundiced impression of Jesus. Even to hear the name mentioned makes us feel cynical, weary or bored.

As adults, we realize we may have accepted a twisted version of what's actually been written, but by then we've lost the inclination to go back to those primary sources and do the research for ourselves.

We may be attracted to less authentic narratives – by the mass of authors who bring out a 'new' theory or 'radical' interpretation of the life of Jesus Christ, based loosely on dubious sources, and who present imaginative fabrications as though they have the authority of original documents.

Or we may simply avoid the entire subject of God the Father, Son and Holy Spirit and shut off all intellectual and emotional responses whenever he gets a mention, producing glib answers to any questions and classing all religious people as gullible fools or loonies.

Then we're no better off – maybe worse off – than someone who's never heard the name at all. At least they have no unpleasant connotations to get rid of before they take the risk of exploring the different avenues of truth for themselves.

So how can someone who has never heard of Jesus, or never been taught to see in him any hint of the personality of God, or who has just been put off the very mention of his name, break through all the negative or oppressive feelings about him, rid themselves of the myths and prejudices and effect a real encounter with the subject of all this speculation?

The answer may be found in some of Jesus' own words. He warned that not everyone who considered themselves a disciple would be given an automatic reception into his kingdom. He said that, at the end of our time here, there would be many people who would claim, 'Oh Lord, you taught in our town, we went to your meetings, we did what you said – preached your message, cast out demons, raised the dead…' who would be told, 'Get away from me, you impostors; I've never known you.'

But he also said that many would be surprised to hear the words, 'Come and claim your reward for loving me, taking care of me when I was ill, looking after me when I was old and helpless, visiting me in prison,' and when they exclaimed, 'When did we ever do anything for you?' would be told, 'When you did this for even the least of my people, you did it for me.'

We're not going to be judged, then, on our spiritual observances or correct grasp of doctrine, but on the fruits of our lives.

Not everyone knows Jesus by name, and not everyone can even face the idea of getting to know him, but everyone – whatever their culture or circumstances – knows someone who is 'the least among people'.

I'd like to listen to Thomas now. He's seventy-nine, a retired hospital consultant and lecturer whose achievements include introducing hospice medicine to the NHS for people with cancer not responding to curative treatment, then day care and home care, at a time when such patients were left in hospital indefinitely with their symptoms unrelieved because doctors believed, 'there's nothing more we can do.'

Here's a man who believed there had to be something more he could do, who listened to anyone with ideas about what needed doing and how to do it, and then carried it out, despite encountering misunderstanding at times.

I've met and talked to a number of his patients, including my aunt, who have said that his care not only eased their pain and relieved their fear but also restored their faith in human nature and gave them real peace in which to live out the rest of their life.

I'm in no doubt, myself, that this man's work has been of great use to God, in being a tangible reminder of the Father who cares, to some of the people who needed him most.

Yet Thomas claims to have little or no faith himself, believes that whether he lives or dies is of no significance to God, and sees Jesus as someone whose life, if it existed, has no possible use or relevance to his own. He does not expect, at his death, to be told, 'You healed my fear, eased my pain and consoled my heart; now come and claim your reward.' He expects his existence to cease and his communication with his beloved family, and with all the patients who would gladly have died for him in return for his kindness, to be abruptly cut off.

I hope he may be in for a nice surprise...

Thomas

I say my prayers because I'm afraid not to, and when I need help I pray a bit harder, but I don't know if I really believe.

My first experience of religion was through my mother. She was Church of England, but she'd go into any church she saw, always to pray for other people. She was also a spiritualist. I remember her taking me, as a five-year-old child, to meetings where the clairvoyant would pick someone out and give them a 'message'. I believed in it all at the time; I'm more cynical now! My mother would hold seances in the kitchen with her friends and you could feel them willing the glass to move, and pressing the table!

My mother was very ambitious for me and sent me away to school. We were taught divinity as part of the School Certificate and as a boarder I had to go to church every Sunday; I found it terribly boring and used to sneak something in to read. But my abiding memory of my mother is of her saying, 'Let's kneel down and say our prayers.'

I felt Jesus could do no wrong and he would help you. Then when I was older I wondered where the help was. I believed he was the son of God. I don't now – but I don't want to not believe; I'm frightened not to; I want to have something to depend on. Everyone needs to find meaning in life – the meaning in love and suffering.

When my wife had cancer, six years ago, I found my colleagues medically helpful, but I was sick with worry and there was no one to talk to. So at nights I used to pray, apologetically: 'If it's your will, please…'

I find it hard to believe in this unseeable, linkless God. I don't see the person of Jesus as a link. I had the traditional impression of him as a good man who came from God, suffered for his faith and died for us, but if you start asking searching questions, like why he said he was the son of God, I don't have any answers for it.

I don't think it's possible to see him as a person; he's almost a mythical figure. It's the purpose of living and the spirit of his beliefs that's important; he's written a law of Christianity: you don't harm people; you try to be good.

You don't have to pray every day; saying prayers doesn't make you into a Christian. There are good and bad doctors and nurses, among believers and non-believers. What I'm conscious of is the fact of trying to help people. As a doctor, you can't just treat physical problems. Patients have pain and sickness – but also depression, fear, anxiety. There may be a rift in the family, a son who's rebelling, a husband who's having affairs. There may be financial problems, spiritual problems. What's needed is total harmonious care.

I drifted into wanting to be a doctor. I was an only child – a North Country child with a broad Lancashire accent. In our environment it was quite an achievement, to become a doctor, and as it was what was suggested, I went to Cambridge and did medicine. After the war, when I was demobbed from the Navy, what I wanted to do very much was go to drama school and become an actor, but I knew it would cause a real crisis at home. But I think I brought some of that acting into what I did: certainly in lecturing – talking, quoting, miming, holding an audience – and as a doctor at times, on the unit, making the patients laugh.

Life as a hospital anaesthetist was very rapid: I saw so many patients there wasn't time to suffer with them; there was an accident, then an operation, then a delivery... I became a consultant anaesthetist, and later became more interested in hospital administration, the development of medicine, resources and services, and was on the hospital management committee. It was at a regional meeting that someone suggested, 'What you need at your hospital is a terminal care unit.' It sounded awful! Terminal care? I didn't know what it was.

At that time, surgeons had problems in dealing with cancer patients who weren't cured. They saw them as failures sometimes or as a 'blocked bed' – an occupied place on a ward that could otherwise be used for a patient they could cure. So they were in favour of setting up a separate unit in the hospital.

Also, doctors aren't necessarily trained in pain control, so a lot of these patients weren't getting their symptoms treated and were suffering distress and fear. I knew there was a need for a different kind of care. I went to see one or two hospices, but one thing I was determined about was not to call our unit a hospice because the image at that time was, 'Once you get in there, you never get out.' I wanted to get people's symptoms controlled, and get them home. Ideally, I felt, GPs should refer patients earlier, not keep trying treatments that obviously weren't being effective.

What we aimed for, on the unit, was a state of peace, purely by removing fear and pain. There were no invasive treatments, no one rushing around with resuscitation equipment. And if a nurse was sitting on a bed listening to a patient, she was doing her job. She didn't get called away by Sister saying, 'Oh, nurse, if you're not doing anything…'

One of our earliest patients was a lady in her late forties who hadn't married, because of looking after her mother. She had nursed her through her final illness, and when it was all over and she was ready to start living, she was struck with cancer, with secondaries everywhere.

She came to us, but I had to send her to an orthopaedic surgeon because she had a spontaneous break in her femur, so she was away for three weeks. When she came back, she said, 'They were very kind to me there, but it's good to be back!' She felt it was like coming home. She had this terrific faith; it humbled me. She said, 'When God wants me, I'm ready to go home. As soon as that door opens, I'll rush towards him!' We controlled her symptoms and she used to sit up in bed and read; she stayed in bed and was nursed, till her time came and she died very peacefully.

All the staff, from the youngest probationary nurse, were taught to listen, to spend time with the patients, to hold their hands – but if a patient had a problem that was beyond them, they were to call on someone more experienced. We had a social worker and a chaplain on the unit as well as the medical team.

There was also physiotherapy, hydrotherapy, occupational therapy and diversional therapies such as pottery and painting; we had an aviary in the garden, and a fishpond: everything was designed to help people relax, take their minds off the worry, and make them comfortable.

You can always give hope: not always for a cure, but to make life livable. Care of the dying is care of the living. Some patients were under our care for only a few days, and some for years – the longest was nine years – but for everyone there was always 'something more we could do' for their quality of life.

Not everyone was ready to talk about dying. The nurses and I would try to encourage them, to give them the opportunity to do so. Sometimes they were afraid of upsetting their families, and the family was afraid of upsetting them, so everyone pretended they didn't know. But it's better to get it out in the open.

I would go with the home care sister to do the first visit at home, and we'd talk to the patient and the relatives for about an hour, before getting down to business. I tried to make them realize I was there to help shoulder some of their troubles, really wanting to help them, and that together we could get through this. It tired me sometimes, and saddened me often. You can't delve deeper into a man or woman's heart without being touched by it.

I got support from home; I had a good home life – when I was home. My wife was wonderful, and my two daughters. One of my regrets was that I didn't spend enough time with them.

I couldn't bring my troubles home with me, because I had to begin a home life when I came in. The troubles only appeared through the night. With problems within the hospital and the emotional problems of the patients, there were times when I felt like crying at night.

I never liked that phrase, 'dying with dignity'. There's nothing especially dignified about dying – not even when it's a heroic death, in battle or something. But what turns death into something horrific is pain, ulcerations, loss of memory, mental changes, not being able to hear or see or swallow: all that lessens the dignity of the patient, but by good teamwork you can restore dignity, treating the physical and social needs.

I wouldn't strive to keep someone alive; I would certainly give enough medication to ease suffering, whether it was antibiotics or morphine; if it turned them over the edge, I'd still give it. I never found it difficult to make a decision like that. I just did what came naturally, whatever eased the patient's suffering.

But this euthanasia: I think it's very dangerous. You hear of doctors being tempted, 'to make the suffering stop' – but if a patient's referred to a special pain control unit, where they have the expertise, most times the physical suffering can be eased, either with drugs or with nerve blocks, epidurals and so on, for the really awful pain. And once the pain's relieved, it becomes less important, and the patient is free to sort out other problems that may be weighing on them.

There's a close relationship between physical pain and anxiety. People have different pain levels. If a son is drinking, or a daughter's rebelling, perhaps because they're afraid of the mother or father dying and don't know how to cope with it – how can the pain go? You must treat the family as well. Our nurses are in and out of people's homes, seeing the patients in their own environment. It's a great privilege to be involved in people's lives in that way.

If you don't get to know the patient, you can't know their needs; you can't gauge their potential and help them to help themselves and attain their goals; and you can't love them. That's what spiritual care comes down to: love. You can't avoid emotion. There's emotion involved in having an incurable disease, and to love you have to suffer.

The original hospices were in monasteries, and the care naturally had a spiritual foundation. You need kindness, goodness, empathy – and professional expertise as well. It's no good being nice and smiling, if you don't know how to control pain. There must be physical and spiritual care. I found it an advantage having a chaplain on the unit: he was a professional, but outside the medical profession.

Ours was very good. He didn't always wear a collar, and he was just as good talking to the man who didn't believe in God and swore like a trooper as he was with the people who had faith. He took everyone at their own level. If you impose religion, it's cloying; it puts people off. But he would pray with people if they wanted it, or hold a service for a family in the day room. I didn't find his sermons boring; he'd make his point well. One patient remarked that she noticed a lot of patients turned back to their faith. But it was never forced.

We had one young fellow in who was quite violent. He'd lived life his own way, and I think had been in prison. He was in pain, depressed and frightened. We got the symptoms under control and he asked to go home, on the understanding he'd call us when he needed to. So he left, then came back for a few days, having some discomfort, then went away again. This happened three or four times. Each time there was no 'thank you' to anyone – just, 'I'm off now.'

Then once, as he was going, he said to me, 'I hope you don't mind me using you as a refuge.'

I was delighted! That was just what I'd wanted us to be – a refuge, like a church, where people go to seek sanctuary.

I don't think I'll mind dying, myself. I don't want to leave my wife by herself, and I don't want to be a burden on her. If a person gets Alzheimer's or something, they don't know their husband or wife any more, and that's a terrible suffering for the other partner.

I say prayers, usually while I'm walking to the newsagent, or in the car. I pray that my wife doesn't have a recurrence of cancer, and that the children are safe. I only pray for myself to the extent that my wife won't lose me and my help; she'd manage very well, I'm sure, but I don't think she'd like it much. Beyond death, I don't expect very much. I'd like another life, a different life up there. I think it would be wonderful to meet your family again, but that can't be possible; I just don't believe it. But if I'm wrong, I'll be delighted.

17
· · · · · · · · · · · ·

Uncle was impatient for me to leave home; he was planning to move again, and was having a house built in a village near the coast. It was to have only two bedrooms, one for him and one for my mother. When my mother asked where my sister and I would stay during the holidays, he said, 'What do they need to come back for? Let them make their own way in the world like I had to.'

My sister was nearing the end of her first year away from home, at teacher training college, and although she'd felt ill-prepared in some ways for an independent life, she'd survived, made friends, and was keeping up with the work. She was finding it hard to manage on the money; Uncle had never considered himself responsible for our financial welfare, and made it clear that once we left home he didn't expect to feed us during the holidays, but it wasn't always possible to get holiday jobs. My mother was drawing social security and trying to hoard it for when we came home, to pay for the extra food. She also put her foot down and insisted that Uncle's new house should have a spare bedroom for us to stay in, and to all our surprise, he listened and changed his plan.

When we did go home for visits, he seemed quite pleased to see us, even though after a few days there would be increasing complaints that we left doors open or lights on or forgot to leave him the cream on the milk, and we'd know it was time to leave. But I wondered if his determination to cut all ties with us once we left home was a way of rejecting us to avoid the pain if we rejected him and never went home again. When he was a teenager, in his first apprenticeship, his parents had emigrated, and he never seemed to get over the impression that they'd left him to sink or swim, even though an older married sister – my mother's mother – had also stayed in this country and kept an eye on him.

I prayed for my sister to be able to make her own life; she had a poor image of herself and found it hard to stand up to people. And I learned from her, how she coped with her unaccustomed freedom, and was encouraged by her success. I had a fear of 'not being able to cope with life' or 'cracking up'; my image of the worst that could happen was being admitted to mental hospital, unable to work or survive in the outside world. I prayed fervently to be able to pass my A levels, be accepted by a university, and be free to leave home. Beyond that, I didn't dare to think much.

When the day came, I nearly didn't make it. Uncle had been fretting and fuming about the slow progress in building the new house; he wanted to move as soon as it was finished, and my mother was trying to insist that I shouldn't have to leave school till I'd completed my A level exams – but thankfully, the builders didn't finish their work before I was due to leave.

I hadn't been accepted by the university I'd decided to go to; another proved to be too inaccessible from our part of the country, another didn't offer a place, and one turned out to be in the middle of extensive building works. I felt confused; I'd asked God's help to choose the right place, my exam results were good, but it wasn't working out. Only my final choice was left, and I went up to see it. As soon as I got there, I felt a great sense of relief and answered prayers. Compared with others, this university had a very casual, relaxed atmosphere with few restrictions, and people seemed friendly. After the rigid control at home, it seemed perfect.

There was one further hurdle, before I could get there: my boyfriend of two years told me, the day before I was due to leave, that he was finishing the relationship and didn't want to see me any more. I spent all day crying and got home late that evening, with a headache, still not having packed.

I wasn't used to travelling alone and had written out the details of the journey, which was quite complicated: train to London, tube across London, train north, bus to the university campus – carrying a large suitcase laden with books.

My sister came in and found me studying the route, and crying. 'I can't do it,' I said. 'I've waited so long to be able to leave home, and it just feels too much: I can't do it.'

She went out of the room and came back again. 'How about if I come with you?' she said, 'No one'll know I'm not a student there, will they? I'll stay in your room the first night and go back to my college the next day.'

She did more than that. She talked to everyone we met, invited them to meet us later in the bar or my room, read through all the literature I was given and helped me decide on which groups and societies to join and which concerts to go to, and left with some parting advice: 'For the first three weeks, talk to everybody, go to everything and join in everything. After that, people form into cliques and it's harder to make friends.'

I'd never thanked God so much for her as at that time; she gave me a real head-start, and I didn't look back.

There was a lot to thank God for there. The friends I made in the first term stayed friends for the whole three years; they were kind, sane and supportive, and refreshingly honest about their feelings, their fears and failings.

It was a relief too to have my own room and privacy. The modern language course I was on involved fewer formal lectures than some, with a lot of individual work assignments, and I'd spend hours at my desk, in the daytime quiet of the hostel, working on essays or translations, knowing that no one would come in without knocking. The peace was unimaginable.

My confidence was low and I still expected to be told I was doing everything wrong. At the end of the first term I went to see my tutor to say I knew I was below standard and could he give me some pointers for catching up on the work during the holidays? He looked surprised, said I was doing well, and told me to go and enjoy the break from work.

There were a few shocks, after the gentle atmosphere of convent school. In the first week at university, we were told where to go for an abortion, how to avoid police drug raids, and the procedure for reporting our cleaning ladies if they overstepped their authority and remonstrated with us for having a boy/girlfriend in bed with us in the morning.

When I went to sign on with the campus doctor, he asked me why I wasn't on the contraceptive pill; a couple at a concert had sex on the floor right next to me, in the middle of the crowd; and a boy I spent one chatty evening with asked me whether the reason I didn't plan to stay the night was because I was frigid, a lesbian, or had been brainwashed by religion? I was so surprised I started laughing, and said it was because I didn't know his surname!

It made me think, though. I had realized it would be difficult to hold on to my faith in God, in an environment and an era – the science-idolizing early 1970s – where cynicism was regarded as a badge of intelligence, and belief in a personal God a sign of gullibility. I realized now that it wasn't going to be enough to turn up at Mass every Sunday and say brief, weary prayers at night before falling into bed. I was going to need the support of a community.

This wasn't as easy as it sounded, although there were several Christian groups on campus. The obvious choice was the Catholic chaplaincy, since I was a Catholic. There was a lively Sunday evening Mass in the garage-turned-chapel of the priest's house, followed by a buffet which always included hot sausages and chocolate biscuits – a big attraction for underfed students! But this was the prelude to the evening meeting, a talk or a debate, and I wasn't attracted to that.

I was ignorant about many church issues, had barely heard of the Second Vatican Council – beyond the welcome fact that it had changed the language of the church services from Latin to English – and felt intimidated by the students who voiced their views so confidently and argued so loudly. To me, it was no different from student political meetings, which I avoided.

So I used to attend Mass, sneak a quick sausage, and leave before the debates started. The chaplain, an elderly smiling man with an artificial leg from a war injury when he was an army chaplain, used to greet me warmly as I tried to leave unnoticed, but I felt too guilty about eating his food and not staying for the meeting to respond to his obvious friendliness.

The Anglican chaplaincy was an alternative – my mother's family were all Church of England so I felt I could have reasonably fitted in, but the chaplain was a 'trendy', dressed in flowing caftans, involved in a dozen social causes, left-wing to the point of anarchy, anti-authority, and usually to be seen rushing off with a minibus full of socially committed students, to some event or rally.

Again, it seemed a politicized religion, though more active and less academic than the Catholic group, and although I could see that religion and politics overlapped at times in the area of social justice, I felt there wasn't a need for both, that in fact the two approaches conflicted, and I couldn't always see where those boundaries were.

The third major Christian community at the university was an evangelical group, who placed more emphasis on personal commitment to Jesus and a living-out of the gospel message, but they were heavily into converting people. After a while, I grew wary of any unknown student who approached me, smiling determinedly, and started up a conversation, in case it soon changed from friendly small-talk to the question of whether I'd 'been saved' or 'accepted Jesus as my personal saviour'.

My culture as a Catholic hadn't prepared me for this, and I found it alarming and intrusive. Evangelism, for Catholics, tends to be very low-key – perhaps partly through fear, from a fairly recent history of being a persecuted minority, but also because of a belief that conversion is an activity of the Holy Spirit working within a person's own life and experience, and that although a believer must be ready to explain their faith if somebody asks about it, the only 'witness' required by a Christian is the wordless example of a godly life.

It seemed to me, too, that this group consisted mainly of young people who were ill at ease with themselves and with student life. Their manner, with students outside their own group, was either brash – claiming that others were missing out on something – or awkward, as if embarrassed about approaching people but feeling compelled to do so. Most seemed unconfident about their personal appearance and sexuality, wearing 'camouflage' clothes as if afraid to look attractive; and their nervousness of ordinary social activities gave the impression of a fear of becoming contaminated.

I could sympathize with their wariness of getting drawn into a lifestyle which was easier to drift into than to resist; I was beginning to see for myself how persuasive the 'easy' culture was – easy highs, with drugs, drink and the party atmosphere; easy sex; easy answers to difficult problems such as poverty, in the world beyond the campus... And I admired the evangelical group's commitment, meeting early every morning – before the general panic to rush out of bed and run, half-awake, to lectures – in order to pray together and read the Bible. I was still half-keeping my options open and wasn't ready to be accountable to a group for what I thought of as my private morality.

But this group wasn't for me – and even if it had been, it was a shock to realize that I wouldn't have been allowed to join, unless

I'd been willing to be 'converted', because their idea of 'Bible-believing Christians' excluded Catholics.

I'd come across misconceptions about Catholic beliefs, among other Christian denominations – based mainly on out-of-date concepts from pre-Reformation history lessons at school, perhaps spiced up a bit by caricatures derived from the Dave Allen Show! – but it was my first encounter with real anti-Catholic prejudice from other Christians, and it made me feel very alone.

I felt like a freelance Christian, while knowing very surely that there is no such thing, because following Christ requires being fully involved in community. I had no links with a church at home, since 'home' had now moved to another part of the country, only tenuous links with the church at university, and my only sense of support came from the knowledge that my mother was praying for me constantly at home, and that I was still part of the eternal and universal 'communion of saints' – that community of spirits of all the believers in God who have ever lived and will ever live, beyond our narrow band of present-day time and space.

When I prayed, I knew God was there, but he didn't always feel close. Much of the time, I felt very alone. One weekend, early on in my time at university, all the students I knew well had gone home or gone away on some activity, and I felt a desperate loneliness, the worst I'd felt since I was a child, hiding from Uncle in the spare-room wardrobe.

By the time the first friend returned from his weekend away with the sailing club, I almost mugged him and forced him to come and have coffee, to keep me company! I realized then that I was becoming dependent on friendship to meet my needs, and that was dangerous: not only are friends not always available when you need company, but nothing strangles a friendship more than need.

After that, I planned my spare time to include some independent activities, including contact with people, and returned to some old resources for spending time alone – reading, going for walks or listening to music. The constant companionship of university life was one of the main attractions for me, but it could also be tempting to let it become a source of security, and that security was illusory.

Although the Catholic chaplaincy wasn't a source of support for me, I began to be more affected by the chaplain himself. He was an odd choice of priest for a community of lively, anarchic students. His age and his disability, his training as a lawyer, and the old-fashioned gravity of his manner, all made him seem out of place.

I often saw him limping around campus, stopping to chat to any student who was alone or seemed depressed; he never asked about their religious beliefs, and every conversation ended the same way: with an invitation to supper within the next week.

When asked to account to the university administrators for the way he'd spend his year's budget, he wrote 'sausages' in large print across the detailed form, and sent it back. It was a fairly accurate assessment of his religious policy towards students: feed them!

He invited me several times a term. His guests at supper were often shy and taciturn, and he was adept at drawing them out, and warmly appreciative when another of his guests tried to do the same, even when they were rebuffed at first. I began to see how he worked, and to study him.

Every night, after his supper guests had gone home, he'd sit in the lighted window of his front room, reading, till three in the morning; the postgraduate student who lived in the house told me that that's when a lot of students, seeing him sitting there, called in and talked to him about their problems.

He employed an ex-homeless alcoholic as chaplaincy cook: it didn't require much expertise to cook sausages. The cook was a gentle man whom most of the students got to know and like, but every so often he'd get drunk, fly into rages of frustration, and retire to his room with a ferocious headache that sometimes lasted for days. The priest wouldn't let anyone go and bother him, apart from taking him coffee and trays of food, and the students took over the cooking till he emerged and took up his post in the kitchen again.

The chaplain was involved in a soup-run around the derelict buildings in the city, and encouraged us to offer our services, but I was too scared. When the charity set up a night-shelter, though, I ventured along. Nervous at first, I soon found the people were mainly very sensitive souls who'd been hurt by life and let the hurt turn to vicious rage or hopelessness, rather than channelling it into ambition or a thirst for justice, as some did.

I remember being there one evening, before the television was stolen, watching an item on the news. A group of miners had been trapped by a fall in a mineshaft. The reaction of the men in the shelter was revealing. Even very drunk, as most of them were, they took the news to heart and really identified with the victims; they were genuinely upset by the incident, as though it had happened to themselves. One said, 'I never worked in a mine, but I've worked underground laying sewer pipes; it must be terrible being trapped like that.'

One evening, one of the homeless men turned up at the chaplain's house. I was leaving surreptitiously, after the Sunday Mass, and heard him say to the chaplain, 'Can you give me a bed for the night?' The priest raised his eyebrows quizzically at him. 'What happened to the place I sent you to, in the church crypt? They can't be full up yet, at this early time of night?'

'They're not,' the man said, 'but it's full of drunks, and the mattresses are hard. Last time I came here, you gave me your bed and you slept on the sofa, and it was more comfortable.'

The priest threw back his head and laughed with real enjoyment. 'You're right,' he said. 'I'd rather sleep in my bed than in the crypt of a church! All right – but just for tonight, and this time I'm serious!'

I began to think about how I could do what this chaplain was doing, in my own circumstances, because I could see in him something that made me think of Christ.

One of the less positive aspects of the university's no-supervision, do-as-you-please policy was that meals were not provided as a compulsory part of student expenditure; there was one three-ring cooker between sixteen hostel occupants, and a refectory offering meals that few students could afford. Many parents couldn't or didn't top up their children's grants; casual jobs were hard to come by, and towards the end of each term, a lot of students were suffering from mild malnutrition.

The ones who knew how to cook were at an advantage; those who didn't queued in the campus supermarket for one-person tins of steak and kidney pudding. I began to recognize some of them, and to ask if they'd like a shared supper: I'd cook, if they shared the cost of ingredients and brought their own knife and fork.

It worked quite well; as I had fewer lectures than the science students, I'd get the bus into the city and go to the market for cheap meat and veg, and make huge stews. My friends had reservations at first about 'outsiders' coming into our group, but soon softened – except on one occasion when I got a bit carried away and invited seventeen people; then they sensibly set a limit of eight! We ate late, so as not to get in the way of the other hostel residents, and everyone washed up.

I had three very happy years at university, until the very end: I was sharing a huge flat with twelve other students, and it was fun at first – like a big community – but with the pressure of final exams approaching, everyone seemed to withdraw into themselves, and personal success became the only goal. Relationships became competitive; it seemed it wasn't enough for each one to achieve their own potential; there was resentment of one another and speculation about who would do best.

Anything that took time away from studying was resented; cleaning and tidying the flat was a source of argument; and food even began to disappear from the fridge and cupboards, as people raided each other's stores rather than waste precious time going out to buy their own. It was a very difficult atmosphere.

For me the low point came when the girl in the room next door to me gave up on university and left, and the student tutor asked us to take in a girl who had tried to commit suicide after finding her boyfriend in bed with one of her flatmates. The first night she arrived, very tearful and upset, the boys in our flat sat in the kitchen and discussed whether they fancied her and what they thought of her legs.

I had been ill, on and off, through my time at university, partly because of a common teenage problem of painful periods which caused me to faint every month, and partly because I was afraid of running out of money and, even worse, of getting fat, and wasn't eating much. I became very weak and dizzy and couldn't get out of my room for three days. Finally, I crawled out, found one of my flatmates working in his room and said, 'I've been ill for three days and had nothing to eat; can you help?'

Without looking round from his desk, he said, 'I might have a bit of cheese in the fridge. Sorry, I've got to finish this work.'

On my way to the kitchen I fainted and was found quite a long time later and was carried back to my room and left there.

I managed to get to the campus surgery. For some reason, the doctor gave me tranquillizers and sleeping pills, although I'd explained I felt dopey and could barely stay awake.

One afternoon, I went out to go to a lecture and found my vision was so blurred that the ground appeared to be moving like ocean waves. I went back to my room and started taking pills. The idea in my mind was to have a good long sleep, and wake up feeling less unwell and confused.

When I'd tipped out large quantities of pills, suddenly a calm descended on me and I heard a steady voice saying to me, 'What are you doing?'

I looked down at the handful of pills I was about to swallow and felt horrified, then enraged at the doctor for handing out suicide-mix to stressed final-year students without even enquiring into their health or eating habits.

It was rage that propelled me down the corridor to the toilet, where I flushed away all the pills. Then I went back to my room, sat down on the bed, and cried for five hours. I thought I would never stop, and it frightened me that I didn't seem able to. But every now and again, that calm would come down again, and I'd draw breath and feel all right, before starting crying again.

By the time a flatmate came in and found me, I looked like something out of a horror film, with swollen face and eyes. He insisted I call the doctor, and only accepted my refusal when I agreed to go to the chaplain instead.

The chaplain was finishing saying weekday evening Mass in the student union building. He had a meeting to attend at the chaplaincy, but took me, with the friend, to the house, installed us in the sitting room, put the television on, and asked the resident postgrad student to bring us coffee and chocolate biscuits. My friend said he couldn't stay, he had work to do, but the chaplain looked at him firmly and said, 'No, stay with her.'

It was peaceful in the house, and the sugary coffee and food made me feel better. By the time the priest returned, I was able to say, 'I'm all right now. But I think I'm going to leave here; I can't take it any more.'

He didn't argue with me, just said, 'I'll come and see you tomorrow. If you still want to go, I'll drive you home.'

'You can't do that!' I said. 'It's on the south coast!' It was a long drive for anybody, let alone an elderly man with a gammy leg. But he just laughed.

Three days later he drove me home. He'd advised me to see all my tutors first – 'just in case you decide to come back and take your exams' – and I'd done as he said, but I had no intention of returning, and had packed all my books.

As we came closer to the coast, I felt very nervous and said, 'I don't know why I'm going home; I won't be able to stay. My mother's only a housekeeper there, to my great-uncle. It's not my home any more.'

He reached out and patted my hand and said, 'It'll be all right.'

When we reached the house, my mother had prepared lunch and he sat down and ate with us. Uncle was silent, and straight after the meal, he went out. The chaplain thanked my mother for the lunch and said, 'I'd like to have a look at the sea. Would you care to show me?'

Slightly flustered, she agreed. I went to follow them out, but he turned round and smiled at me, and I knew I wasn't meant to go too. I don't know what he talked to her about, but no questions were asked of me and I was allowed to stay as long as I wanted.

After two weeks, my mother was showing signs of stress. I was sleeping for sixteen hours at a stretch, waking up to eat, trying to study but falling asleep again, often in the middle of a sentence. The village doctor told me to go for walks, so I walked along the cliffs every day, but my mother was nervous until I returned. I thought she was afraid I might kill myself.

She said I was having a nervous breakdown, but personally I didn't feel it was that serious and that I could be just exhausted. I also felt food was involved in some way; I was getting cravings for sugar, eating it by the spoonful out of the sugarbowl, and it seemed to ease the dizziness.

After two weeks, a friend asked to come and visit me, and my mother flew into a rage about all the trouble I was putting her to, even before expecting her to feed 'all my friends' as well. It was clear I couldn't stay at home indefinitely.

An item on the local television news revealed that a schoolgirl killed in a car crash had been identified as the sister of my ex-boyfriend. I was sitting down to write to the family when the phone rang, and it was him. He said, 'I just had a feeling you might be home. Can I come and talk to you?'

I met him outside and we walked along the cliffs. He was very distressed, and desperate for a break from all the mourning at home. I invited him to come and stay a few days at the university, as it wasn't possible for me to invite anyone home.

After he'd left, I realized that must mean I was going back to university. I wondered if the chaplain had prayed for me. When I returned, he didn't seem at all surprised to see me.

My flatmates had not been expecting me back, and had eaten all my small store of canned food. The girl in the next-door room had locked herself in, after a week in mental hospital, during which time no one had visited her. She only let me in when I told her I'd been in much the same state that she had. After that, she used to talk to me and we lent each other music to listen to; she said she found it good 'calming down therapy'. It did help to concentrate on the music, refusing to let my mind stray to worrying about the future. I also went to Mass every day, and ate a meal every evening. It was a strategy for survival.

My expectations of God were still quite low. I asked for help to get me through the day, but it didn't occur to me that he would be concerned about how I felt and not only about what I did. I thought he wanted me to be useful, to care for others, and to count my blessings. I worried about people starving and tried to eat little, want little, and help others. I strained myself to the limit, and constantly asked for his help so I could strain myself further. I didn't have any concept of a God who was compassionate, or generous enough to provide for everyone's needs. I certainly didn't think he wanted me to enjoy life, just to earn my keep and not be a drain on the world's resources.

I'd already changed my plans once for my future career. I'd been going to put my language skill to use by training to do commercial interpreting, but I'd taken careers advice and the advisor reckoned I was on the wrong track. My heart wasn't in it, I had no ambition to make money, and he felt I'd be more suited to social work. So I'd taken a job with the charity that ran the city project for the homeless – but I was having second thoughts. The nineteen-year-old girl who worked at the night shelter told me she was regularly left in sole charge. She showed me where she slept: in a curtained cubicle, with no door, under a filthy blanket. The toilet was at the other end of the shelter, reached by stepping over the forms of twenty men in stages of drunkenness ranging from dangerous, through violent, to unconscious. The toilet had a broken door and no lock.

I agonized over whether God intended me to do this job. Were the risks an occupational hazard of doing this kind of work? Or was it criminal carelessness on the part of the charity's organizers? I wasn't sure. I was more sure years later, when I heard that one of their untrained volunteers, left in sole charge of a hostel, had been murdered. But at the time, it was one more worrying question I didn't know the answer to.

It was the chaplain who provided the answer, one evening when I was sitting in his kitchen. 'Are you able to do this job?' he asked. I looked at him, and it suddenly all seemed simple. 'No,' I said. 'Would you like me to let them know you won't be joining them next month?' he offered. 'Yes please,' I said. It was settled.

I applied for probation traineeship, but funding had been withdrawn and there were no vacancies, so I wrote for details of a job in a children's home and was asked if I'd consider instead filling a vacancy in one of their homes for disabled young people. I'd asked God to find me the right place, and I hadn't planned this; it had just happened, so I said yes.

I was only there four months before I fell ill again, but it was a time I wouldn't have missed for anything – a privileged insight into the lives of people who, in the face of serious disabilities, prejudiced attitudes against the disabled, crippling symptoms and embarrassing disfigurements, made a real life for themselves, encouraged one another through times of bitterness and depression, and had affection and interest to spare for everyone who worked with them.

For the first time, I began to see the meaning of the word 'saints', and it didn't seem a far-fetched or fanciful concept, like other-worldly figures in medieval stained-glass windows.

I was squeamish about dressing wounds and coping when people were sick, but on the whole I was happy with the work. Like many charities, though, the organization treated its clients quite well and its staff quite poorly. Accommodation and food were provided, but the food was only whatever was left over from the residents' meals, and only for the staff who were working that shift, and the salaries were too low for the care staff – mostly school-leavers waiting to start nursing training – to buy more than the occasional snack for themselves. I wasn't the only one who became dizzy and light-headed at work, but I was the only one who fainted, and that got me the sack.

They were quite nice about it, explaining it wasn't safe to take the risk, as I was lifting disabled people – and asked me to vacate my room as soon as possible, so they could lose no time in appointing my replacement. I understood their position; it was just that I had nowhere to go.

I prayed for help and felt, deep down, that things would work out okay, but I'd been given a date to leave and although I was applying for every job I could, time was running out. To complicate matters, I wasn't entitled to sick pay because the doctor had said I was fit to work and the home had refused to accept that, and after I left, I found they'd said I'd left voluntarily, so I wasn't able to claim unemployment benefit either.

A schoolfriend had a flat and would probably put me up for a while if I asked, but she was living with her boyfriend and they were getting on very badly at the time. My sister had a small rented room in a family house, and a job that paid barely enough for her to live on, and she was engaged. I didn't want to intrude on anyone's life. And most of all, I didn't want to go home. My boyfriend had said I could move into the flat he shared with a colleague, but I hadn't known him long, couldn't pay very much for my keep, and I was determined to be independent.

I never wanted to rely on anybody because I was afraid I'd be too much for them and drag them down. My mother had always said I was a difficult character, too much to cope with, and I'd found it alarming, at home, during the times when she didn't seem to be coping well with life's demands.

I had the impression I'd be too much for anyone to cope with, even maybe too much for God, a strain on his patience and goodness. It worried me that he had to keep giving me help, and I could never do anything to help him. Children of single-parent families feel a heavy responsibility for the parent, and I think I still saw God as the single parent of a huge family, who mustn't be troubled with too many demands!

The day came for me to vacate the job. There was still nowhere to go except home. I cleared my room, packed my bag, said goodbye to everyone, got on the train, and arrived on my boyfriend's doorstep with my suitcase. It somehow felt less immoral than going home. I hoped against hope that God wouldn't blame me too much.

18

. . . .

God didn't seem to have abandoned me. Within a month I had a job I enjoyed, as caseworker for a charity organization, visiting people with social problems, going to their homes or hospitals, assessing needs and arranging support services, and helping run a club at a day centre once a week.

It involved three hours travelling a day, to and from my work district, then covering about six miles a day on foot; I had no car, and the bus services were slow. To avoid wasting visiting time by going to the office, I did all the paperwork at home in the evening. My boyfriend complained I worked too hard and he didn't see enough of me; I'd moved into a flat shared with three girls by that time. But the time we did spend together was good; we were getting on well and beginning to think about getting married.

I was in the enviable position of looking forward to going to work in the morning, and looking forward to coming home in the evening and seeing my boyfriend. I thanked God every day for looking after me so well.

But the childhood teaching: 'count your blessings; don't make a fuss; think how well off you are,' still took its toll of my prayer life. I continued to pray for strength to be of use to God, to help people and to forget about myself. So I didn't mention to him how ill I felt and how much of an effort everything was, beyond asking his help to ignore it, to get on with life and not make a fuss. Then one evening my flatmates found me unconscious and called an ambulance.

At first it seemed clear what the trouble was: I had all the symptoms of low blood sugar. The diabetics in the ward knew it; the doctors recognized it at once; the tests confirmed it. Everyone was supportive and sympathetic – till some of the test results didn't match up. Then I was told there was nothing wrong, I should live a normal life and forget about it.

The abrupt change of attitude left me confused. I felt guilty, as though I'd wished some imaginary illness on myself, and upset: I'd thought doctors were naturally compassionate and would persevere with patients till they found the cause of their sickness, and a cure.

The social work agency arranged an appointment for me with the medical consultant on their board of governors. He saw me in his private clinic, a top floor room in a huge empty house, with a receptionist far away on the ground floor. In the course of an extensive examination, smiling widely, he asked personal questions that had nothing to do with health, involving considerable sexual innuendo. I left as soon as I could, clutching a prescription for some kind of medication, but never told anyone what had happened.

I felt in some way it must be my fault; I'd been abused as a young child, in one of our temporary homes, then had twelve years of verbal, sexual and physical violence from my great-uncle for all those years, and I assumed there was something about me that people recognized as bad and treated with contempt, even when they had a good reputation and appeared to treat others with respect.

I also wondered if I'd imagined the incident, as some people were beginning to suggest I was imagining the illness.

Then it happened again: the GP I'd signed on with made comments which, coming from anyone other than a medical professional, would certainly have sounded lecherous. This time, there was confirmation from other patients; a couple of young women I met mentioned that their GP was a 'creep' and a 'lech', and it turned out to be the same man.

My sister asked her doctor to take me on instead. He was a blunt, no-nonsense Irishman, who looked at my hospital notes and said, 'What are they messing about with? Sounds exactly like low blood sugar to me.' Then he said, 'It's up to you where you go from here. I can send you back into hospital; they'll do a million tests on you and put a name to your illness, but you could get used as a guinea-pig in the process, and there's no guarantee they'll send you home feeling any better.'

I didn't know what to do. I felt dizzy all the time, had had a number of episodes of going unconscious, felt sick, had a lot of pain, and everyday tasks took enormous effort; each step was like wading through treacle. A date had been set for the wedding now, and I desperately wanted to get well. I saw no alternative to going back to the hospital.

I was X-rayed and tested from head to toe. Test after test was negative, borderline, or inconclusive. The doctors were fascinated, each time there was a new hypothesis, especially if the condition they suspected was unusual, but once the tests didn't confirm it, they lost interest.

I learned a lot about the hospital process, through my own treatment and from talking to and observing the other patients, and I began to feel the approach was naïve. If illness was closely connected with stress, then the system of tests and treatment did nothing to relieve it. Most patients were very nervous of being in hospital, and nervous of the doctors, who were so rushed and so clinical in their attitude that no relationship formed between them and their patients.

I began to feel that healing could only take place between humans; drugs and treatments were only implements. But the doctors only seemed interested in disease: curious about its causes and eager to meet its challenges and defeat it on its own territory. They didn't have time to be interested in human beings, in all the complexities of their unique and individual lives, and they didn't want to get drawn in. It was a fast-food approach to healing, with quick stop-gap remedies to stave off the pangs, then on to the next customer.

I saw too that the doctors' and nurses' private lives affected their relationship with their patients: that in fact someone's private life is not at all private, because it affects their personality, and they bring that to work with them. To the extent that they compromised their integrity in private, giving way to ambition, desire for money or success, or lust, or snobbishness, or pride – to that extent their spirit was tied up and unavailable to their patients.

And when a doctor wasn't able to get down to the level of the patient's real suffering, because he or she was avoiding that depth in themselves, then they could only apply superficial cures that removed or covered up physical symptoms. It often seemed that when the doctors were lacking in depth or perception, the patients took on the task of trying to heal *them* – trying to make them listen and understand the nature of illness and take a real interest in people.

Some of the tests were like torture, particularly for someone who was already unwell, and some of the drugs were so harsh that the side-effects they caused were worse than the original symptoms.

There was sympathy, and there was attempted kindness, and well-meaning efforts to cure, but that isn't the same as love, and I couldn't imagine how anyone could be healed without being loved. It seemed to me that a person's desire to become a nurse or doctor comes from God. Even when it's mixed with other motives, such as desire for social status, the inner prompting to heal the sick is a real calling and, coming from within the spirit, it can't be ignored.

But because it comes from God, it can only be effective if it's carried out under God's authority, which means that the doctor or nurse's whole life – private as well as professional – has to be subject to God's law and draw very heavily on his guidance, perception and help. If not, then the person does have some measure of natural ability to heal and to discern, and may have some measure of success in overcoming the signs and symptoms of sickness. But it's limited, and the danger is, the 'cure' may take away the signs of a deeper unease and send the patient away, apparently cured, without ever approaching the real person and their real need.

That's how it seemed to me, but at the time there wasn't much choice but to be a hospital patient, within the current medical system. I was married at twenty-one: the round of hospital admissions and clinic appointments was to continue until I was twenty-eight.

Finally, in confession, I admitted that I was failing to accept my life as it was, and rebelling against God for letting my youth be wasted in illness and causing a strain on my marriage. The priest told me there was no need to try and accept it. 'Some people find that their illness brings them closer to God,' he said, 'but if that's not the case with you, and it's making you feel farther away from him, that's the last thing he wants. Why don't you ask to be cured?'

'I've been in and out of hospital for the past couple of years,' I said wearily, 'and they can't find what's wrong.'

'Ask for a miracle,' he said. 'People think they're few and far between, or that they only happen in places like Lourdes, but they happen every day – and right here in this parish, I'm telling you.'

I came out of the confessional, knelt down and prayed, 'Lord, give me a miracle and cure me.'

During the next week, a woman offered me a place on her group trip to Lourdes. I told her I wouldn't go now; I'd go as a thanksgiving when I was cured, because I believed the Lord was going to cure me here, at home. She didn't agree with me, but I was convinced. After all, I hadn't become ill in a vacuum, but in a certain environment, with a certain history, and surrounded by certain people. Therefore, my illness had something to do with all of those, and my healing had to include them too; otherwise it would only be partial and not fulfil its real purpose.

Also within the next week, I noticed a change in myself: the fear had gone. I'd been afraid of what was wrong with me, feeling sure it was something serious. I still felt there was some quite serious physical illness, and that more suffering lay ahead of me, but there was no fear about the outcome.

I'd also been afraid of losing my job, and that happened, after a couple of months. And I'd been afraid my husband would get fed up with me being ill or would turn against me and believe what some of his friends were implying: that this illness was purely neurosis or a convenient excuse to get out of things I didn't want to do, and that he'd made the wrong choice of wife and was to be pitied. And that happened too.

I wasn't afraid of dying, but I was afraid of living this half-life of being ill all the time, indefinitely. I was afraid of the future, of being unemployable, useless and having no place in the functioning world. I was afraid of my husband not loving me, and my mother's prediction coming true when she'd said so often, 'I pity your poor husband if you ever get married.' I was also afraid of committing my life one hundred per cent to God, cutting myself off from 'normal' priorities and being seen as a holy fanatic out of touch with reality.

And all that fear went. I couldn't remember why I'd felt that those things would destroy me. What mattered was that, through all these unpleasant and undesirable circumstances, God had a purpose, and he'd help me find out what it was. I didn't hear him as a voice, but my prayer felt answered. He would heal me; I'd be all right. In the meantime, a sentence kept running through my mind: 'You may get hurt, but you won't be harmed; you won't be damaged; the Lord has got hold of you.'

At the end of the week, I was sent an appointment. I'd asked for a second opinion, when the doctor discharged me after the last stay in hospital. I'd been found to be jaundiced, and though he dismissed it as unimportant, he'd agreed to refer me to a liver specialist. When I went for the appointment, the specialist confirmed I had a liver condition, causing jaundice and blood sugar imbalance. The treatment proved ineffective but at least I had an answer for those who implied I was malingering, and I felt more confident.

I was in my early twenties by this time; it was six years since I'd left home, and one day my mother packed a small bag, told Uncle she was going away for the weekend and left him and never returned. There was consternation, and anger, in the family, and anxiety that neither of them would cope alone. In fact, Uncle discovered a new independence, learned to cook, and became much more amenable to accepting and appreciating people's help. His bitterness with my mother stayed with him, though, till he died. After nineteen years of her looking after him and humouring every whim, all he could remember about her was that she'd deserted him, and he never forgave her.

My mother was unsteady for a while, then took a living-in job with people who paid her a salary, gave her the use of the car and a weekly day off, and even sometimes thanked her for her work; her confidence increased enormously and she began to regain some enjoyment of life.

My sister was married with two young children, who were a delight. I hadn't conceived, and though everyone made arch comments every time I fainted or was sick, pregnancy was never the cause of it.

I decided to try an alternative to conventional treatment; it wasn't controlling the symptoms, and I was being sent to three different clinics in two different hospitals. The pain now was almost constant and I passed out whenever it became unbearable; I was often sick, had constant infections, and the episodes of going unconscious were becoming frequent. On a friend's recommendation, I changed to homoeopathic treatment, and was given pills and a diet to regulate the blood sugar levels, which helped me feel more alert, but the pain was persistent.

I was in a job, only part-time now, at my husband's suggestion, but even that was too much and my boss was severe about any time missed due to sickness. After collapsing at work and being taken away in an ambulance, I didn't expect that job would last much longer.

At about this time, I changed the way I prayed. I stopped begging God to help me keep going, and said instead, 'Lord, I can't go on like this, and I can't see a way out of it. Please, just do something.'

I began to get the feeling that, as I was even more distressed about not having children than about being unwell, perhaps I should go for tests for that. My doctor was discouraging. 'Wait till your health is better,' he said. 'You're in no state for more investigations, and you wouldn't be well enough to look after a child at the moment anyway.' Most of the people I spoke to said the same. But each time I prayed, the idea came back again.

'Lord,' I prayed, 'I don't like the idea of these tests; I don't want them, and the doctor doesn't recommend it. So where is this idea coming from? Is it what you want?' I felt a strong sense of encouragement, and I began to feel this was coming from God. After all, it wasn't logical, and it wasn't my own inclination: I wasn't at all anxious for more tests and more stress! I discussed it with my husband, who told me to do whatever I thought was best, so I began to attend yet another clinic at the hospital and enter another programme of tests. I was put on the waiting list for an investigative operation.

A friend offered me work in a business he was setting up, and said,

'Come in when you're well and stay home when you're not.' This took away all the stress of worrying about letting colleagues down or losing my job, and I was able to really concentrate on the work; the quality of it was praised and my absences were not criticized.

After a while, I was offered freelance work by other companies as well; my husband warned me against taking on too much, but it felt good to be enjoying work again, and for the first time contributing a reasonable salary to our joint budget, as commercial work paid much more than social work for charity organizations. It provided an insight, as well, into a different lifestyle. The charity workers I'd worked with were motivated by people's needs, and would put up with poor salaries and working conditions in order not to take valuable resources away from their clients. The charities sometimes exploited this.

In the commercial field, employees seemed to exploit the company, using it to further their own ambitions and provide them with a higher lifestyle, and their work and commitment were only guaranteed for as long as the company gave them what they wanted; if a rival offered better conditions, there was no hesitation in changing to that one. Employers complained about lack of 'company loyalty' but they had no more loyalty or responsibility towards the people they employed, and were ruthless in finding legally watertight excuses for making them redundant if they weren't quite productive enough or the company's top line weren't making enough profit. It was a different system.

I was more involved in the church now, at least in its prayer life, attending a weekly group, and reading the gospels at home and praying more from the heart than I had before, seeing Jesus more as a person and less as an authority figure mirroring authority figures from my childhood. I was coming to understand that the purpose of his life was to love, and that that was the purpose of everyone's role here, in whatever circumstances they found themselves.

I visited my great-uncle, after my mother left, and my sister and

I wrote to him regularly. We sent him news of ourselves, our careers and husbands and families, but all his replies were about my mother, how ungrateful she was and how she had let him down. Finally he wrote and said contact with us was upsetting to him and he didn't want to see or hear from us any more.

Then my aunt died, and the memorial service was in the village where Uncle lived. He didn't attend it; his neighbour was there and told me Uncle had shut himself in the house and refused to see anybody. I asked how he thought Uncle would react if I went to see him, and he shook his head sadly and said, 'He talks about you girls and the past with fondness, but I think he has too much pride to let you know he misses you.'

I decided to give it a try; he could only throw me out, and it had happened so often before that I should be used to it.

The house was in darkness, with all the blinds pulled down, and no one answered the doorbell. I sensed someone looking out through the blind, and knew he had seen who was there. I rang again, but he didn't come to the door. Suddenly I became angry: I'd been trying all my life to get through to this man, and for all those years he'd shut himself in a dark house of bitterness and anger, when all he had to do was open the door and let people into his heart. I began banging on the door and shouting: 'Let me in!'

Then I remembered him banging on the bathroom window, at the bungalow, threatening to break the glass, and I stopped – partly because I didn't want to do the same thing, and partly because I wondered why I was bothering, why I cared about him at all. If he wanted to spend his life wallowing in bitterness, let him, I thought.

As I was about to move away from the door, it opened, and there he was – looking older and smaller and much less frightening, but still with the same grim set to his face. He said, 'I'm not seeing anyone today; I'm in mourning.'

I said, 'Okay,' and he said, 'You'd better come in. Would you like a sherry?'

It was rather a surreal meeting, sitting drinking sherry in the blacked-out sitting room, searching for something to say. In the end I asked, 'Are you still painting?' and he said, 'I've been going to a class. Do you want to see what I've done?'

He consented to let me open the blinds and make him a cup of tea, while he stacked pictures round the walls. Then he sat there, in the house where he now lived alone, this rich old man surrounded by antique furniture and his own beautiful pictures, sensitively drawn and painted in the most delicate watercolours, and he talked about a past I didn't recognize, where we had such happy times together as a family and life was such fun.

Soon afterwards, he moved into a residential hotel and was looked after for his remaining years. We visited him there, but whenever he looked at me his eyes would fill with tears and he'd look away and direct all his conversation to my husband. When I had my first book published, I sent him a copy – not because he was ever likely to read a novel, but because I thought he might like to have it on his shelf and tell people his great-niece had written a book. But my cousin, who visited him sometimes, told me Uncle had read it three times, cover to cover, knew all the names of the characters, and told everyone he met to buy it!

I kept in touch with him then, but in the last few months before he died he became angry again because I couldn't visit. I explained I was ill but he didn't believe or forgive me.

After all the years of living with him in poverty, he left a fortune in his will, divided among his wider family. I didn't want my share; I wanted to either give it or throw it away, and my sister felt the same, but one evening when I was praying, I felt the Lord telling me this would be revenge. He said, 'Buy something to remember him by, something he'd value himself, then give the rest to your husband to do as he likes with.' So I bought a plant for the garden, and left it to my husband to decide how to use the rest.

I'd been admitted to the homoeopathic hospital by this time, for more tests to try and find out why I was going unconscious. In the course of this, they'd tried to actually bring on the comas so they could monitor the process, and had told me to do all I could to make myself ill before I went in there – to fast or eat foods that normally brought on symptoms, and to get exhausted. I wasn't sure about this; it felt wrong to deliberately cause illness, but I went along with it. Sure enough, I was soon in a coma and they did a series of tests, before reviving me with glucose. Unfortunately, they lost the most important test result.

I went home to find I'd been given an appointment for the investigative operation in the other hospital. I was going to cancel it, because it was so soon after these induced comas; I felt very ill, and the doctor said it wouldn't be safe to have an anaesthetic. But when I prayed, the encouragement was still there: no, go ahead.

Because my GP was in homoeopathic practice – even though he was also fully qualified in conventional medicine – the anaesthetist wouldn't accept his recommendation to put me on a glucose drip from the beginning of the period of fasting, not just at the moment of giving the anaesthetic. I knew I couldn't fast for that long without going unconscious, and said I wouldn't be willing to have the operation without the drip. The anaesthetist showed some hostility at this, and said, 'It's my decision, not yours or your GP's.' I said, 'But it's my life, and I'm the one who dies if you can't bring me round afterwards.' He slammed my file down on the bed and walked out, but shortly afterwards the Sister came and fixed me up with the drip.

I was unnerved by the argument, and lay awake praying that night. I said, 'Lord, I know in an operation I should trust myself into the surgeon's hands, but I don't trust the staff here. So I put myself into your hands. Please be with me through this.'

In the early hours of the morning, I began to feel strange, the way I usually felt before I lost consciousness. This seemed odd; I couldn't see how my blood sugar could have dropped below the safe limit when I was on a glucose drip. I rang the bell several times, but no one came. So I got out of bed and dragged the drip stand after me, out of the ward. When I came into the light, I saw the tube was full of blood; the drip had blocked. A nurse came along and helped me get back to bed before I passed out, and another needle and drip tube were inserted; I fainted again while it was being done. I was awake all night then, with liver pain.

I was first on the operating list for the morning, but it was delayed, and by the time I went down, my vision was blurred and I felt really ill. I asked the Lord if he wanted the operation to go ahead or not, but I didn't get any feeling that I should refuse it, and although the ward sister expressed doubts when she read my notes for the night, no decision was made, and the porters arrived to take me down to the theatre.

I felt almost unconscious before I was given anything, and when the time came for the anaesthetic, it was as if a huge lead weight dropped on to my chest; it was very sudden, and my breath stopped. I can remember thinking, 'Something's wrong; it shouldn't happen like that,' then there was a sudden whoosh, and I was in the presence of God.

I can't find any other way of explaining it. It was like coming into a vast arena of light, seeing the Lord there and knowing, as a sudden and amazing revelation, that he really was God, and Jesus was really Lord of everyone, and every word in the gospels was right. And I was all right too: I was meant to be who I was, just as I was, and he had made a place in the world to fit me. As I realized that, and the words kept going through my head, 'It's all right! And all of it's right, all the gospels, everything's true!' I became aware of a lot of other people there, all around me, and they were all laughing. It seemed that they were laughing at my amazement, because all of them had been equally amazed themselves.

It's hard to explain the sense of revelation. I'd believed in Jesus Christ all my life, and I had no doubt of the basic truth of the gospel accounts of his life. Yet, from the sophistication of twentieth-century life, I'd assumed a more-or-lessness about the details; after all, they were written – or dictated to others, possibly at third or fourth hand at some later time – from the word-of-mouth accounts of uneducated fishermen. I knew the details disagreed at times, but that had never bothered me; if anything, it made it more authentic, as with any eye-witness accounts where everyone remembers the same event differently.

But modern analysis inclined towards extracting the essential message of the gospel accounts, while warning against accepting the form and style too literally, and I suppose I'd accepted that emphasis.

But now I saw that the truth of those gospel texts was perfect; it was our minds that tried to neaten it up in accordance with 'superior' logic, and that that wasn't right; there was no need to alter it or interpret it. It was our understanding that was lacking, but if we could just accept what we found in those books, we would later understand how right it was – every 'non-essential' jot of it. It wasn't the basis of some negotiable way of arriving at the truth; it was the truth.

And each person was just right, as they were, with an individual place in the universe carved out by God to fit their particular shape, and each person's life had to be just that shape, with all its frustrations, loose ends and inconsistencies. Every so often, I saw the crowd change formation: someone would move forward and push a person out of their place – but that was all right as well.

The person who was pushed might feel, at the time, that someone was stealing their place, but it couldn't have happened unless God allowed it and it was progress: their time to move on now, and as they moved he prepared them another place to occupy, and as they adapted to it they changed to a slightly different shape. But they weren't becoming distorted, and their lives weren't falling to pieces; it was just that it took them a while to adjust, but as soon as they accepted the change they were able to settle comfortably into this new stage of becoming themselves.

I saw that everything in life was taking place in the context of God, in the light of his presence and his watchfulness. His design for our lives was so flexible that, however bad the choices we made or however rigid we were in refusing to adapt to new circumstances, he would adjust his design to accommodate all our intransigence, and all we did by resisting him was to increase our own frustration and make life more of a fight for ourselves. In no way did we interfere with the smooth running of his household, in which there was room for everyone, and everyone was encouraged to become more fully themselves and settle more happily into the shape he'd designed for them.

I understood that he really had created me out of love, and that every moment of every day he was maintaining me, like an artist lovingly adding delicate touches to a canvas that already looked okay to anyone else, but which, once those details were added, definitely enhanced the picture.

I had often felt that I'd arrived on earth by accident; I'd been told that my birth was due to a failure of contraception, so nobody had invited me; then I'd been told that I got in people's way, upset them and failed to do what was expected of me. But my life had been meant to begin exactly when it did, and my character was no accident either; it didn't consist of a collection of faults and I wasn't a 'difficult person' after all; I had talents and gifts that God had given me, some of which needed practice to manage and develop, but all of which had a positive potential – and this good news was the same for everyone.

Just as I was getting used to this delicious sense of harmony and companionship, I could feel myself starting to drift back again; God was telling me it wasn't time to stay here. I felt very sad and unwilling to go back, and wondered why I had to, whether I wasn't yet fit for more than a few seconds of perfection; at the same time,

I realized that if I'd known before what I knew now, I could have done much more, because I'd have been more confident, both in the reality of Jesus as portrayed in the gospels and in my own value. I felt as though I hadn't done anything with my life yet.

Of all the people who had surrounded me in this place – which I thought of as 'the outskirts of heaven' – I hadn't recognized anybody known to me on earth, although everyone felt familiar. But as I began to come back to ordinary life, I saw the figures of my mother and my husband. I wasn't sure if that meant I was coming back for their sakes, or whether they were there to make sure I landed back safely! Either way, it felt as though they were drawing me back to normal consciousness.

I woke up as abruptly as I'd gone out, to find somebody pulling a tube out of my throat, which was sore, though not as sore as my stomach. The pain hit me as soon as I woke. I was waving a hand at the woman doctor there, trying to tell her I'd seen God and he was real, but she turned away and sat down with her back to me, writing. The pain intensified. I tapped her on the shoulder and croaked, 'Pain!'

'You'll be given something when you get back to the ward,' she said, without looking round. I was glad I hadn't mentioned God.

I've had some vivid dreams at times, but this wasn't at all like a dream; it was so real that, by comparison, our normal material existence seemed only half-real. It was an experience that didn't fade, and I was going to need that inspiration to get me through the next few months.

After this reassurance that I was all right, exactly as I was, the surgeon came round the next morning and told me they had found something very wrong: the internal organs were swollen with growths, to eight times their normal size; the disease had probably spread further but they could only deal with one area at a time. As my liver was too weak to tolerate steroid drugs, the only answer was to operate as soon as possible, to remove the growths they could see. Then I should return for further tests and probably more operations.

As I didn't react very much when he told me this, he thought I hadn't taken in what he'd said, so to convince me of its seriousness his registrar showed my husband and me the slides that had been taken by the internal camera during the operation and pointed out how wrong everything looked. I remember feeling betrayed by this, as if no one had the right to tell my husband I wasn't all right as I was. But we discussed it, and I talked to my mother and sister, and decided to go ahead with the first operation as the surgeon advised.

I doubt very much whether I would have coped, without that experience of the presence of God overseeing everything; it helped me to know he was involved, and to feel more certain of myself. But it also left me feeling very homesick for 'God's household', and that feeling has never really gone, though it's strongest at times when I can't see much evidence of Christ in the situation I'm in or in the people around me.

If that was a taste of heaven, it increased my longing to be there, and it made me impatient to live through whatever time I had left on earth.

And if it was just a different view of the way we actually are on earth, at a deeper level of awareness, then I wished I had enough faith to see that reality always, in every person, and to know that whether we're conscious of it or not we're in the presence of God all the time, living out his plan for us, each in our own assigned place in the world.

19

. . . .

Chris and Elizabeth are a young married couple from very different backgrounds: Chris, thirty-three, was brought up in a devout Baptist family in Scotland, and Elizabeth, twenty-seven, who is Indian, grew up in a wealthy Bombay family with parents who were Sunday churchgoers but didn't let the gospel challenge their personal lives. The couple met through their work with street children in Bombay, and are about to return after a one-year course in Bible and pastoral studies in England.

Chris

The good thing is that I was brought up by committed Christian parents and went to church on Sunday from as early as I can remember, and read the Bible from as early as I could read. There were family prayers at weekends, and we each had our own mission to pray for. Sunday was a special day; we didn't work or go to shops or watch television; we'd usually go out for a walk, and to two church services. I don't remember having an opinion on it, but it wasn't a killjoy day; it was still fun.

In an evangelical church, a lot is made of 'becoming' a Christian, and at the age of seven or eight I remember becoming aware, perhaps through my Bible-reading notes, that we all need to come into a relationship with God. I only saw it as a friendship thing at that age, but I remember asking him to be a friend. I felt he wanted me to ask him.

I had a clear idea I had to do something about it: it wasn't just going to happen. That was the point at which I felt I became a Christian. I tended to pray to God, but I always knew Jesus was God.

There was nothing much to say I was a Christian when I was at school and getting into fights and so on, except going to church, which I never completely rebelled against.

God has had his hand on my life, and I slowly came to understand that it had implications: that I should be sharing my faith. I approached that with fear; I was fairly shy.

As a university student, I was more a part of a Christian clique: quite introverted. There was a guilt feeling that we weren't sharing our faith, so we would go and sit in a bar and try to witness to people. Looking back on that now, I don't think you can separate out the spiritual from the non-spiritual side like that. I was concerned that my friends might burn in hell, but that's not really friendship.

Now I think that if your faith's real, it will come through, but at the time I felt I wasn't being an effective Christian. I don't disagree with that; it was the method that was wrong. We weren't involved with people in the ordinary way, and that's no good.

I had plenty of Christian friends who couldn't hack it and left their faith, because they weren't learning how their faith was implicated in the real world, so they just forgot it. But there were also students who could have a good time at university and have lots of non-Christian friends, and yet not compromise.

I feel much more secure in my faith now and really know what it means. But even through all this I experienced a grounding in the faith and always read my Bible. And at university and afterwards, I was in circles where I heard good speakers, who had things sussed out. I left university and home at the same time, moved to a different area and found a job, and got involved in a church for myself; everything was at my initiative now.

Since the end of my student time I've led a number of Scripture Union camps. I remember when I started to organize it we didn't have any of the people we needed – a canoeing instructor, cooks, a lifesaver, an abseiling instructor, etc – and I just prayed and asked God to provide, and he did. That was encouraging in my faith.

I think I also began to realize there's a hurting world out there and faith has something to say to that. Certainly in the last five years or so, since I've been concerned about the poor, I have more awareness of Jesus as a person, as a man, someone who walked the earth. It's meant more to me.

Early on, prayer was a lot of asking for things; I'm getting better now at praising and thanking, rather than presenting a shopping list. But prayer was always rather informal: in a Free Church, there's no background of liturgy or a particular form of words for prayer. That has its disadvantages, but its benefits as well.

I wasn't taught to expect Jesus to answer back when I talked to him. I had an awareness of his presence, and a sense of peace that you get when you know you're doing the right thing. At times there's been a feeling that I must go and do something.

One of the most dramatic answers to prayer was over the Christmas Cracker project, which was set up by the organization I now work for. The idea was for young people in different areas to take over empty shop premises in the run-up to Christmas and sell Third World food at First World prices.

My group had got everything together, but we couldn't find a place; we tried everywhere. The local newspaper had run an article on the project, and in desperation I rang them to ask if they'd run another one because we couldn't find premises. The journalist I spoke to said they would, and he also suggested somewhere to try.

His suggestion kept coming back to me till I went there. They gave us the whole upstairs floor of their shop and we made £8,000 in three weeks.

It wasn't a voice I heard, but something was pushing and prompting me till I took notice and went and did it.

People are prompted by the Holy Spirit, but I would see the Bible as essential to my faith and would be sure the Holy Spirit wouldn't prompt anyone to do anything that's not consistent with the Bible.

I worked for five years with British Telecom, but I think even before that I had an awareness of a call on my life, and I had an increasing frustration with just doing a job and being caught up in the rat-race, going after promotion and so on. I have no problems with anyone being a Christian and working full-time like that, but I felt I wanted to do something different.

I think it was prompted by some conference or youth event that I went to: there was a talk about the Christian's responsibility to the poor, as part of the gospel. The Christmas Cracker project came up at that time too and that made me more aware of the issues of the developing world. I went to India for three weeks, with the organization that ran the project. Then they had another programme for three months, and I resigned my job to do it.

At that point, I was fairly sure I wouldn't go back to secular work. But being single with no commitments, that's a lot easier.

To start with, I was involved in youth work, just straightforward meetings and discipleship, but there were also opportunities to go into slums and see other things, and that was increasingly important to me – to see and understand the needs and, where possible, to help.

A boy on the streets came to live with us for a while; we were taking some street kids into hospital to get treatment, and we started a small boys' home for six of them.

At this point I saw how the kids who became Christians progressed to becoming aware that there was a personal God who cared for them. They prayed for food or shelter, and they saw it work. There's no question about the difference it makes to them; it's exciting, and you can see how the gospel message of showing concern for the poor enriches your own faith too.

The different things that Christ did came alive for me: his healing, spending time with widows, tax collectors, prostitutes – spending time with people, taking time to go and heal Simon's mother-in-law when she was ill... The people who were there at the time were important to him, not just the crowds but the individuals. And he didn't just heal, he forgave them as well, restored their relationship with God.

When you tackle a problem with Christ's help, it's at a much deeper level. You can feed and clothe someone, but if you can point them towards their own relationship with God, you can start tackling the greed and the selfishness that are there.

I think a block to the relationship with God is trying to do it by your own strength. There has to be a humility: we're not God and there's something about us that's not right. Coming into a relationship with him involves asking for forgiveness. If that's not there, we have the wrong attitude to God; we're always going to be arguing and complaining.

Something that New Age thinking claims is that we're all God, but I don't agree with that. We're not all God. He's distinct from his creation.

People say it's not essential to pray and go to church; what matters is to lead a good life. But I just don't think we have the strength to lead a good life. I'd like to ask people who say that whether they really are. I know that even as a Christian I don't always lead a good life, and we just can't do it on our own.

I'd go even further and say God has created us so that we can't do it on our own. We need the relationship.

By saying, 'I can do it on my own,' someone is choosing to say, 'I want to do it without God.'

There have been things that have made me doubt God, and if you believe in him then you tend to blame him when something unpleasant happens, because he's meant to help you out with things and it's not fair! I can remember in my late teens or early twenties being dumped by a girlfriend, and it was horrible. But then you realize he has other plans for you – good or better.

I was pretty keen to get married; I was looking, and also waiting for God's timing. I wouldn't ever have said, 'I must get married.' I know God knows best. I never demanded it of him.

But he gives us choice and allows us to make decisions. Some people wait forever, because they're looking for flashing lights and signs of God's will. I don't think marriage has to be prepared in heaven, put it like that.

But it was fairly clear, when I met Elizabeth. We enjoyed each other's company and loved each other and we were ready to get married, and we shared the same work as well.

I am very grateful for the upbringing in a Christian home. It was vital to my personal development of faith, although the need was still there to make the faith my own and make a personal choice, and I probably have a very different faith from my family. But there has been encouragement all the way, from the family, very strong support for what I'm doing.

Elizabeth

I come from a Catholic family, a large family, and my father is a quite wealthy businessman, in Bombay. I was brought up going to church, but Jesus wasn't the only one for me, just one of many gods. That wasn't what I was taught, but it was the environment; I was at school with people of different religions and, to me, the Hindus had their gods and the Catholics had theirs.

My life began to change when I was thirteen and my friend's sister died of cancer, and that affected me. I was always having some physical pains and I grew up thinking I had cancer and I was going to die. It was a horrible fear and I couldn't share it with anyone.

Sometimes I even wanted to commit suicide; I was very depressed as a teenager. I just lived for the day; I wasn't making plans for the future, and I wanted to die because I thought there was nothing left for me. I never went to the doctor to check whether I did have cancer; it was a phobia.

When I was sixteen I heard about a gospel concert with a YWAM (Youth with a Mission) outreach, and I went to it. There were people from Europe and America there, drug addicts and all kinds of people, talking about how Jesus had changed their lives. I got excited and thought he must be real if he had changed people's lives.

I contacted them after the concert and they came to my house and started to explain the Bible to me and they talked about their own lives as well, and I wanted to know more about this person, Jesus.

After the team left, there was a lady who followed up on me and she would teach me from the Bible. But I still had the fear and I couldn't share it. I think it was just growing pains, now, but then I thought it was cancer. It didn't change. I'd thought there would be a miracle and my pains would go away. I really prayed to Jesus to take it away, but nothing happened.

I began to doubt Jesus. Maybe he was real for those people but he wasn't helping me, and he was my last hope. I decided, instead of going to the Bible class, to commit suicide.

I had a favourite niece and I wanted to take her for a last walk before I committed suicide, but just as we were coming back home, this lady who took the Bible class came to visit me. I said to her, 'What are you doing here, instead of taking the class?' And she said, 'God told me to come.'

I started crying and said, 'Even God can't help me,' and for the first time I told her I thought I had cancer and was going to die. She asked me if there was someone who could take care of my baby niece while we talked.

She took what I said seriously and said there would be some symptoms and signs, if I had cancer. She prayed with me, and told me not to do anything foolish, then she made an appointment to take me to a doctor, and he explained it was a common teenage hormonal problem.

For me, Jesus proved himself. There was no turning back. I was seventeen then. I regained the will to live, and I began to change. I was materialistic and I didn't care about the poor; we always had servants, and I thought the poor were meant to be servants of the rich, but that changed.

I had a lot of opposition from my parents and for two years I wasn't allowed to go to the Bible class. They were upset because I joined a different church and also because I started work with street children, and they had different plans for me – to be a chartered accountant or something like that.

I spoke to my parents, and my father asked me to leave home if I was going to go on with this, but I didn't have anywhere to go. Some of my sisters tried to talk to him; they said at least I was going to God rather than drugs or something, but my parents felt it was a cult. I don't blame them now for feeling like that. They didn't know what it was, and they really cared. So that's why I stopped going to the Bible class.

I was training for a BCom (Bachelor of Commerce) degree and I had one year of study left to do, to get my degree, but I felt God wanted me to be a nurse because I could use that to help the poor. I started the nursing course, but to make my parents happy I did the final year of the BCom degree by correspondence course, at the same time as doing the first year of nursing training. That meant a lot to my parents.

When I joined nursing I was living in the hospital itself and I joined a church then; I was more independent. But even then, I told my parents, and my family had a meeting. I said, 'If you don't want me to come back home, I won't.' My parents agreed then that I was independent and could decide for myself; they didn't want me not to come home. But all this did damage the relationship with my parents.

I had never dreamed of becoming a nurse: I was very scared of blood or wounds. But there was a verse in scripture – Paul's letter to the Philippians, chapter 4, verse 13: 'I can do all things through Christ who strengthens me,' and God got me through it, and I found I even began to enjoy nursing. I wanted to do it, because I could use it among the poor and because it would make me independent of my family, but without his help, I wouldn't have been able to. I was always top of my class, in all the three years, and that was an indication to me that God was with me.

I learned to thank him; he had been faithful in so many things. Praise and worship and thanking were very important to me. Another area that became important was confession, because I began to realize my bad habits and I felt the Holy Spirit prompting me to change certain things in my life. I would fight with my brothers and sisters, use bad language, and my life centred around going to dances, watching TV... not that that's wrong, but I needed to change my priorities.

After I finished my training, my friend and I started working with the street kids. In India, you can live with your parents till you're married, and now they accepted my faith, my father wanted me to come back home. So they met my basic needs, and my friend, who was an older lady, used her housekeeping money to help the children.

We started with the families who live on Bombay railway station – that's their home. We provided basic health care, dressing wounds and sores or taking people to the doctor, and taught literacy – just the alphabet to start with – and nutrition, gave them snacks, and also taught the gospels, sharing the faith.

When you find children who are so hopeless, you can see how the gospel makes a difference to their life. We weren't there twenty-four hours a day, but we taught them to pray for their own needs – for instance, if their father was in prison, wrongly charged, or if they needed food – and Jesus demonstrated his care for them. When we came back, they would tell us what had happened, and it was encouraging for us as well.

We went there three times a week, for three years. My friend now continues to run this work with the street children and also the boys' home, and I started to work alongside Chris's organization doing medical clinics, but I still keep in touch with my friend.

Chris and I met at my work on the railway station. One of the kids wasn't well, and Chris helped me to get him admitted to hospital and then to transfer him to another one.

We seemed to spend a lot of time with this child at the hospital, and through that I began to know Chris well. Some time later, Chris said that he liked me and would like to have a relationship. After consulting a few friends, and also as I got on very well with Chris, I felt that I wanted to marry him.

In Indian culture, you go out with someone with a view to marriage.

It's not hard and fast – you can change it – but you enter the relationship with marriage in mind. In a cross-culture marriage you have to make a lot more adjustments; I considered that seriously. But because Chris and I knew there would be adjustments to make, perhaps we were more prepared for marriage than some people who marry within the same culture. My father really grilled Chris, before we were married, but apart from that my family didn't interfere. The Catholics in Bombay are mainly from a Portuguese background; they're much more Western than the Hindu culture, and all my brothers and sisters have chosen their own partners.

Chris had always had it in mind to do this course, and it was one of my dreams to go to Bible college – though I never dreamed it would be in England! Nine months after we married, we were on the course.

I felt I needed Jesus more, coming to England, and he was there for me. Bombay is a city of contrasts, with a lot of poverty, and I was afraid that in a developed country I would get comfortable, so I prayed to enjoy the year but to be prepared to go back to the poor of Bombay – and I am looking forward to going back now!

The course helped me to broaden my mind; I saw people of different denominations having such a close relationship with God. They weren't necessarily charismatic but they had a real faith and love for the Lord, and that helped me.

I have never actually heard God audibly, but something often strikes me through a book I'm reading, or through reading the Bible daily, and also through his faithfulness in everyday things: like, when I was here, I really liked the daffodils and I was wondering whether to buy some, then someone brought me a bunch. And even financially, God has brought us through this year. I'd thought, 'What are we going to do for money?' But each time we needed it, a cheque has come in, from friends or from people from Chris's home church, or somewhere.

At times, we had spoken about what we were doing, and about our needs. It's difficult to do that at first, but it's part of the way God provides, and it involves other people in our work.

About the future, we're not sure yet: when we get back to Bombay we'll see what the plan is, but I hope to use my nursing more, in community development in the slums, maybe a medical clinic.

Chris and I would live at the level of a person with a normal salary, not extravagant, but not in a slum. I don't think it's necessary to live at the level of the people you help; you can get overwhelmed by the needs. But our home is always open for the street children to come for a meal, and once a week we have a Bible class there.

At first I was a bit apprehensive about having them in my home; it was something I had to pray about, then it was all right. They didn't know how to use the toilet and would mess up the home, and I was careful about leaving cupboards open and things like that, but slowly they learned and settled down.

There have been difficult times. The first time I took some clothes for the children and gave them out, there was fighting over it and they were tearing each other apart. After that I would wait till I had enough for everyone and I'd wrap one thing in newspaper and write the name on it and say, 'That's for you.' And when I gave tablets or a plaster to one child, they all wanted some, so I had to get shrewd about who really needed treatment and who just wanted attention.

I teach them to write the Hindi alphabet. I'm not fluent in Hindi; I learned it at school but the Catholics usually speak English at home. My parents speak to each other in Marathi, but they speak to their children in English. Some of the street children speak Marathi, which is Bombay's language, but they all speak Hindi. They come from everywhere: some are orphans, some live with their families on the street, some have run away from their village – from the age of seven upwards.

If we have a family, which we'd both like, that would be my priority. I'd like maybe to do both things side by side. But I trust God for the future. I feel life would be so impossible without him, but he has been so faithful – and I know he's there in the future too.

20

. . . .

When a tragedy happens in someone's life, it can either destroy their faith or strengthen it.

For me, being told I had a serious illness was a shock but also something of a relief. I had felt for a long time that I was ill, but every time someone said it was 'just your nerves' I felt guilty and pushed myself harder to keep going. Now, there was the stress of facing an operation, and probably a series of operations, but one positive result of the diagnosis was that people who had been cold or judgmental and said, either behind my back or to my face, that I was not really ill, changed and became more friendly.

My symptoms hadn't changed, but a physical illness with a medical name is treated with more respect than nameless pains and distress – even though I believe now that emotional and spiritual distress lie behind any illness, and the physical pain is often the most manageable part of the suffering.

My husband became a great source of support, insisting that others let me make my own decisions about what treatment to accept. I was by no means prepared to accept the whole package and was taking it one step at a time. My aunt, when she was dying of cancer, had told me her treatment had caused as many problems as the disease and, given her time again, she would have refused further treatment, once she'd found out the first operation had failed. I had the feeling at the time that she was telling me this for my benefit, and I 'stored it up and pondered it in my heart'.

So when, a few months after the operation, it was becoming clear that it hadn't controlled the problem, I was prepared to re-think the situation. I never took a conscious decision not to return to the hospital; I simply postponed my next appointment, to give myself a break from the stress-inducing round of waiting for tests, waiting for results, and waiting for the next admission to hospital. I needed time to call my soul my own.

But it was a nightmare time. I spent most of each day alone, coping with pain and trying to stay calm through bouts of panic. It reached the stage that I was afraid to open my eyes in the morning and find out what else had gone wrong, because each day seemed to bring a new problem: another lump or a new area of pain, or an infection, or finding that my legs wouldn't hold me up.

One day I collapsed on the way back to bed from the bathroom, and woke up on the landing, too dizzy to stand. The ladder to the loft was folded flat against the ceiling, and I saw an image of angels climbing up and down it: hordes of them, passing each other – only, because it was horizontal, there was no way of telling which was the top of the ladder and which was the bottom. I lay and watched this happening, hazily, and it occurred to me that it's not clear in life who's at the top of the ladder and who's at the bottom, and maybe when we're right at the bottom of the heap, we're nearest to God.

At the same time, I heard a gentle voice saying, 'Yes, I was left without a leg to stand on too!' It was such a reassuring and humorous tone that I felt I wasn't going to come to any harm, and was able to wait quite calmly till my husband came home.

So, ten years later, when I met Francis, sitting in a wheelchair at the end of a pew in church, I had some idea of how he felt.

He had developed a crippling and incurable disease two years before, when he was thirty-six, and had already lost the use of his legs and hands, and his speech was very slurred. The illness had progressed fast; he had been forced to give up both his work and – which meant more to him – his band; he was a talented musician.

I asked him whether, with all that had happened to him, he still felt like himself, and he said, 'Not really.'

In my own experience during those past ten years, it seemed that half the trauma of illness was this deep change: all the old securities would go. A person who asked to be healed by God would have their life turned upside down; having already lost their health, they would be asked to lose their whole identity, before they experienced God building them up again. If they accepted the process, they would become more of a person than the person they had been before. But it was hard.

Francis seemed to be halfway through this process. He was still living in the nightmare world of being afraid to wake up in the morning to find out what else had gone wrong with him while he slept; he was preoccupied with the progress of physical symptoms, and not ready to talk about, or think about, his feelings, or to examine his life before he got ill.

He was happy to agree to my going to pray with him at home, and to take other people with me – as long as the prayer was confined to requests for God to relieve his physical sickness. But as the Spirit began to prompt one person after another to pray about his life, his fears and doubts and insecurities, his family and his relationships, he began to refuse prayer.

It was a worrying time. So many people were praying for him, but his symptoms were steadily worsening. I didn't know what the problem was; there seemed to be fear of letting anyone get too close to him. I wondered how close he was letting God come, or if he was holding him too at a distance.

He resisted suggestions of getting as many of the family as possible around to pray with him regularly. He said, 'They get upset – even the children. And I get emotional.'

I asked what was wrong with that. Which emotions was he afraid of?

By this time – I had known him about eight months – his speech had deteriorated so much that his only way of 'speaking' was by use of a board with printed letters on it. He would look towards a letter on the board; the listener would follow the direction of his eyes and say the letter aloud; then he would look at the next letter.

He spelt out now: 'Crying,' then after a moment's thought added, 'I feel very angry. I can't express anger or sadness, using this board.'

'Angry with God?' I asked, but he said emphatically, 'No. About not being listened to.'

I said, 'Are you sure you haven't given up listening to yourself? Would you be willing to express to God how you feel – even if you can't find words for it? St Paul says if you're open to the Holy Spirit, he comes and expresses our feelings to God even if only in groans.'

He tried, but couldn't. He seemed to feel it was wrong to complain to God, as if this was questioning his will.

I asked if he'd be willing to give the Holy Spirit permission to let me know how he felt, so I could express it and pray for him in those terms. He was hesitant. I asked if there was something about his life he didn't want me to know. He said no, but got very angry. For two months, he made it clear I was not welcome in his house.

I believed that every illness had a physical, a mental, an emotional and a spiritual dimension to it and that Jesus could only be invited to heal all of it – not just remove the physical symptoms. And Jesus was present in other people, and worked through them, as well as making himself known to the person directly. At the moment I felt Francis was keeping Jesus – and me, and the others who came with me to pray with him – at arm's length. My impression was that this illness of his had a strong element of emotional distress, as well as a backlog of sheer physical weariness.

His defence against depression had always been to keep busy, often to the point of exhaustion. Now that physical activity wasn't an option, his defence against those feelings was to keep his mind occupied and avoid any deep thinking.

Several people, including the priests who visited and prayed for him, suggested he'd do better to face the despair and anguish he was trying so hard to suppress, express it openly and let others share it, but he wasn't ready to do that, so there was little that could be done about the exhaustion. But I felt he was beginning privately to make some connection between his own emotional history and the apparently sudden onset of this very distressing illness.

When he allowed me to visit him again, I told him I wasn't going to put any pressure on him but I believed he was carrying an awful weight on his heart, all on his own, and I'd really like him to tell me what had happened to him, to cause such a long history of concealed depression.

He was very hesitant, then suddenly flicked his eyes over to the letterboard. I fetched it and he started to talk, and didn't stop for a couple of hours.

I'd like to be able to say that it turned the tide of the illness, but it didn't – or not that I could see – even though Francis believed in God's power to heal the incurable, and so did I: I had to, since he'd cured me and I'd since then seen him cure a number of other 'incurables'.

After he opened up and talked about himself, the prayer with Francis did begin to have more obvious results: he'd feel heat going through him and the pain would subside; he'd tell me how bad the depression was and what his fear was about at that time, and during the prayer he'd feel the weight of it lift and he'd sometimes get really radiant with joy; he even, several times, moved his legs and arms quite naturally, with movements that were completely controlled.

But when I'd return in a couple of days, he'd often have further injuries and feel tired and heavy again.

'Do you want to give up?' I asked one day. 'Aren't you fed up that the prayer's being so ineffective?'

He nodded towards the board and spelt out: 'It is effective. I am able to cope.'

I knew each person could only be healed in their own way; the kind of healing I'd had myself might not suit the next person at all, and only God knew Francis, and all his circumstances, well enough to decide what to give him and what to withhold. But I had serious arguments with God when I prayed.

At the same time, it was obvious that Francis' relationship with Jesus was changing. He'd always had faith, but God had seemed so distant to him that he'd been on the brink of believing he didn't exist. Because his faith was deeper than that of most of the people in his life, he'd kept all his doubts to himself, for fear of affecting their faith with his own despair. He'd tried every way he could think of to make God more real to him: more prayers, extra devotions at church, penances, fasting; he helped people as much as he could, used his musical gifts in the service of the church, and had every video of every major film made about the life of Jesus Christ.

But the Christ he loved and wanted to know stayed distant from him. Francis said he had never felt any warmth when he prayed, never had any sign of the presence of God, and never felt any response from him.

His feeling of isolation from God was matched by his feeling of isolation from other people. He said he'd felt as though everyone was on a different planet, together, and he was on another one, on his own. Several close personal relationships with girls had done nothing to remedy the isolation. They'd seemed more interested in having a relationship, being a couple, having a social life, and eventually in marriage, their own house and babies, than in him as a person, he felt.

Adding to his struggle now was the fact that a past girlfriend had returned and said she intended to leave her husband and move in with him, to look after him in his illness.

At first he was elated; he said, 'I don't dare even look at myself now: I dribble, my neck is twisted, my body is so thin – and she wants to come back to me, even as I am.'

He was sick and tired of being tired and sick; the proposition was a flash of colour in an otherwise dismal picture of the future, and he was seriously tempted.

Then reality began to impinge on the fantasy. He had tried to live, all his life, by staunchly Christian principles, and he didn't want this on his conscience, especially if he was close to dying. In addition, he had a niggling doubt that she might not be accepting him 'even as I am now' but perhaps 'only as I am now' – helpless and unable to make any real demands. So he thought it out for himself and dismissed the option, but it took it out of him.

He was very tired by this time, very thin and very unwell. Everything seemed to drain his energy: people arguing or not getting on with each other, or running themselves down, or boasting, or being angry, or getting materialistic. One member of his family wouldn't speak to another; another one was hyperactive, constantly talking about activities and plans, and even being in the same room with them, Francis would start to look drawn and have trouble with his breathing or develop aches and pains. But always, however tired or ill he was, someone only had to mention Jesus' name, and he would light up.

A priest suggested some meditations for me to do with him – visualizing Jesus and asking him to come closer and to speak to him – and at first Francis found it hard to do, but after a while it came more easily; there would be such a sense of God's presence in the room that I didn't want to breathe, for fear of interrupting it, and at last Francis began to feel how close Jesus could come. Once or twice, I had the feeling of eavesdropping on a private conversation. It was sometimes quite a while before Francis would open his eyes again, and when he did, they shone.

He liked to talk, but he had a real hunger for prayer. If I stopped praying with him and said, 'Aren't you tired?' he'd signal, 'No,' even when he looked exhausted, and if I said, 'Well, I am, even if you're not!' he'd nod to the board and spell out, 'Get on with it!'

The hardest moment was when he asked if the Lord had revealed whether he would cure him or not. I hadn't received any assurance of it, only that Francis would not die, as some who had the same disease did, either choking or in a state of panic, and that he would not need to be doped up on morphine in order to dull the hunger pangs from not being able to eat.

Francis had one very troubled patch where all he could think of was being dead. I asked him what exactly he was afraid of, because the fear took different forms at different times, and he said, 'Afterwards – the coffin, the mortuary...' then, 'Am I being silly?'

I told him I'd had the same thing, at the time when I kept on falling unconscious and it was no use trying to deal with it by being logical, reasoning that if you died you wouldn't know anything about that side of it. So I spoke to a priest about it, and he came and said Mass for Francis and his family and the people who were praying for him, and after that Francis said those fears didn't come back – though others emerged.

His determination to keep his fears and doubts from the family was understandable; he felt he had to have faith for all of them. But I wonder whether, if we don't let each other in on the worst of our doubts and fears, we can really let Jesus into the whole situation, or whether all our prayers stay superficial.

'How long have I got?' he asked one day, and I said, 'Fairly soon,' and he turned his head away.

I said, 'I had a glimpse of where you're going, when I nearly died, and you certainly don't end up dead; it's more like coming alive. If you don't want to go, give me your ticket and I'll go instead of you!' and he laughed and signalled, 'No way!'

Another day, though, I went in and he asked immediately, 'Did the Lord say anything to you about me?' and when I said, 'He said he's coming soon,' his face lit up. I asked how he felt and he said, 'Excited.'

He wasn't ready yet to die, but his enthusiasm for this life was waning. He no longer saw himself as someone who had once had everything and had it taken away, and was beginning to feel that the best, for him, lay ahead.

I had arranged to go to Rome for a few days to visit a priest I knew; I'd prayed about it and I knew God was telling me not to cancel the trip, but it was hard to leave Francis. I felt fairly sure he wouldn't be there when I returned.

The day before I left, I went to see him. He was too weak to cough and his chest was congested. His courage was wearing thin; he was fretful and restless and kept calling for his pillows to be arranged.

But as I was saying goodbye, he nodded towards the wall, which usually meant that he'd slipped sideways and needed to be lifted upright. So I put an arm round his shoulders and a hand behind his head, which had to be supported carefully when he was moved, because his neck was so weak. And he smiled this brilliant smile, sheer joy, and I knew that wherever he was going and however he would experience this place that no one could tell him about, he was going to be all right.

That was my view of Francis and how Jesus came alive in his life, what he did for him and what he didn't do. I would have preferred a different ending, because he became a good friend, a real ally in faith, and I miss him. But there's no doubt that what he went through and the way he handled it had a lasting effect on the faith of many other people, and I've asked some of his close family to tell their version too: his elder brother Joseph, fifty, his wife, Katrina, forty-one, and their eighteen-year-old son Simon.

Two years after Francis' death, Joseph has just visited Medjugorje, the village in Croatia where, since 1981, a group of children – now adults – have claimed to have daily visions and conversations with Mary, the mother of Jesus.

21

......

Joseph

When Francis was really bad, I wondered why God made him suffer: I asked a priest when I was in Medjugorje, and he asked if I was angry, and I was. It's not bad to have an argument with God. Jesus himself questioned, 'Why have you deserted me?' and said, 'Let this cup pass me by.'

I've always had strong faith, but what gave me faith when Francis was ill was that he never moaned at God. 'Your will be done' – that was his attitude to life.

Going on pilgrimage to Medjugorje recently made me want to go to daily Mass, not just Sunday Mass. At Medjugorje I heard the visionaries saying the way to help the world is to pray more, and I've got time because I don't have a regular job any more. It's only forty minutes, and it's like nourishment, receiving holy communion. God is there – Christ is there.

If you don't pray, you can never attain faith and find God. The faith comes to you through the prayer.

I felt this great change in attitude to faith, while I was in Medjugorje. There are a lot of young people there, praying; no one is ashamed. The Mass lasts three hours, but it feels as though you've only been there an hour. The church is packed to the rafters, and all the Croatian families come in to pray the rosary.

It's good to teach a child to pray from a very young age, as young as three – just a simple prayer.

I always saw God as loving, someone you could talk to. And if God doesn't want me to have something, then it's not for the good of me. Even Francis – God had other plans for him. It's God's plan that Francis suffered, maybe for the sins of the world, because I don't think anyone suffers for themselves alone.

But I did wonder, 'How could God do this for someone like Francis?' because he had so much faith. In my brother's family, the youngest child is the only one who prays; the older children laugh at her. My brother says you can't force them to go to church; they've got to do it for themselves. On Sunday I tell mine, 'If you don't want to come to church, don't go because of me going – but give that one hour to God, to talk to God and ask him to help you, and always ask for his will.' I won't question his will.

I prayed a lot more when Francis was ill. Just to see him was a suffering: it stripped his dignity. He was a private person; at first he resented letting the nurses help him, but he had to accept it. That disease strips a man right down. Someone has to wipe your very tears when you cry; he couldn't even do that for himself. That's a brave man, for me, but he always had that smile, and he didn't give up going to Mass and holy communion, not even when he was in the wheelchair and people stared. Another person would have turned against God.

I think it's affected our family: the children felt sad but they didn't feel bitter against God.

Sometimes you look with envy at people with success: I try to be good and I get nothing! But the priest in Medjugorje, he suffered, under the communists: eight of his friends were shot and their bodies burned, right in front of his eyes, and this priest asked God why he let this cruel thing happen to him, when he was the one looking after the children – the visionaries who had been persecuted for saying they'd seen Our Lady. But through it his faith built up.

I don't understand some people in the Church not accepting Medjugorje: if it was just a pretence, how could the children keep it up for fifteen years? And how could it be evil when the only message is to pray and be at peace; would the devil tell you to pray for peace?

Satan blesses people as well, with success and wealth, so that people turn from God: they've got everything, so they don't need to pray. It's often people who are dying or suffering who turn to God and pray.

There are a lot of hypocrites, but a lot of people too who are really suffering. You've got to suffer to achieve real peace; the ones who have nothing and are happy are really successful; the ones with all the material things are failures.

People are so proud to say to you, 'My child is doing this or has that,' but they're not worried about their children's souls.

Francis had such an unwavering faith; a lot of people told me their faith had been strengthened by him. There was only one time he made a complaint: he said, 'No one knows what I'm going through.' And, two weeks before he died, he had to stop having holy communion because he couldn't swallow, and he was crying then.

I met a man in Medjugorje who had had a brain tumour and a mental breakdown, and his mother and two sisters had died of cancer, and he cursed God. But he's been to Medjugorje ten times now; he was there leading the singing and telling everyone how great God is and how great Our Lady is. You could see the faith in someone who really didn't believe before. He said he never blamed God again. And everyone I met there had that type of faith.

I was the one who was with Francis when he died, with the priest, and we were praying as he died. He died in peace, with the rosary in his hand, and we buried him like that, and the children put little letters in the coffin with him. That's the effect he had on everyone.

Faith like he had is hard to come by; some people just don't find God. But he certainly suffered for it.

Simon

My faith started with going to church when I was young, and I remember hearing some of the Bible stories that Dad would read us – Samson, and Joseph's coat of many colours.

I really learned about God at school, studying for my first communion. But maybe it was when I went to high school that I changed to talking to God – asking for help, and thanking. I helped out with playing the music for school Masses as well, and that made me think about what the songs were about. Usually when you sing in church you don't think about it much, but when you have to play it, the meaning of the words comes out and you think about it more.

I've never felt that God doesn't exist. We go to Aylesford shrine every year, and I went to Lourdes with the young adults' pilgrimage, and it was nice to be with so many young adults who have faith in God. In school, not many of my friends have a strong faith; a lot of them don't really go to church often, and some of them feel against God because they're poor or things have gone wrong for them.

When I went for my interview for the sixth form, one of the questions I was asked was whether it made a difference, being in a Catholic school; it doesn't really, because half of them don't have faith by the time they get to seventeen.

I don't know why some people have faith and some don't. I feel I have to pray and I have to go to church; if I didn't I'd feel empty inside. I have to have contact with God. Although I feel he's around all the time, he's not as close.

People think church is boring and parts of it are slow, but because they're not going to church they're not close to God. There are parts of it – and certain priests – that drag on when they don't have to. But recently a visiting priest gave a sermon – a sixty-second sermon – and he got his point across and everyone went away thinking about it and no one was confused.

I feel God's probably got my life set out for me. I'm not rich or anything. I'd like to play music; that's my ambition. I have to believe in God and trust and have confidence in him.

When Uncle Francis was ill, I seemed to keep my faith. First of all, we didn't really realize what the disease was about and how bad it was going to get. I asked why it was him, because he'd always had so much faith and he'd always done so much for God. I don't know if I saw it as a punishment. But I suppose because he kept his faith, it helped us. I can't say how I would have reacted if it was me.

I kept thinking of all those Bible stories, and about Lourdes and how Bernadette had to suffer. Probably all the saints have suffered. Our Lady said to Bernadette, 'You can't receive happiness in this world, only in the next.' So maybe everyone has to do some suffering, and Uncle Francis had to do his here.

Maybe what happened to him wasn't worse than anyone else but just different; maybe some people suffer in the next life.

I can't really remember him very well before he became ill; he worked during the week and played in the band at the weekend, so I only saw him perhaps once a week, after Mass. I have more memories of him when he was ill, and then it was hard to converse with him.

I always saw Jesus as he is in the Bible: he was a man, but the son of God as well. Physically he wasn't any different. He was trying to set an example to others, showing a good way.

I suppose he had to accept what happened to him; he knew what his task was. And I suppose God does ask things of us sometimes. A few months ago, I went to a reunion for the people who'd gone to Lourdes, and the priest asked me and a few others if we'd help promote next year's pilgrimage. I could have said no, but I thought it was a good thing because it might help someone back into the Church or to regain their faith. So maybe that was something God was asking me to do.

Katrina

I was born a Catholic and went through thinking that's all there was; I didn't realize there were so many other faiths, except that my dad was high Church of England. My sister asked him why we didn't all go to the same church, when we all believed in the same God, so that's when he started going to the Catholic church. To him, there wasn't much difference between them, except that in the Catholic church Our Lady came into the picture more. He liked that; she was someone he always turned to, and he made her important to us. She's not that important to some people, even if they're close to God.

As a child, I didn't think too much about God. Then when I was thirteen my mum and dad took me to the shrine at Aylesford for a day of prayer, and it deepened my faith. My dad had been ill and came near to death quite a lot of times; my mum was crying and praying a lot, and I remember thinking he'd be all right; God was going to bring him through, and he did.

Then I went to Lourdes, when I was fourteen, and what impressed me most was the people who were caring for the ones who were ill; they were engrossed in them, and in God, and in Our Lady, and it seemed like a whole package – that's where they were getting the strength from.

It's quite easy to have a deep faith when you're in a holy place, then when you come home you feel different, and it enlightens you. I don't know if it would change everyone, going to places like that, or if it would only last while you were there.

But I didn't think about having a real deep faith till Francis became ill. When he first got ill I was very cross with God. Francis was such a good person, never did any harm to anybody, and there are all these horrible people out there, sailing along and nothing ever seems to happen to them.

But later on, I wondered if there was a reason: in the family there had been quite a lot of upset, brothers and sisters not talking to one another, and I wondered if God was telling us something and we all had to look into our lives more. We can all be hypocritical and criticize other people for things we might do ourselves.

When Francis died, I felt I didn't want things to go back to how they were; if they did, he'd have died for nothing. I don't think his illness would ever have been cured; I don't know if God can stop something like that or not, but I feel it would have made a big difference in Francis' case if the family could have accepted each other. Some of them were cruel to Francis when he was ill, but he was willing to forgive, and if he could, then the others should have done as well. It might not have made a difference to Francis' health, but to his mind. When you're dying, you think about who you're leaving behind.

There had always been arguments in the family; little things cause big arguments, and it's hard to see who's at fault. In a big family, the mother has to split herself in so many ways, and maybe one gets more attention than another, then some weren't entirely honest either, because they didn't want trouble. So some felt pushed out and got bitter, and there was a lot of niggling, then the others got fed up and stopped talking to them. And when I tried to put things right, what I said was taken the wrong way and made it even worse. There was a big row; it was horrible.

It was probably a few months later that we heard Francis had this disease. Francis said he wanted to see his brother's family, but it was about three and a half years before they came round. Because one of the children was his god-daughter too, I think it hurt him more that she didn't come to see him. It was like a breakthrough when they did come, but it was almost too late; the last six months of his life were so downhill.

I used to pray a lot, for the argument to be over, but it went on and on.

My faith was up and down; I thought if God was out there, why wasn't he helping, and why couldn't they have come sooner? I've never really doubted God but I have thought, 'You're just not listening at the moment.' A few days after Francis died, I got up one morning and thought, 'How could you let him die?'

But as the days went on, I started looking at it in a different way and thinking, 'I know he's free from all the pain.' The minute he died, there was no sign he'd ever had anything wrong with him; I thought, 'There's someone there who's taken him to another place.'

I didn't like seeing him in the last three months. I was around there one night and he asked for the letter board and said, 'No one can understand what it's like having this disease.' And I said, 'Maybe that's why you were picked: you're a really strong person; if it happened to one of us, we might have just given in to it and died, but you've kept going with strength and faith, and you've lived for four years with it.' He was crying, and Mum said, 'You shouldn't have said to him about dying.'

I sometimes felt I'd have liked to talk to him about it, but I felt no one in the family wanted to bring that word 'dying' up. But he could maybe have said what he felt about dying, and talked about his faith. There was something very strong in him; it wasn't just going to church.

It was a bit of a taboo within the family to talk about death. He was upset, and I would have been too, but if I was in his shoes I'd have wanted to talk to someone I was close to, to give me strength. I think he wanted to talk about it.

Now, I have very mixed feelings. I have a lot of belief and strength but it wavers from time to time; like if Simon doesn't get a job now, I'll be questioning God, not thinking, 'Is there another reason why?' Sometimes I wonder why it is that some people never lose their job or have down moments; they seem to have it easy, while others struggle for everything they do. Maybe it's your faith being tested – how easily you'll give up on God.

I see God as standing there in the wings to guide you a bit, but not to tell you which way to go. Joseph thinks things have to be a certain way: there's one pathway to heaven, but I don't think like that. I think you use your free choice to do things that either help you or hinder you. We blame God for human things that go wrong, but we don't thank him so much for things that go right.

I pray for things to happen if they're right, but when something does go right I do feel all the praying has made a difference.

I think Francis became ill for a reason; whether it was from up above, I don't know. Even though they say there's no cure for his disease, Francis believed in healing power, but I think certain people are chosen and that's their lot in life.

Some people come through car accidents because they're not chosen to die at that moment, and some people have an out-of-body experience and nearly die and it makes them come closer to God, or they talk to other people about it and it helps them. A friend of ours actually died four times; they said if he came through it his brain wouldn't work, but he's fine. But it didn't make him turn to God. He's a nice guy and he'd do anything for anybody, but he's not like Francis – and one was taken and the other one lived.

When I'm praying for the children, I feel God is guiding me, as a parent. I want my children to have a free will and not push them to go to church or anything, but like you teach them manners and other things, I want to teach them the value in life. In a family, some go one way and some go completely the other, when they've been brought up the same way. And some people have an inner faith in them that others don't have. I think when someone has an experience of God, it's a complete gift. In the last six months of Francis' illness, I felt very close to God, perhaps because we were praying constantly for him.

Although people say you don't have to pray or go to church to be close to God, if you do then it's like if you keep going to see your favourite rock star: you go to all the concerts and get to know all the songs. If you're not in touch with God you're not going to get to know him.

We make excuses for not praying – no time – and it's true, but you have to make time to do certain things. Sometimes God does pick someone who's got no faith at all, just to show that he's there, but I think you have to get close, so that when he does show you that sign you can acknowledge it; otherwise you mightn't know it when it comes.

When my dad died, I was writing a letter to him and hadn't finished it. So I finished it anyway and sent it to my mum and asked her to tell him what I said, even though he'd died.

I was looking at this picture of my dad, and I tried to visualize God and talk to him, in the same way I'd talk to my dad, and it really felt as though I was looking at God and talking to him. I'd never had that experience before. I suppose we can talk to him, in just the same way.

22

· · · · · · · · · · · · · ·

St Paul said that whoever has the spirit of God is a child of God. It's clear that the spirit of God isn't limited to people who go to church, or people of particular denominations or religions. As several people have mentioned, there are plenty of kind, compassionate people who don't profess any belief in God but who love him 'in the least of their brothers and sisters'. And there are plenty of 'religious' Christians, Muslims, and so on, who have no compassion or kindness at all, except to their own friends and families and people of their own kind – but Jesus himself said there is no virtue in loving only those who love you; even pagans do that.

So what difference does it make to someone's life, to have a 'live' experience of Jesus Christ, or to develop a deep relationship with God? To outward appearances, at least, it may not always seem to make them a better person. They may even be more at risk of upsetting people, as Elizabeth upset her family, or as the early apostles upset society, healing incurables and denouncing other people's gods and idols.

I believe there may be two main differences between the person who meets or wants to meet Jesus Christ and the person who has not met and doesn't want to meet him. One is the desire itself: the desire to know God more accurately and more intimately, not settling for a received idea of who he is and just accepting or rejecting it, but wanting to search and research and find out who he really is.

The second is very similar: the desire to love and to be loved. Our first reaction might be that everyone wants this; it's an inborn desire of all human beings. And it is – it's in our nature as beings made in the image and likeness of God, the great lover who also desires us to love him. But it also has to be a choice.

Both are equally difficult to choose – to be loving and to be loved. When it comes easily, it's not the real thing. Any parent who has sat up all night with a sick child, comforting its distress and cleaning up the mess, will tell you that afterwards their love for the child has a deeper dimension than it had before, when the child was easy and rewarding to be with, all dimples and smiles.

Then there are people who give a lot of love to those who need care – but they may not be very good at being loved. They may love 'at arm's length', doing everything that's needed, giving generously of their time and their patience, always with a kind word and a smile – but when it's their own time of need, instead of giving others the opportunity to be the giver for them, they shut themselves away and try to sort out all their own problems themselves, 'protecting' from their troubles the very people who are most able and willing to give them love and help. They are generous givers of their niceness, but reluctant sharers of their suffering self. There are others who are eager to receive love and friendship, who welcome compassion and sympathy – but when they see someone else in need, somehow they're never quite ready to give yet; however much they've received, it's never enough to start giving to other people.

My conscience attacks me on reading both these profiles, because both of them are me at different times. It's very hard to get the balance right, between loving people and allowing them to love me – when they're not always the people I feel loving towards, and they're not always the people I'd choose to be loved by.

What difference can Jesus make to this? All the difference in the world, I believe, because he is the balance.

He got the balance right, in his own lifetime. He gave love and he received. He let the 'bad woman' of the local town hug and kiss his feet and weep all over them, in the company of some of the most critical religious leaders with the most power to destroy both his reputation and his life. And he promised to be with us for all time. With someone like that with me, I can take the risk of both loving and letting myself be loved – especially by 'unacceptable' people.

If I only receive love from people I find acceptable, and I only give love within certain predefined limits – within my family or the context of my caring professional job – then I'm still keeping God at arm's length, repressing my innate desire to know him as he really is, because there's so much about God that's unacceptable.

If his son takes after him, then it's all too easy to see in Jesus Christ the hard-to-accept face of God. There are countless examples in the gospels of Jesus behaving in ways that were seriously disturbing to the ideas of the people around him, including their idea of what it is to be a good person. Neither did he meet the normal criteria for being a strong person. He wasn't afraid to cry in public, as when his friend Lazarus died. He wasn't ashamed to show his fears in public, and even his moments of doubt about the love of God for him, as when he cried out on the cross, 'My God, my God, why have you forsaken me?' He was tired, hungry, angry, impatient; he sweated, he bled, he died. He refused to use his powers to save himself from death. He was not, by any stretch of the imagination, a super-hero – or even a 'nice guy'.

If Jesus, as revealed in the New Testament, is unacceptable, how about his Father, as portrayed in the Old Testament – constantly pleading with his people to listen to him, and when they wouldn't obey, letting them be struck by all kinds of disasters and plagues?

Not a comfortable character to invite into my own home and allow to be in charge of my daily life.

And how about the third face of God – the Holy Spirit – as revealed in parts of the Old Testament and throughout the New? He prompted people to act in peculiar ways – people thought the disciples were drunk when they started speaking in foreign languages and preaching publicly about the power of someone who'd just been executed.

Anyone who claims that religion is comforting hasn't done their homework about who God really is. The way to God by means of Jesus Christ has very little to do with comfort or feeling good about myself. The more contact I have with him, the more he can do for me, and some of the things he can do are extraordinary. But he does it to help me to be extraordinarily fruitful. He does pick some people out for favours never experienced by others – but never only for the benefit of the person who's picked out; it's often to equip them to do more for the benefit of other people.

Let me tell you how I got healed.

It didn't happen overnight, but I can remember the day I knew it was working.

Leading up to that day were six months of staying at home doing very little except dealing with the bouts of pain and the panic. I'd been doing freelance work for magazines, and because I was writing an article for a newspaper about the experience of infertility, the doctor at the hospital had let me have some extracts from medical textbooks to help describe the form of disease I had. From that I gathered that, if the disease had advanced to the degree that I had it, it was probably either pre-malignant or already cancerous. I asked him what would happen if I left it and had no further treatment, and he said, 'In your case, the next stage would be that the bowel would rupture.'

It didn't sound too attractive, but weighing up the pros and cons I decided I needed peace even more than I needed treatment, so I decided to wait, keep calm, and pray – and stay at home. If and when there was a rupture, no doubt I'd be taken into hospital as an emergency, even though I'd cancelled my clinic appointment.

I did get bouts of terror in the middle of the night, waking up with my heart pounding, thinking, 'I have this horrible disease, it's not getting any better, and I'm not having any treatment – that's really dangerous,' but every time I prayed, the same instinct returned: that my deepest need was for peace, and I wasn't going to get that by running to and from the hospital for tests and treatment.

As well as my own and other people's prayer, another source of help was the editor of one of the magazines I wrote for. He had been a volunteer for the Samaritans and had none of the usual hesitancy about commenting on how ill I seemed and asking straight out if it was cancer. When I said it probably was, he asked if I'd told my husband or any of the family and when I said no, he said, 'Phone me any time you want someone to talk to – but especially at three o'clock in the morning, because that's when people have their worst crises.' As it happened, I never needed to phone him at three in the morning, but only because I knew I could; he had really meant it.

My husband, at the time, was also ill, which was why I didn't talk to him about my own fears. I did try once or twice, but as soon as I started, he would quickly and loudly start talking about something else. My mother did the same thing, and although I thought my mother-in-law had a shrewd idea of what was wrong with me, she didn't ask me any questions, so I concluded they just weren't ready to hear it.

My husband had possibly, the doctors said, had some kind of viral infection, though there was no sign of it now; he had symptoms consistent with stomach ulcers, and also signs of nervous breakdown. He suffered a great deal of fear, and a great deal of anger.

It was not an easy time, for either of us. We were worried about ourselves and about each other, and felt guilty and upset when the other one clearly needed to be looked after and we were not in a state to do it. In an ideal world, when one partner in a marriage is going through a crisis, the other one is there to love and support them.

In the real world, husband and wife are often so close that when one is at their weakest, so is the other. That's fine, as long as the strong partner in the marriage is God. But where one or both of the couple leaves him out, it's disaster. For my husband, God was the very last person he wanted in his house, because God had allowed him to get ill and risk losing his job.

But it was through my husband that my healing started. A friend of his had been visiting faithfully; I knew he was praying for him and wanted him to get well. That doesn't sound unusual, in a friendship, but some of his friends and colleagues were not so straightforward in their reactions; there was an element of, 'Look at the state he's in!' and 'Thank God I'm not like that,' and they would react to his signs of weakness by showing they were capable and strong, talking about their work and activities, responsibilities and plans. They didn't mean to emphasize the difference between themselves and him, but everything they said, and even their body language, made that point.

But this man would come in, most days, for a short visit, making it clear he wasn't going to stay long and expecting nothing in the way of hospitality or even conversation, just sitting with my husband and accepting him the way he was.

One day he came in, and said to him, rather embarrassed, 'Look, you're not getting anywhere with the hospital, and you've said yourself the hardest thing is to get them to take any interest. I wouldn't normally suggest this, but my sister-in-law has some kind of gift – call it what you like – for healing people. She's not a spiritualist, she's a practising Christian. She says she has no special powers; it all comes from God – and I've seen with my own eyes people who were in a terrible state and have tried everything else, and once they started going to her, they got well, over a period of time. If you want her phone number, here it is.'

My husband was equally embarrassed and said words to the effect of 'thanks, but no thanks,' and I said, 'I'll have it!'

So I phoned her later that day and told her my worst concern, which was being unable to have children. She asked if I had ever suffered from any illness, and I gave her the long history. She explained that what would be done was spiritual; there was nothing I couldn't be helped with, but it would happen according to the way God directed, and that wouldn't necessarily match my own priorities. The illness would have to be dealt with first.

She sounded confident and I was impressed. Then she asked how soon I could come down to see her. She lived a long distance from us, a four-hour journey by train. There was no question of it, I said; I couldn't even walk up the road without getting faint. If it was spiritual, I asked, was it essential for me to be there physically? Couldn't I be healed without her seeing me?

She sounded a bit hesitant but said yes – but I'd have to stay in close contact, phoning her every time a symptom occurred. I said, 'I can't do that! I'd be phoning you six times a day; I'd drive you mad!' The confidence returned to her voice; she said, 'Only to start with.'

So that's what we did. I'd wake up in the morning, feeling sick, phone her and say who it was and, 'I'm feeling sick,' and she'd say, 'Okay; leave it with me,' and put the phone down. Later on in the day I might ring and say, 'I have pain round the area of the operation scar,' and she'd say, 'I know, you've got an infection. Leave it with me,' and that would be the end of the conversation.

There was no small talk, no sympathy, no psyching up. She went away and did whatever she did, and I got on with my day. After a while I would notice that I'd done something I hadn't felt capable of, and that the symptom, whatever it was, had eased. Then something else would occur, so I'd phone the next day and say, 'The sickness went after an hour – thanks very much – but now I'm in a lot of pain.'

After a while, I interrupted her familiar, 'Leave it with me,' and said, 'Can I ask what it is you're doing? Is it prayer, or what?'

'It is prayer,' she said, 'but it's also quite hard work. It's from God, but I have to use the gifts he gives me. What happens is that I get an image of what's wrong: I see the part of the body that's sick and it looks the wrong colour. So I go and look up the anatomy, and what might be the appropriate remedy for the problem, and I send you the medicine – in spirit. If I get it wrong, the Lord tells me, in no uncertain terms, so I don't send it out till it's right; I have to go back to the books and learn. Not everyone who has a gift for healing does it this way, but it's the way that's given to me, so that's how I have to do it. The power comes from God, but I have to co-operate; I have to do it his way.'

It sounded strange to me. But then she found it hard to work with me at first, because I was so used to hospital clinics and specialists that I'd assume she couldn't deal with a certain problem, because it wasn't part of the condition I'd already told her about, so if I had something extra, like flu, I wouldn't mention it. That would apparently make her work more difficult, because she could 'see' symptoms in me she couldn't account for and was trying to find out how they fitted in with the illness I'd told her about, when I'd known all along there was a flu epidemic and I probably had it, and hadn't told her.

So it took time to adjust to this new system, where symptoms were not grouped together and given a name and then treated by the appropriate specialist, who would show no interest in the other symptoms because they didn't come into his territory.

After a while, cautiously, I mentioned a non-physical event: I was getting waves of anger. She adopted that quite happily as just another symptom: 'Often something to do with part of the brain, and the liver,' she said briskly.

I asked if there was something I could do to help heal myself. 'No,' she said firmly. 'Healing comes from God. If you try to do it yourself, you can get in the way. People talk about mind over matter, but the mind isn't any stronger than the body. You leave it to me, and I'll leave it to God.'

'What about praying?' I asked. 'Does it help if I pray for myself, or not?'

'Oh, praying,' she said, 'yes. Prayer always helps. Of course.'

I was determined not to be too easily convinced. By this time, I'd been ill, on and off, for a number of years; I was in my late twenties, and had had more medical diagnoses and confident predictions of successful remedies than I could count, and I was not inclined to be optimistic this time – especially not about someone with an interest in medicine but no medical qualifications. I think I would actually have found it easier to believe if this lady had had no interest or faith in medicine; I could have accepted something purely 'spiritual'; it was the physical aspects of the gift that I found confusing.

Once, she even sent me a packet of pills: the little dummy sugar pills used by homoeopaths, who then soak them with the appropriate medication – only these, she said, contained no form of physical remedy at all; if they were analysed in a laboratory they'd be found to contain nothing – 'or nothing found on this earth'. But they were the best way of receiving healing at the present time, she said, 'because your spirits are low'.

I felt sure she was mistaken. Maybe somebody else might find this kind of thing would help their faith, or take it as a psychologically reassuring sign that something was being done for them, but I found it an obstacle to belief.

The only thing that made me think again was that my husband was also phoning her for help by that time, having seen a difference in me, and she also sent him a packet of pills, with his name on it, telling us not to mix them up and take each other's by mistake, because they were not the same.

Because we were told to take one a day and I thought my husband might forget to take his, I counted the pills in each packet – there were thirty in each one – and every night as we went to bed, I swallowed one pill from my packet (feeling rather a fraud, as I didn't believe it could have any effect) and handed him one from his packet, which he took.

After I'd finished mine, his lasted another ten days.

I picked up the phone. She was unsurprised by this. 'Yes,' she said. 'Not everyone gets healed at the same pace; I told you, it's individual.'

When I'd been phoning her regularly for a couple of weeks, and thought I was feeling better as a result, I put the healing to the test – not as a cold experiment, but because I happened to particularly want to be well one day, and I woke up feeling very ill.

I'd decided, cautiously, to resume some work. I'd been offered a freelance job producing an in-house magazine for a company, and had accepted it on the understanding that I would do it as a job-share. My work partner was a friend who was capable and intelligent but had never done this kind of work before, so she needed a certain amount of behind-the-scenes help. She would go round the various workplaces and gather information for possible features, and I would write out questions for her to ask the interviewees and help with writing up the articles. When the first issue was due to come out I'd been in hospital, just conscious after a coma, and we'd had all the page proofs spread out on the bed trying to work out the best way to edit and repage them!

Now I decided it was time to participate more actively, and as one office was not far from home and the photographer we'd asked to do the pictures had a car and was willing to pick me up on the way and do the driving, I'd arranged to do a couple of interviews there.

The trouble was, as the day came nearer, the manager kept ringing up to say he'd found another person we should really have a word with as they had something to tell that would make an interesting article; also he'd arranged a meeting among representatives of various departments and wanted me to attend it. My friend agreed to be there, but she couldn't do all of it – and I woke up that morning very dizzy and very sick. I was on the phone at once, but I didn't have much hope that the healing could work that quickly, so I phoned the photographer and asked if he'd go in alone and take the photos; I'd try to do the interviews later in the week.

He wasn't keen, as he'd never met the people before. He asked if I'd just go in with him, introduce him to the managers, then he'd run me home and go back to do the work. I felt it wouldn't be fair to refuse.

When we arrived, I introduced him to the manager, who introduced me to the first person I was due to interview. I explained I wouldn't be doing the interviews that day, but she seemed really disappointed, so I took out my notebook and said I'd take down the bare facts now, and talk at more length later in the week. She talked with great enthusiasm about her special interest, for three-quarters of an hour.

As I hadn't fainted or thrown up, I decided to risk the first ten minutes of the meeting, just to give my friend some back-up because she was slightly nervous about discussing policy with all these heads of departments. We got through the meeting fine; I felt fairly sick, but nothing went wrong.

After that, I decided to push my luck a bit. After all, since I'd phoned the lady and heard the, 'Leave it with me,' the usual warnings I'd had that morning that I was about to go into a coma hadn't materialized. And if I did go unconscious, it wouldn't be the first time it had happened while I was working with this particular photographer; he'd called my husband and got me home before, and still appeared willing to risk working with me, so presumably he'd get me home again, if the worst happened.

I carried out all eight interviews, then went home, made tea for the photographer and his assistant, supper for myself and my husband, then my friend came round and we worked on the magazine until midnight – without a symptom in sight.

This woman had a lot of people phoning her and the phone was often engaged. After a while I found that when I couldn't get through, if I sat down and prayed for twenty minutes, the symptom would go by itself. Once, I was reaching for the phone, and the symptom went. I began to think perhaps I'd outgrown the need for an intermediary.

I knew that this process had had a profound effect on my faith. Finding someone so prepared to put her own life aside and spend so much time trying to help people made me see God differently. Not only did whatever gifts she had come from him, but surely if one of his creatures was so endlessly patient and willingly available, then God must be even more ready to receive our calls – and his phoneline would never be engaged, because he could deal with all of us at the same time!

When I prayed, I began to see him as being there, available and listening and only too willing to help. And the more help I received, the more my expectations rose. God could do anything! And he wanted to be allowed to do it!

By this time I'd asked the woman to tell me what she saw as being wrong with me. She didn't want to, saying, 'It'll all get dealt with,' but I insisted, so she told me she could see a lot of growths. They were not tumours, she said, which are hard, but soft growths, but still it was a form of cancer and because it was in the bloodstream it had spread to every part of the body, including the brain – which was why I'd been going into comas – and caused millions of growths, some large and some very tiny, but all growing.

It confirmed what I'd felt myself: that there was only one

problem accounting for all the symptoms, not separate conditions as I'd previously been told. I'd thought that must be the case because when the pains started they occurred in one part of the body after another; it didn't seem likely that this would happen by coincidence, if the problems were unrelated.

But cancer is a very emotive word, and I suppose however well you've been warned by your own suspicions, it's always a shock to hear it applied to yourself. The effect it had on me was that for a couple of weeks it was all I could think of. It was as though a large neon sign with the word 'CANCER' written on it was flashing in front of my mind. And afterwards I found I'd lost track of a whole month: I had no memories at all of what had happened during it. I only knew we'd spent Christmas with my sister's family because we had the photographs to prove it.

It was obvious, though, that the disease was coming under control; I felt quite different. My husband was also getting better, though he claimed to have no faith at all and only phoned the woman because I insisted he did, to give me a break when he complained! A few hours afterwards, I'd ask him if he still had the symptoms, and he'd say grudgingly, 'It's not too bad.' But he clearly had more energy, was much less depressed, and was going back to work.

After eight months, I felt that the illness was no longer in charge of me; I was stronger than the disease was. So I told my husband what it was, and also that it was on its way out. It was harder to tell my mother; she still talked loudly about something else whenever I tried to mention it.

Finally she found out from somebody else, and was very hurt and angry – and worried. She said, 'How can you say you're all right now, if it's cancer and you haven't been back to the hospital?' I said, 'Look at me. You can see I'm not like I have been, the last few years. I'm staying conscious, I'm not sick, I'm working and going out, enjoying myself. When did you last see me like this?'

She agreed, then thought for a few minutes and said, 'You can't have been really ill, then. It must have all been in your mind.'

I showed her the scars on my stomach and told her if that was the case, I kept my mind in a pretty funny place! She said then that the operation must have been a success after all, even though I'd had pain and infection afterwards and I'd been warned the adhesions from the surgery would probably cause as many problems as the growths had. I started to point out that I hadn't even begun to have operations on the other areas, nor had any of the usual drug treatment to control the disease, then realized there was no use in arguing. Let everyone believe what they chose. The main thing was that I was well. I was well!

Probably the only way to prove it to someone else would have been to go back to the hospital and have more tests, but that would be stressful and I was fairly sure that what triggered the illness in the first place was stress. I did pray about it and was willing to go back if it seemed to be God's will, but it was eleven years, in the end, before I went back to the hospital.

Even then, with the date booked for the same investigative operation I'd had in the first place, I had last-minute doubts about whether to go ahead. I knew Francis by that time, so I asked him if he'd mind praying for me and asking God for guidance.

Two days later, Francis said although he could never hear anything about himself, he had had an answer for me: 'Go for it.' So I went, and the results were great: no sign that there had ever been anything wrong, no growths, no adhesions and – especially unusual after such extensive surgery – no lumps and bumps in the layers of muscle and flesh.

I wasn't so sure about the mental damage. After all, I'd spent a lot of time unconscious and had had memory lapses. I didn't feel like asking for a brain scan, so I did the entrance exam for Mensa, the organization for people of high IQ, instead. When I passed the test I didn't think it was worth worrying about brain damage!

The only thing that wasn't healed was what I'd originally asked for: I didn't conceive. My husband and I had the programme of tests re-run, eleven years after the first time, and nothing was found to be wrong. I was offered IVF but after taking the initial steps began to feel seriously uneasy about the ethics of it, and when I'd read up both the scientific research behind it and the theological research, I decided I couldn't accept it.

One day, after eighteen years of praying to have a child, I heard God say, 'This is not for you.' It felt to me like an answer to prayer – certainly not the one I wanted, but at least it sounded clear and I felt no doubt it had come from him. I certainly couldn't have coped with hearing it from anyone else.

In the meantime, though, he started to send me his children: people of all ages, who needed healing. At first, it disturbed me a lot. I didn't have the same gift that the woman who had healed me had: I had no medical interest and no facility for 'seeing' illness in terms of colour variations. I knew God was sending the people, and he was giving me knowledge of what was troubling them, but I didn't know what to do. I did talk to the lady who'd healed me, and she confirmed that this was the way it started: feeling God prompting you to do something or say something to a person, and keeping on getting the same insight into their life, however often you dismissed it, then finally telling the person and finding they confirmed it.

I was scared it might have a connection with clairvoyance or being psychic, in which case I wanted nothing to do with it. The occult, in all its forms, is firmly forbidden to Christians, and for good reasons – I've encountered people who, although they're not fully 'possessed', are definitely restricted in the use of their free will by the overriding influence of a stronger spirit which they've unwittingly invited into their life, through getting involved in a seance or something as seemingly harmless as astrology or fortune-telling or 'nature rites'.

I knew it was not always easy to tell the difference between the prompting of the Holy Spirit of God and the interference of some demonic influence. We think of good and evil as black and white but it's never as clear as that; evil mimics good and can appear benign and helpful. Just as lust can be camouflaged by feelings of love, and rage and bitterness can pose as a thirst for justice, so occult forces that draw people into spiritual bondage can offer feelings of freedom and knowledge and power – and even remove physical symptoms. Human discernment just isn't up to sorting out the genuine from the counterfeit.

All I could do was stay close to the Church. I needed it as I never had done before. Nearly 2,000 years have passed since the birth of Christ, and the Church he set up then, under Peter, is still going – as shaky and flawed and full of mistakes and bitter experiences as Peter was himself when Jesus picked him – but still going and still learning. I reasoned that it must know something, at least, by now about the boundaries between good and evil.

So I stepped up my churchgoing, read the Bible every day, and prayed more, both privately and in church groups with other people, and I listened to advice from everybody who seemed to me to lead a godly life – not just people who did good deeds, but people who had a real love and desire for God, who followed his will when it went against their own, and tried very hard to be loving to everyone, including people who were quite nasty or unjust to them personally. The advice they gave was good, and their prayer for me and with me was even better.

I began to feel more confident about offering to pray with people, and to be more cautious about telling them what I felt or 'heard' was troubling them, till they showed they were ready to hear it. I also became better at saying no, at realizing that not everyone who needed to be healed by God needed to receive their healing through me, and at acknowledging that I couldn't be all things to all people: if one person got out of a wheelchair and walked about, it didn't necessarily mean God would ask me to pray with every other wheelchair-user I came across.

I read the gospels differently now. I put myself into Jesus' shoes and noticed when he did or said something I wouldn't do in those circumstances. The stories ceased to sound like stories, when I saw similar things happening around me, here and now: someone getting healed of measles, instantly, or a person stopped in the middle of an epileptic fit. And when it didn't work, I no longer felt inclined to give up in despair and doubt everything that had happened before, but took it as a cue to learn more – to go back to the drawing-board and consult the Architect about his design for that person's life, not just their health.

The gospels also began to shock me more. Some of the things Jesus said, I found shocking. Some of the things the disciples did, as recalled in the Acts of the Apostles, were disturbing. Some of the letters they wrote were outrageous. The 'naughty child' in me from long ago began to feel more at home. There was a place for her here too, as well as for the calmer, well-behaved adult I'd grown into.

I believe now that to encounter the real Jesus, the real Father, and the real Holy Spirit, we have to go through a process of being distilled. So much of my image of who I am had come from other people's ideas of me. As a child, I'd accepted it, as children do accept what they're told by adults. As I grew up, I had to learn to separate the reality from the fantasy, from the projections of other people's ideas and difficulties, their prejudices, and the way society judges its members. In order to get back to being the person my creator had made me, designed in his image and likeness, I had an awful lot to lose – and I'm sure I still have.

In the same way, coming to know the real God meant throwing out a lot of false images and learning to recognize what is an essential teaching (even when it's taught by someone who's less than perfect) and what is of optional interest (helpful to some people but by no means a fundamental teaching of Jesus Christ) and what is just sheer rubbish (even when it's taught by someone sincere and convincing).

Marianna had to learn that priests and nuns are not God and may not resemble him very much at all, in order to move on and learn that a particular priest or nun can be sensitive and helpful. Bernadette had to discover for herself that 'the Church' was not a collective tyrant who would disown her for being married twice, but a collection of individuals, some of whom would be willing to help when she asked for help. Dean had to find out that not all church groups were claustrophobic or dominating.

There's a weeding-out process to do on the ideas we've received over the years, from teaching or from personal experience, about Jesus Christ, about God, about religion and about the Christian churches. And we're not only entitled to question everything; if we really want the truth, we're obliged to go through the work of threshing out for ourselves what's plausible but wrong and what's hard to swallow but true.

Jesus had referred to the Temple of Jerusalem as his Father's house and had spent three whole days in it at the age of twelve, entranced by the teaching of its elders – but in his early thirties he went through it with a whip, driving out the exploiters. If he can do that, then we can go through our accumulated history of ideas about God and be ruthless in separating truth from prejudice and self-interest. But the only place to do it is not alone – when, as Dean says, we can convince ourselves of anything – but 'in the Temple', in the presence of God, who understands everything and is only too willing to guide me as long as I refer all the questions to him.

It's not easy to let go of ideas learned early in life; it feels disloyal to me, to decide that what I was taught by a much-loved and respected relative or an admired teacher was not quite right, and even more so to accept that their well-meaning acts of kindness may have been misjudged and not really quite in accordance with what God wanted of them at that time.

And it's possibly harder to acknowledge that somebody I resented or found hard to like might have got the theory right, or at least some of it, despite an uncompromising manner that made them impart that knowledge in such a dry or unappealing form.

It's humiliating too, to realize that someone unremarkable or a figure of fun or a 'church caricature' might have something I haven't found yet – that the acne-sufferer youth who claims to be 'born again', the headscarfed old woman mumbling over rosary beads or lighting candles in the church or the skull-capped Jew bowing and intoning Hebrew, or the Muslim with his head bent to his knees, praying five times a day might have some little incomplete but vital grain of a truth so incredible it's beyond anyone's comprehension.

23

•••••••••••••

Janice is someone who struggled to make sense of her jumbled religious history of myths and mysteries and truth, and found God more clearly in the ordinary social interactions and daily challenges of life than she could in the spiritual teachings of the Church. Janice is in her forties, married, with two grown-up children.

Janice

I just accepted everything I was told as a child: it was true and I didn't question it whatsoever, until I suppose teenage years, when you start rejecting things. I didn't want to go to Mass because it was boring, but when I went to college I chose a Catholic one to go to – I'm not sure why; maybe because it was secure, something I knew. It might also have had something to do with the fact that there were three times more men there than women!

I didn't have to get up early and go to Mass at a certain time there. Church was more like a community, more friendly and more a part of everyday living. At home, you lived, then slotted a bit of religion in.

At that point, I started getting rid of things that were laws and rules: about going to church on Sunday, fasting, different grades of sin. But once I started rejecting one thing, I wasn't old enough to tell the difference between the important and the not-so-important things, and I felt I could end up rejecting everything.

There was an extra Mass on a Wednesday at college, and I always went to that. But then when I was teaching, in my first year, I didn't like going to church by myself and neither did my flatmate, who was Anglican, so we took it in turns to go to each other's church.

At school, I'd played the guitar and so did a friend, who was Methodist, and I used to go and help out at her church. In those days, Catholics weren't meant to take part in other church services – it's different now.

I felt that church was a community thing and there wasn't any point going if I didn't know anyone in the community. So for a few years I didn't go. But when I had children I felt that wasn't fair; they should at least have the option, and also with children I was a community and I was included – though my husband didn't go because he's agoraphobic. It was very child-based: preparation for first communion, and activities for children and families. We'd sit and chat after Mass and it fitted in with life more.

I'm not particularly regular now the children have left home: I don't go every Sunday because I don't feel it's the be-all and end-all of my faith, going to church. It's a nice extra for me but my life doesn't stop so I can go to church. My daughter has carried on going and my son hasn't.

The Jews don't celebrate Passover, they relive it, and that's what we're meant to do in the Mass – relive Christ's sacrifice on Calvary – but it isn't always possible.

Having accepted everything, then rejected a lot, I looked at what I still had, and I felt guilty that I didn't believe all I'd been taught. I didn't see it as my role to sift out the previous generation's misconceptions; I never thought of it like that. I thought you either believed or you didn't.

When I was teaching young children in a Catholic school, I had to bring it right down to something simple so they could understand it, and breaking down the meaning of the ten commandments, or the words of the 'Our Father', helped me realize what it meant for me.

I don't think I've ever thought about my faith; I've just lived it. I didn't isolate Jesus from God; I don't know how I'd describe him to someone who'd never heard of him. But then if I had to describe myself, I couldn't.

I think how you treat other people is how you treat God, and in a way that's how my love of Christ has developed, through loving other people and through always looking at what's lovely about them. I can't do that all the time, but trying to has made me a happier person. Things that have been really hard to cope with in my life aren't so hard now.

I live a lifestyle that's not how I would naturally want to live – quite socially isolated, and that's not me, so it's really hard and I used to get quite miserable. But now I can find more happiness in what I have rather than in what I want and can't achieve. I suppose that's come from finding Christ in other people. It's something that's evolved very slowly, over years.

My husband Michael has a mental illness and can't cope with travel or going out; we do manage now to go on holiday but always to the same place, not too far from where we live. So, for instance, if we're on holiday and it's a nice sunny day, what I'd like to do is go on a long walk and take a picnic, or stop at a nice pub somewhere along the way. I can't do that with him, so the alternative is to do what he wants to do, which is to sit indoors at the holiday camp, doing the quiz or the shove-ha'penny, and it's upset me and I don't want to do that, but I've done it for him.

It goes against the grain, and it's not enough. But if I visualize these lovely walks, and other parts of the world I'd like to visit, and think, 'Maybe one day I'll do that, but not yet,' then I can look at the person I'm with and enjoy being with him. Enjoying being with him rather than looking at what I want to have is finding the Christ in him. I don't mean being a martyr and forcing myself and saying, 'I'm doing this because I'm a Christian.' It has to be more than that. Somehow I have to put aside what I want and say, 'I can't do that,' and accept what I can do. It's the same thing with my love for Jesus: I have to be able to put aside all the other things.

When my husband gets cross or is being really unreasonable, I can say nothing and resent it, or I can feel that this will pass and not let it upset me. I used to feel, 'I'll forgive him when he apologizes,' but now I try to see behind it and beyond it; really it's a very small thing that's happened. I have to be able to see it all as a whole. I can't say, 'It doesn't matter; let him have his own way,' but it's not something that's going to affect my life in this world, or my life in the next world.

I don't mean it's good to be a doormat and let everyone do what they want to do, but sometimes you have to give way when you don't want to.

I remember, at school, seeing a film of the life of Jesus. One of the nuns asked what I thought of it and I said I felt sick, seeing the nails going into his hands, and she said, 'He did this for you, and you can't even look at it. If he suffered for you, you must suffer for him.' For me, that's the wrong attitude: that you have to be a martyr for Jesus. It's much better to think, when things are bad, 'This is only a small thing.'

I don't pray for things to happen; I pray more for support. When I was a child, I remember playing a game with my sister and saying she was cheating because she was praying to win – and she was! I'm very much anti this idea that if you pray enough you'll get your reward. With the chanting of prayers, there's still something of that element around. My praying is more a time of being with Jesus, rather than asking for things. I don't ask for a sunny day, or for God to take my arthritis away. I do ask for my children to be happy, but not for myself. I don't think I need to ask for that, because I am happy being with him. If things are very difficult, I ask God to be near me, but I don't ask him to take it away.

I frequently don't know what to do, and I suppose I do ask for guidance, but I don't ask and wait for an answer. I tend to just have a time for God but I don't wait for some kind of revelation because it doesn't happen for me like that: it's more a feeling of what's right. But sometimes I don't know whether I'm persuading myself that something's right, or even if there's a dividing line between what's right and what's wrong.

I never put time aside for prayer; I always think of something else I'm meant to be doing. I can't sit still; I need something to distract my hands, like driving or peeling the potatoes. That's my time for being with God.

I have a very poor memory, and RE at school was just another lesson. It means more to me now, when I hear it as one of the gospels read out in church, and if the sermon isn't very good I'll re-read the readings, and I get quite a lot out of that, and I enjoy sharing it with the children I teach.

When I teach the children about Jesus, I try to let them know that he's always there for them and that he's their friend, and he's always pleased with them, and pleased for them. I don't want to give them the impression I was given – that God suffered for me and in return I had to do certain things.

I get upset with people who cause injustice, but I don't think we should blame God for things like an earthquake killing people. I think there must be a reason why it's happened and we can't always see or understand the reason. If I could understand the reason and didn't agree with it, then I could be angry with God.

I don't agree either with the view that some people have to suffer. Some things that happen, there doesn't seem to be a reason, and it doesn't seem fair, but just because I can't find someone to blame for it, that doesn't mean I can blame God. I can't turn round and blame you because some child in Ethiopia died, so why should I blame God?

What I feel will happen when I die is that I won't need my body any more and I'll go on living without it, with God – so life here is just part of the continuum of life. Why I believe I'll have life after I'm here, and not that I had life before I was here, I don't know. A friend of mine believed she lived here before, as a monk, but I don't personally believe that.

I really don't know what the point is of being here. There must be a reason.

24

It seems that doubt and questioning are an essential part of the search for the real Jesus, and faith can never be more than a second-hand experience without them. But when doubt hardens into cynicism, and a one-time believer rejects all the received beliefs but doesn't replace them with a real search for truth, that cynicism can trap the person into isolation, pessimism and contempt for people.

Paul is someone who felt the force of that trap closing in on him. Now thirty-seven, he recalls clearly what happened to him, as a young student in the seminary (training college for priests) when he experienced the loss of all the faith he'd ever had.

Paul

I always knew God was there as a vague presence, but not as a person. I remember, when I was seven, the Mass moved from Latin into English and I heard for the first time, 'Christ has died, Christ is risen, Christ will come again,' and that really struck me.

My aunt was housekeeper to a priest in the country for years, and as children we'd go and stay there in the holidays. I used to be in the church when no one else was there, or I'd go up in the morning and open the doors, and it was nice; it felt like it was mine. I used to go in and sing, because I liked the echo! And there was a presence; I did feel I was in the presence of God.

I was twenty when I joined the seminary because I was thinking of becoming a priest. I'd developed an interest in God, through a book about prophecy a friend had lent me, and I'd started reading the Bible. I felt, if the Bible was really true, about the coming of the kingdom of God, it would change my life altogether; I couldn't think of anything more important, so my joining the seminary was a search for truth. I was full of questions about Jesus and God.

When I entered, I was told by a student who was ahead of me that the seminary was a place of human weakness and sin, and it meant I'd have to confront all my own, and the community's. There was the ideal, then there was the reality, which was pitted with disappointments and egos.

It was within that context that my thinking became very negative. I started doubting the eucharist, and that was a short step to doubting God himself.

After a few months of that, I felt I had lost my faith – but I couldn't avoid God because everything there spoke of God, and it was a real time of turmoil. I felt I was battling with myself and with God.

There was a prayer group in the seminary, set up by some of the students; it was charismatic, and some of the students laughed at it, and others regarded it with caution. There were no superiors there, and I found it was an opportunity to pray from where I really was; it was all right to say I wasn't so happy with the situation, and it was a place to pray with other people.

The group did an eight-week 'Life in the Spirit' course, and at the end of it everyone was prayed over individually. There were about eight of us, and I waited till last because I was feeling very angry at being in this situation, rebelling against being prayed with. I was angry with myself and with God. When my turn came, I thought I'd just go along with it; I wanted it to be over and finished with as soon as possible.

People started praising God and asking for renewal in the Holy Spirit, and I sat resisting it. Then someone leaned over and said into my ear, 'Jesus loves you,' which angered me even more because I didn't feel loved by God; I felt he'd disappeared and didn't exist. I was judging everybody else's prayers as insincere. Because I felt a hypocrite if I praised God, I couldn't imagine anyone doing it and really believing it. To praise, God seemed such a precious thing, I was afraid to do it with no meaning in it.

I thought this student saying Jesus loved me was a whitewash job; he didn't understand the pain I was in. So I turned to him and said, 'Fuck off!'

The group intensified the prayer, and it began to be prayers of deliverance. All of them laid hands on me and began to pray that the love of God would penetrate my heart and that any evil that was within or had attached itself to me in some way would be cast out.

At this point I felt I was about to cry so I closed my eyes and I could see, in my mind's eye, a shield around me. As the people were praising God and singing, I could see their prayers hitting this invisible shield, bouncing off it and not reaching me, and I had a sense of my own vulnerability and helplessness: I couldn't make myself believe, or get rid of this shield around me, and there was something insidious and evil that had attached itself to me.

The student who had told me at the beginning that this was a place of weakness and sin started singing a hymn that had a line in it about trusting Jesus, and I realized that was the one thing I hadn't done; I'd tried to reason things out for myself, to understand, and to put God under the microscope, and I'd brought on myself this darkness and confusion.

I knew this was the answer – that I couldn't break out of this myself. There was a moment, that seemed like an eternity, when I felt that Jesus couldn't do this: he mightn't be able to reach me. So I told him I trusted him to help me. And with that, this dome – or whatever it was – shattered, and the prayers felt like rain falling in a desert; I could feel them penetrating me, deep in my heart, and it was as though Jesus was as present as the person next to me, but even more real.

He was the risen Lord: what I mean by that is, he was powerful but he was humble; his presence wasn't intrusive, it was comforting, life-giving, supportive and gentle.

At about 11 p.m., I went down to the prayer room, off one of the corridors: the seminary was a cold place, full of corridors. I was afraid of being caught by the superior for not being in my room at that hour, so I didn't turn on the light in the prayer room; there was just the candle burning in front of the tabernacle, because the blessed sacrament was there.

I was worshipping God – but it felt like Jesus was worshipping the Father and I was caught up in his worship.

But I'd only been there five or ten minutes when the atmosphere in the room changed, as if something evil entered. I wasn't expecting that at all; it was the farthest thing from my mind, and I'd never experienced anything like it before, but the evil presence was as real as the presence of Jesus, and as intense – so much so that I wasn't aware any more of Jesus being there. It was like a sudden invasion.

I stayed kneeling in front of the tabernacle and stopped my prayers; the hair stood up on the back of my neck and there was a sensation of terror. Without knowing how or why, I identified this presence as the person of Satan. I reminded myself to go on praying, so I started praising and worshipping God. The more I prayed, the more intense the presence of evil became; it felt as if the devil was claiming ownership of me.

I was very frightened, confused and sweating. I decided to face the fear and address Satan directly, instead of trying to avoid his presence and focus on God. So I said, 'Jesus is my saviour; he's my salvation; I belong to him. You have no power or authority over me. I don't belong to you; I belong to Jesus – and in the name of Jesus I command you to leave; get behind me.'

Instantly, he left; the atmosphere in the room changed, and I began to praise God, Jesus and the Holy Spirit.

After a while I went to my bedroom, which was a dingy, depressing, dark little place, and the beautiful thing was, Jesus was with me, in my room – and he never left my side for two weeks; that intensity of his presence remained. I knew in my heart and my mind that God is real and that Jesus is the risen Lord – risen from the dead. I know because I've met him. And I knew without doubt, and still do today, that the eucharist is truly the body and blood of the risen Lord. I still don't understand it, but that's not a problem now.

The sense of that encounter has remained solid; both the positive and the negative experience confirmed for me the providence of God.

After the two weeks, I was able to get on with my studies, without all those doubts beating me over the head – though some things troubled me. For instance, I'd met many missionaries back from overseas and they talked about the churches they'd built and so on, but I'd been reading books about healing – Francis MacNutt was one I remember – and I wanted to know why people weren't getting healed. I couldn't see God's healing action in the world today and I wanted to take Jesus's command to heal seriously.

A year after this experience, at the age of twenty-five, having completed five of the six years of study, I was sent to work in a parish for a month. Two newly-ordained friends of mine were there, in their first placement. I could see a strain there. Among the older priests, parish administration seemed the main concern, and while the young priests had enthusiasm, they were working within well-defined limits. I was keen to get involved in ministry while I was there, but all I was asked to do was visit hospitals and count money.

I was thinking about the people being the body of Christ – that we're all the body of Christ – and I asked the parish priest if I could at least be involved in giving out communion.

It was while I was giving out communion at Mass one day that I had one of the strongest religious experiences I've ever had. It's hard to explain it, but what happened was that the line of people came up to receive communion and as I was looking down at my hands, ready to pick up the next host, I could feel the presence of Jesus, so strongly that I was almost frightened.

I thought, 'This is a public situation and I have to act responsibly.'

But I knew the person standing in front of me was Jesus, and I wondered how I could give the eucharist to Jesus and say, 'This is the body of Christ' when he is the body of Christ? That's how real it was.

I looked up and saw a woman parishioner who I recognized, and then she changed and I could see Jesus standing there. He looked totally vulnerable, but in this vulnerability there was enormous power, radiating from him. His hands were slightly outstretched, as if he was totally empty, with no resistance to God the Father, and this power was love; it filled everything and it filled me, and I felt very small and humbled. Then, it changed back to the woman, and I offered her the body of Christ.

Soon after, I returned to the seminary for the start of the academic year. I wanted time to reflect on this experience because it had been so powerful, but there was no time for reflection. I felt I was nearer to ordination than I was to God. I needed to know more about God's love. How could I preach the gospel otherwise? I wouldn't have anything to give.

I prayed about it, and decided to leave the seminary. I had some savings, so I left Ireland, came to London and found a place to live. I prayed for a couple of weeks about whether to get a job, and the response was, 'Do what you see me doing.'

What I saw the Lord doing was healing the sick, raising the dead, and setting prisoners free, so I asked him, 'How do I do this?' and the response was, 'Be available to my people, love them where they are and as they are.'

Part of the way I did this was by offering to pray with people, for healing and for guidance and self-knowledge and peace. After the experience in the church, I saw that God's love for me was real and I began to pray in a new way, writing in a dialogue fashion, asking God questions and writing down the answers. Before I prayed with someone, I'd ask God what the problem was and how to pray with them.

Because I was available, I was called out one night to pray with a friend of someone I knew, who was depressed. I asked the Lord about this lady and received very detailed instructions: don't treat it as a social visit, no chat, get right down to prayer, and leave immediately it's over. He said the lady had been abused in childhood and felt evil inside, but that she wouldn't tell me this; I was just to pray for her to be delivered, and for God to enter into that event in her childhood.

I set out at about 10.30 at night; it was snowing heavily and there were no buses so I had to walk. I reached there about 11.15. Both ladies were delighted to see me and insisted that they put the kettle on. I knew Nora, who had phoned me, and I hadn't seen her for some time; the other woman, Jill, seemed quite well and happy and sociable; what I'd had in the writing made no sense, and it seemed unkind not to chat with them. I felt angry with God. But I followed his instructions.

So Nora and I began to pray with Jill. I spoke the words the Lord had given me, into her ear so Nora wouldn't hear, and as I did, Jill fell to the floor, saying she felt very ill and wanted to vomit. I thought, 'Oh fuck, what's happened?' but the Lord told me not to panic, Jill was all right, so I went on praying with her as she lay on the floor, groaning.

The groaning soon stopped and I helped her up into the chair. The prayer had lasted about twenty minutes. I told them to stay quiet in the presence of the Lord for a while, and I'd leave. It was midnight by now and snowing very heavily and Nora was telling to me to stay the night in her spare room, but I insisted on leaving.

When I returned home I spent about two hours praying for Jill, because I was in a state of panic and thought that it was all a load of nonsense: that the writing was wrong, I was fooling myself, and I'd made things worse and disturbed her in some way; that if there was any evil there, I'd caused it.

A week later, Nora phoned me. She said Jill was very well and had told her that when I'd started to pray, she'd felt this terrible sickness in her stomach, then felt the touch of God, taking evil from her stomach. She'd never told anyone, but she'd felt she was evil ever since she was abused in childhood, and now the evil had gone. They'd gone on praying for about an hour after I left, and Jill was really happy.

My savings lasted a month or two, but as soon as I ran short of money, people would send some, even though I hadn't told them it was short, and I lived like that for four years.

But I've had a struggle with my faith, in that the personal experience of God left me for about five years. On a very deep level, I've known that God is real and in some mysterious way has been guiding my life, but I lost that feeling of his presence totally. I don't know why; I think it was a type of test, to strengthen me. I've met a lot of Christians from other traditions who emphasize the experience of faith; if they don't experience God as real, there's something wrong and they search for some sin in themselves – and it can be true, but there are times when God withdraws his face from us, so that we grow. And I had five years of searching in darkness, and a sense of emptiness within, where God just seemed not to be around and seemed almost irrelevant.

This was very difficult for me, because I'd gambled my life on God. Jesus had promised that if you give up home, money, wife, family, he'll give it back a hundredfold. And, at the age of thirty-three, the jewel of faith I'd sold everything to buy seemed to have slipped through my hands. This was more painful than my previous experience, because this time I knew God existed.

It became so bad that it was impossible to pray. I could only say formal prayers like the Our Father and Hail Mary. Those prayers do have a value. After all, Jesus gave us the words of the Our Father and he said pray it; he didn't say you must feel it! So I kept saying them, and each day God would be on my mind.

I kept on receiving the sacraments and going to Mass because, as a Catholic, I believed it was something God wanted to do for me, no matter how little I was prepared to receive. I think he was happy to feed me, and happy for me just to be there, and slowly my experience of God began to come alive again. I now see that period of blackness and darkness as just as much a religious experience of God as the others I've described.

I completed my theology studies for myself, and I tried another religious order for a year, but I've worked now for several years alongside people working long hours for bad pay, some of them men aged forty to sixty who have been made redundant. The economic movement in the world that's taking away people's jobs and their dignity is an injustice which has crept into every institution, including the Church, and I feel that the Lord is calling people in the Church to stand up for the gospel values, within the Church and outside it. There's a lot to be done.

Now, at the age of thirty-seven, I feel Jesus is leading me to return to the seminary and I feel apprehensive because I'm putting myself under authority, and I don't trust the judgment of some of the people I've seen in authority in the Church. But Jesus can work through that, and on my part the call is to let go of the image of God and of myself that I've got. God is bigger than I imagine him to be, and I need to let go of the image I'm comfortable with and be aware of my own smallness, and submitting to authority is part of that.

There have been things I've been asked to do before by authorities, that I'm not capable of – like teaching, and being with people who are dying – and yet I've managed to do those things and do them quite well.

I totally agreed with the idea of euthanasia; I worked for two years with people whose sufferings were overwhelming: pain, incontinence, confusion, agitation, hallucinations, aggression, weakness, slowly dying – and I couldn't see why they should be left in that state. Everything I knew about the love of God, these people seemed to witness to the opposite.

Then I discovered that I was afraid of the weakness and vulnerability of my own physical condition, and it wasn't till I looked past the human suffering and the mess to the person that I began to see some value in their life, even as it was. My part was to reach out and touch them and love them as much as possible, and I found that if they could do anything for me they were very pleased – like helping me when I was trying to lift them, or keeping an eye on someone while I went to get them a cup of tea; or the ones who were religious, I asked to pray for me and for others, and they were very happy to do it.

The confused ones were very sensitive and aware of the atmosphere on the ward; if someone was agitated, it would spread like a contagion, but they were very receptive to peace as well. They were completely at the mercy of the nurses and care assistants and their kindness or cruelty or indifference, and they were still very capable of receiving and giving love. Instead of not understanding how God could allow their suffering, I began to see Jesus in them, as he was on the cross.

When I started work in that place, there was one man in his late eighties who couldn't walk and had lost his memory, though he could follow a line of thought. It frightened me to see what the male body could become: beauty is such a fleeting thing. He would always wet the bed at night and I had to change the sheets and wash him in the morning, and the stink would make me sick. But after a few months of having conversations and getting to know him as a person, I developed an affection for him.

After he died, I had to take the sheets off the bed – and there was this ugly distinctive smell that had previously made me sick; nothing could ever make it pleasant, but because I had good memories of him, it was like a remembrance of his presence, and the smell was no longer a problem.

Once I was aware of the person, even their suffering, and the way they were suffering, became very precious. I don't worship suffering, and I think we should always try to eliminate it, but if we can join people in it, there is a bond in being human. It's a shared experience; some just go through it ahead of us.

I certainly don't look forward to old age and death, and I'd rather die quickly than become confused or end up in a nursing home, but however I'm to suffer in my life, even if it's that way, the value is in living it, not avoiding it.

For me, the priesthood is the closest way I can imitate Christ and offer my life for the people I've known and the people who don't believe in God and the people who can't offer themselves, for one reason or another. The most difficult thing is not giving up the things I've achieved but surrendering the things I haven't achieved.

I may end up in a church counting money, or doing very mundane things, but the essence of priesthood is to offer it to God, leaving the results to him and allowing him to use my life in any way he wants.

What sums it all up for me is a few lines from the Old Testament, from the prophet Jeremiah in chapter 20, where he says, 'I used to say, "I will not think about him; I will not speak his name any more." Then there seemed to be a fire burning in my heart, imprisoned in my bones. The effort to restrain it wearied me; I could not bear it.'

I feel like that.

25

• • • • • • • • • • • • •

The people whose experiences of Jesus Christ are featured in this book come from a wide range of backgrounds. Their ages range from seven to seventy-nine; there are men, women and children; they are single, married, divorced, separated, celibate, bereaved or gay. Their nationalities are English, Belgian, Sri Lankan, Irish, German, Dutch, Australian, Portuguese, Scottish, Indian and Pakistani.

Their religions were originally Catholic, Anglican, Anglo-Catholic, evangelical, Baptist, or uncommitted, but their culture and environment have also exposed them to the influences of Buddhism, Hinduism, Judaism, Islam, spiritualism, atheism, Jehovah's Witness and other non-Christian cults, humanism, materialism, communism, cynicism, occultism, and New Age thinking.

They have encountered or failed to encounter the risen Jesus Christ of the gospel accounts, in a variety of different circumstances, in every kind of suffering of their own and of other people, as well as in happy and positive circumstances. They have been impressed or unconvinced, moved or unmoved, by very similar events, to which they have all reacted differently.

They all have the same Father, and each person has certain similarities with their human brothers and sisters, but each also has their own uniqueness and their own repertoire of striking differences in personality and approach to life.

The same God is God of all of us, but each of us knows him differently. One thing is certain: that because we are mortal, we only have a limited time of physical existence on this earth in which to decide where we want to be in relation to the God who created us, and to the person of Jesus Christ.

For the short time we're here, there is a place for us, whatever our culture, experience or views. What matters is to be honest and decisive about my place, in relation to Jesus Christ. Do the attitudes I currently hold really represent where I am and want to be – or are they other people's views, which are of no use to me?

Am I far from having a close relationship with Jesus Christ because I am actually far away from him and don't relate to him at all? Or do I really identify with this person and his life without too much difficulty, and simply don't allow this reality to express itself or show itself in my life?

Is there conflict between what I really believe, inwardly, and what I admit to, for fear of being condemned or ridiculed? Have I simply got on with my life, on auto-pilot, not allowing myself to think about difficult issues? If I don't have the answers myself, have I refused to think about the questions? Am I afraid to show ignorance by going back to the primary stages of learning about Jesus Christ, or ashamed to admit I know very little about him?

What anyone can know about God, anyway, is not very much. What we know about Jesus Christ in his life on earth is dependent on very brief and undetailed documents based on verbal accounts by his followers, all of whom seem to remember the same events differently – perhaps because, as such diverse characters, they experienced them differently.

But, given the little information available to us, do I study it carefully and 'ponder it in my heart' or do I dismiss it, because it's not complete and doesn't tie up all the loose ends neatly or answer my complex questions simply enough?

Do I also dismiss the Church that Jesus Christ founded on the impulsive and unreliable character of Simon Peter, whom he called 'the rock' and in whom he saw qualities that no one else saw, because that Church doesn't meet my ideals of rock-like reliability and perfect humanity?

You might like to try, in the context of all the contemporary accounts of Jesus Christ in this book, to place yourself and your own relationship with him somewhere on the scale from faith to cynicism. You may find, in the narrative of one of the people here, something that reminds you of your own experiences or feelings, or one phrase that's struck you as appropriate – or as particularly difficult to swallow.

And even if you thought of yourself before as someone who's had no experience of Jesus, the son of God, you may find that some memory comes to mind – some occasion when you had an inkling of God's existence or the presence of one of his family, or alternatively, some time when you had an overwhelming sense of his absence and of your own smallness and isolation.

There is no one in the universe who hasn't had some experience of the God who created everyone. Each one of us is stamped with the memory of our origin. But recalling it, in the context of a largely secular and often uncaring existence in the material world, is another matter.

I pray that the Holy Spirit of God will breathe in you and bring your memory of God to life, in the light of the life of Jesus Christ.

And I pray that, as soon as you want it, you will experience the presence in your life of Jesus Christ, who has risen from death and is available to you right now, and for as long as you want his intervention in your own life.

Also by Lion Publishing

Eldred Jones, Lulubelle and the Most High

Clare Nonhebel

'Eldred Jones taught himself to read at the age of five. This would not
have qualified him as a child genius, except for three significant facts:
Eldred had spent the first five years of his life in an oxygen tent, he had
not spoken a single word since birth, and the book he was reading was a
medical textbook.'

Winner of the Betty Trask Award and much-acclaimed author of
four previous novels, Clare Nonhebel has written an extraordinary tale
of three remarkable children. Eldred's parents simply wish he was like
ordinary children instead of dabbling in complex mathematics and
designing potentially lucrative farm-waste-disposal systems. Lulubelle
has outstanding acrobatic skills and wishes her irresponsible mother
would behave more like an adult. And Keith just wishes that the
surgeons who keep trying to correct his severe physical disabilities
would take his opinion seriously.

All three are caught up in a world of adult agendas, and their
determination to break free unleashes past evils and buried memories –
through which they are intimately linked. This story, with echoes of
Roald Dahl and Kate Atkinson, resonates with profound social
concerns and is told with a rare eye for the subtle truth about people.
It confirms Clare Nonhebel as a writer of great originality, verve and
compassion.

ISBN 0 7459 3812 4 (hardback)

Child's Play

Clare Nonhebel

'Profound and credible... *Child's Play* is a menacing tale about a young unmarried mother and her disturbed daughter, which unfolds with the simple deliberateness of an innocuous bedtime story... For all the charm of her writing, this book explores the raw motives behind apparently complex actions and she draws conclusions which, while avoiding the mawkish, carry the warmth of compassion.'

The Sunday Times

'We guess the truth before Clare Nonhebel gets there and are thereby lost in admiration for her skill in handling Lois' trauma. It is a long time since I came across such a marvellous portrait of a little girl as this one in all her incongruities, desperate compensatory tactics, passionate affections, concealments and uninhibited joy.'

Ruth Rendell, *Daily Telegraph*

Winner of the Betty Trask Award for her first novel, *Cold Showers*, Clare Nonhebel has written a gripping story of a young, black single mother discovering the shocking truth behind four-year-old Lois' disturbed behaviour – behaviour which has cost Sonia her job and her home and which threatens to wreck the little stability that Sonia's sheer guts and lucky chance provide. Clare Nonhebel's fourth novel confirms her as, in the words of *The Times*, 'one of the most versatile storytellers of her generation'.

ISBN 0 7459 3930 4 (paperback)

All Lion books are available from your local
bookshop, or can be ordered direct from Lion
Publishing. For a free catalogue, showing the
complete list of titles available, please contact:

Customer Services Department
Lion Publishing plc
Peter's Way
Sandy Lane West
Oxford OX4 5HG

Tel: (01865) 747550
Fax: (01865) 715152